GRADING THE NATION'S REPORT CARD

Evaluating NAEP and Transforming the Assessment of Educational Progress

James W. Pellegrino, Lee R. Jones, and Karen J. Mitchell, *editors*

Committee on the Evaluation of National and State Assessments
of Educational Progress

Board on Testing and Assessment

Commission on Behavioral and Social Sciences and Education

National Research Council

NATIONAL ACADEMY PRESS
Washington, D.C.   1999

NATIONAL ACADEMY PRESS • 2101 Constitution Avenue, N.W. • Washington, D.C. 20418

NOTICE: The project that is the subject of this report was approved by the Governing Board of the National Research Council, whose members are drawn from the councils of the National Academy of Sciences, the National Academy of Engineering, and the Institute of Medicine. The members of the committee responsible for the report were chosen for their special competences and with regard for appropriate balance.

The study was supported by Award No. EA95083001 between the National Academy of Sciences and the U.S. Department of Education. Any opinions, findings, conclusions, or recommendations expressed in this publication are those of the author(s) and do not necessarily reflect the view of the organizations or agencies that provided support for this project.

Library of Congress Cataloging-in-Publication Data

Grading the nation's report card : evaluating NAEP and transforming
the assessment of educational progress / James W. Pellegrino, Lee
R. Jones, and Karen J. Mitchell, editors ; Committee on the
Evaluation of National and State Assessments of Educational
Progress, Board on Testing and Assessment, Commission on Behavioral
and Social Sciences and Education, National Research Council.
    p. cm.
  Includes bibliographical references and index.
  ISBN 0-309-06285-3 (cloth)
  1. National Assessment of Education Progress (Project) 2.
Education—United States—Evaluation. 3. Educational tests and
measurements—United States. I. Pellegrino, James W. II. Jones, Lee
R. III. Mitchell, Karen Janice. IV. National Research Council
(U.S.). Committee on Evaluation of National and State Assessments
of Education Progress.
  LB3051 .G66686 1998
  370'.973—dc21
                                    98-40150

Additional copies of this report are available from:
National Academy Press
2101 Constitution Avenue N.W.
Washington, D.C. 20418
Call 800-624-6242 or 202-334-3313 (in the Washington Metropolitan Area).

This report is also available on line at **http://www.nap.edu**

COMMITTEE ON THE EVALUATION OF NATIONAL AND STATE ASSESSMENTS OF EDUCATIONAL PROGRESS

JAMES W. PELLEGRINO *(Chair)*, Peabody College of Education and Human Development, Vanderbilt University

GAIL P. BAXTER, College of Education, University of Michigan

NORMAN M. BRADBURN, National Opinion Research Center, University of Chicago

THOMAS P. CARPENTER, Wisconsin Center for Educational Research, University of Wisconsin-Madison

ALLAN COLLINS, Bolt Beranek and Newman, Inc., Cambridge, MA

PASQUALE J. DEVITO, Rhode Island Department of Education, Providence

STEPHEN B. DUNBAR, College of Education, University of Iowa

THOMAS H. FISHER,* Department of Education, State of Florida, Tallahassee

LARRY V. HEDGES, Department of Education, University of Chicago

ROBERT J. KANSKY,** Department of Teacher Education, Miami University, Oxford, OH

SHARON LEWIS, Council of the Great City Schools, Washington, DC

RODERICK J.A. LITTLE, Department of Biostatistics, University of Michigan

ELSIE G.J. MOORE, College of Education, Arizona State University

NAMBURY S. RAJU, Institute of Psychology, Illinois Institute of Technology

MARLENE SCARDAMALIA, CACS/Ontario Institute for Studies in Education, University of Toronto

GUADALUPE VALDÉS, School of Education, Stanford University

SHEILA W. VALENCIA, College of Education, University of Washington

LAURESS L. WISE, Human Resources Research Organization, Alexandria, VA

LEE R. JONES, *Study Director*

KAREN J. MITCHELL, *Senior Program Officer*

HOLLY WELLS, *Senior Project Assistant*

---

*Member until October 1996.
**Member until June 1996.

iii

iv

Acknowledgments

The work of the Committee on the Evaluation of National and State Assessments of Educational Progress benefited tremendously from the contributions and good will of many people.

Staff from the National Assessment Governing Board (NAGB), under the leadership of Roy Truby, executive director, and their subcontractor, American College Testing, Inc. (ACT), and staff from the National Center for Education Statistics (NCES), under the leadership of Pascal Forgione, commissioner of education statistics, and their subcontractors, Educational Testing Service (ETS) and Westat, Inc. were a valuable source of information and data on the National Assessment of Educational Progress (NAEP) throughout the project.   Susan Loomis of ACT, Nancy Caldwell of Westat, and James Carlson, Stephen Lazer, John Mazzeo, and Christine O'Sullivan of ETS provided the committee with important information on occasions that are too numerous to mention.   The committee especially extends thanks to Peggy Carr and Patricia Dabbs of NCES and Mary Lyn Bourque and Raymond Fields of the NAGB staff. In their roles as NCES and NAGB liaisons to the committee, they provided important information and perspectives throughout the course of its work.

Committee members and project staff benefited tremendously by attending and learning from discussions at meetings of the National Assessment Governing Board and its committees, the Technical Advisory Committee on Standard-Setting, the NAEP Design and Analysis Committee, the NAEP Subject Area Standing Committees, and the Advisory Council on Education Statistics. We thank all of the committee members and staff for opening their meetings to us and for sharing their knowledge and perspectives.

The Office of Planning and Evaluation Services, U.S. Department of Education, administered the contract for this evaluation. Director Allen Ginsburg provided assistance in planning the evaluation, and Elois Scott, Collette Roney, and Audrey Pendleton each served as the contracting office's technical representative during various phases of the evaluation. The committee thanks them for their advice and assistance as they monitored its work.

Between March 1996 and April 1998, the committee met nine times. At its December 1996 meeting, the committee held a workshop on standard-setting models and their applications to the NAEP achievement-level-setting process. Each of the following individuals made a helpful and insightful presentation at the workshop and prepared a written paper, the collection of which was published in a recent issue of *Applied Measurement in Education* (volume 11, number 1, 1998): Jeanne Goldberg (Tufts University), Lawrence Hanser (RAND), Sheila Jasanoff (Cornell University), Robert Linn (University of Colorado), Robert Mislevy (ETS), Barbara Plake (University of Nebraska), and Mark Reckase (ACT, Inc., now of Michigan State University).

At its May 1997 meeting, the committee held a workshop to examine NAEP's mission, measurement objectives, and possible reconceptualization. The following individuals made presentations and provided valuable insights to inform the committee's deliberations on these complex issues: George Bohrnstedt (American Institutes for Research), Robert Boruch (University of Pennsylvania), Christopher Cross (Council for Basic Education), John Dossey (Illinois State University), Emerson Elliott (National Council for Accreditation of Teacher Education), Raymond Fields (NAGB), Robert Glaser (University of Pittsburgh), Herbert Ginsburg (Columbia University), James Greeno (Stanford University), Eugene Johnson (ETS), Daniel Koretz (RAND, now of Boston College), Alan Lesgold (University of Pittsburgh), James McBride (Human Resources Research Organization, Inc.), Robert Meyer (University of Chicago), Lawrence Mikulecky (Indiana University), Robert Mislevy (ETS), William Morrill (Mathtech, Inc.), Lois Peak (U.S. Department of Education), Andrew Porter (University of Wisconsin), Lauren Resnick (University of Pittsburgh), Lawrence Rudner (Educational Resources Information Center, University of Maryland), Richard Snow (Stanford University), David Thissen (University of North Carolina), Margaret Vickers (TERC), and Wendy Yen (CTB/McGraw Hill).

Early in the committee's work, Stephen Sireci (University of Massachusetts) wrote a paper for the committee synthesizing issues regarding the dimensionality of the NAEP assessments, and NRC consultant Joanne Capner provided analyses of NAEP's current assessment development and reporting strategies. The committee also commissioned new research and syntheses on several key topics to assist them in their evaluation. The following individuals contributed their time, energy, enthusiasm, and intellect to these efforts, and their work is published in the volume of research papers that accompanies this report: Sheila Barron (RAND); Robert Boruch (University of Pennsylvania) and George Terhanian (Harris Black International); Patricia Kenney (University of Pittsburgh); Michael Kolen (University of Iowa); James Minstrell (Assessment, Curriculum, and Teaching Systems for Education); Stephen Sireci, Kevin Meara, Frederic Robin, and Hariharan Swaminathan (University of Massachusetts) and H. Jane Rogers (Columbia University); James Stigler (UCLA) and Michelle Perry (University of Illinois); and Jennifer Zieleskiewicz (Illinois Institute of Technology).

In November 1997, the committee convened a group of experts to discuss and explore the applications of contemporary cognitive and curricular research and theory and instructional practice to assessment development in NAEP. Consultants who shared their perspectives at this meeting included: David Pearson (Michigan State University), James Minstrell, Paul Nichols (University of Wisconsin), Leona Schauble (University of Wisconsin), Alan Schoenfeld (University of California, Berkeley), Patricia Kenney (University of Pittsburgh), Brenda Sugrue (University of Iowa), and Karen Wixson (University of Michigan). The committee's consideration of this topic was greatly enriched by the stimulating intellectual exchange at this meeting and in subsequent interactions with the attendees.

The Board on Testing and Assessment (BOTA) provided especially valuable guidance and feedback at critical stages of the committee's deliberations. The chair of BOTA, Robert Linn, assisted the committee by participating in discussions at several committee meetings and by reviewing and commenting on a draft of the final report. BOTA's intellectual contributions to the committee's work are much appreciated.

Many individuals at the National Research Council (NRC) provided guidance and assistance at many stages of the evaluation and during the preparation of the report. Executive director of the Commission on Behavioral and Social Sciences and Education (CBASSE) Barbara Torrey provided overall administration of the evaluation and shared her contagious enthusiasm for the work of the NRC with the committee. Alexandra Wigdor, director of the Division of Education, Labor, and Human Performance, provided continuing guidance and was especially central to the preparation of the committee's interim letter report on NAGB's proposed redesign of NAEP. Michael Feuer, director of the Board on Testing and Assessment, provided oversight of the committee's work and made frequent important contributions to committee discussions, providing unique and insightful perspectives and helping the committee maintain focus and achieve consensus. We also thank Eugenia Grohman, associate director for reports (CBASSE), for her advice on structuring the content of the report and for guiding the report through the NRC review process, and Christine McShane for her expert editing of the report manuscript and advice on the exposition of the report's main messages.

The committee especially expresses gratitude to the NRC project staff for their intellectual and organizational skills throughout this evaluation. Jacques Normand and Susan McCutchen served as the study director and project assistant during the early phases of the committee's work. They were succeeded by senior program officer Karen Mitchell, study director Lee Jones, and project assistant Holly Wells. Karen and Lee tirelessly assisted the committee in many ways—serving as valuable sources of information about NAEP, organizing and synthesizing the committee's work, keeping the committee moving forward through its deliberations and the report drafting process, and providing energy, enthusiasm, and exceptional good humor along the way. Holly Wells capably and admirably managed the operational aspects of the evaluation—arranging meeting and workshop logistics, producing multiple iterations of drafts of committee writings and report text, and being available at all times to assist with committee requests, however large or small. The committee is deeply indebted to Holly for her commitment to the committee's work, her dedication to meeting the committee's many needs for information and service, her problem solving skills, and her affability in all circumstances.

This report has been reviewed by individuals chosen for their diverse perspectives and technical expertise, in accordance with procedures approved by the NRC's Report Review Committee. The purpose of this independent review is to provide candid and critical comments that will assist the authors and the NRC in making the published report as sound as possible and to ensure that the report meets institutional standards for objectivity, evidence, and responsiveness to the study charge. The content of the review comments and draft manuscript remain confidential to protect the integrity of the deliberative process.

We wish to thank the following individuals, who are neither officials nor employees of the NRC, for their participation in the review of this report: Lizanne DeStefano, School of Education, University of Illinois, Champaign-Urbana; Emerson J. Elliott, National Council for the Accreditation for Teacher Education, Washington, D.C.; Susan Fuhrman, Graduate School of Education, University of Pennsylvania; Eric Hanushek, Wallis Institute of Political Economy, University of Rochester; Lyle V. Jones, L.L. Thurstone Psychometric Laboratory, University of North Carolina, Chapel Hill; Carl K. Kaestle, Department of Education, Brown University; P. David Pearson, Department of Education, Michigan State University; Gloria M. Rogers, Office of Institutional Research and Assessment, Rose-Hulman Institute of Technology; Bruce D. Spencer, Department of Statistics, Northwestern University; David M. Thissen, Department of Psychology, University of North Carolina, Chapel Hill; and Linda F. Wightman, Educational Research Methodology, University of North Carolina, Greensboro. Although the individuals listed above have provided many constructive comments and suggestions, responsibility for the final content of this report rests solely with the authoring committee and the NRC.

Finally, as chair, I would like to sincerely thank all of my fellow committee members, who generously contributed their time and intellect to this evaluation.

Our work covered an exceedingly broad array of complex topics and issues, and committee members exhibited a remarkable commitment to learning from each other's expertise, examining NAEP from new and varied perspectives, continuing the dialogue on some very tough issues, and producing a final report that clearly reflected a consensus among all members. All of this occured in an atmosphere of substantial and ongoing collegiality and cordiality. It has been a professionally stimulating and personally gratifying experience to work with the members of this committee and the NRC project staff. It is my hope that their high standards and expectations have been fulfilled on this evaluation project and by our final report.

James W. Pellegrino, *Chair*
Committee on the Evaluation of
National and State Assessments of
Educational Progress

The National Academy of Sciences is a private, nonprofit, self-perpetuating society of distinguished scholars engaged in scientific and engineering research, dedicated to the furtherance of science and technology and to their use for the general welfare. Upon the authority of the charter granted to it by the Congress in 1863, the Academy has a mandate that requires it to advise the federal government on scientific and technical matters. Dr. Bruce M. Alberts is president of the National Academy of Sciences.

The National Academy of Engineering was established in 1964, under the charter of the National Academy of Sciences, as a parallel organization of outstanding engineers. It is autonomous in its administration and in the selection of its members, sharing with the National Academy of Sciences the responsibility for advising the federal government. The National Academy of Engineering also sponsors engineering programs aimed at meeting national needs, encourages education and research, and recognizes the superior achievements of engineers. Dr. William A. Wulf is president of the National Academy of Engineering.

The Institute of Medicine was established in 1970 by the National Academy of Sciences to secure the services of eminent members of appropriate professions in the examination of policy matters pertaining to the health of the public. The Institute acts under the responsibility given to the National Academy of Sciences by its congressional charter to be an adviser to the federal government and, upon its own initiative, to identify issues of medical care, research, and education. Dr. Kenneth I. Shine is president of the Institute of Medicine.

The National Research Council was organized by the National Academy of Sciences in 1916 to associate the broad community of science and technology with the Academy's purposes of furthering knowledge and advising the federal government. Functioning in accordance with general policies determined by the Academy, the Council has become the principal operating agency of both the National Academy of Sciences and the National Academy of Engineering in providing services to the government, the public, and the scientific and engineering communities. The Council is administered jointly by both Academies and the Institute of Medicine. Dr. Bruce M. Alberts and Dr. William A. Wulf are chairman and vice chairman, respectively, of the National Research Council.

Contents

EXECUTIVE SUMMARY   1

INTRODUCTION   9
Changing Sociopolitical Context of NAEP, 9
Committee Charge, 11
History and Current Status of NAEP, 12
Current Context and Demands, 19
Overview of the Report, 20

1 CREATING A COORDINATED SYSTEM OF
  EDUCATION INDICATORS   22
Introduction, 22
NAEP's Current Mission, 24
Views of NAEP's Purpose and Use from Prior Evaluators, 25
Findings from Our Evaluation: Uses of NAEP, 27
Purpose and Use of Indicator Systems, 35
Potential Value of a Coordinated System of Indicators, 42
Designing and Supporting a Coordinated System, 45
Planning and Managing the System, 51
Summary, 54

xi

2 STREAMLINING THE DESIGN OF NAEP   56
   Introduction, 56
   Overview of NAEP's Current Sampling, Data Collection,
      Analysis, and Reporting Procedures, 57
   Selected Findings from Previous NAEP Evaluations, 65
   The Committee's Evaluation, 68
   Toward a More Unified Design for NAEP, 73
   Summary of Proposed Design Features, 84
   Major Conclusions and Recommendations, 84

3 ENHANCING THE PARTICIPATION AND MEANINGFUL
   ASSESSMENT OF ALL STUDENTS IN NAEP   87
   Introduction, 87
   English-Language Learners and Students with Disabilities, 89
   Efforts to Enhance Participation in NAEP and Other
      Large-Scale Assessments, 91
   Review of Progress Through 1996, 92
   Problem of Consistent and Accurate Identificationm, 102
   Goals for Enhancing Participation and Accommodation, 106
   A Research Agenda, 109
   Major Conclusions and Recommendations, 112

4 FRAMEWORKS AND THE ASSESSMENT DEVELOPMENT
   PROCESS: PROVIDING MORE INFORMATIVE PORTRAYALS
   OF STUDENT PERFORMANCE   114
   Introduction, 115
   Overview of NAEP's Current Assessment Development Process, 116
   Selected Findings from Previous NAEP Evaluations, 122
   The Committee's Evaluation, 124
   A Vision for Assessment Development in NAEP, 157
   Major Conclusions and Recommendations, 159

5 SETTING REASONABLE AND USEFUL
   PERFORMANCE STANDARDS   162
   Introduction, 162
   NAEP Performance Standards and the Achievement-Level-
      Setting Process, 163
   Selected Findings from Past NAEP Evaluations and Research, 166
   1996 Science Achievement-Level Setting, 168
   The Committee's Evaluation, 171
   Achievement-Level Setting in Future NAEP Assessments, 181
   Major Conclusions and Recommendations, 182

6 STRATEGIES FOR IMPLEMENTING THE COMMITTEE'S
   RECOMMENDATIONS FOR TRANSFORMING NAEP   185
   Recapitulation of the Primary Recommendations, 186
   Recent Work That Provides a Foundation for New Paradigm NAEP, 189
   Operationalizing Changes to the NAEP Program, 191
   Conclusion, 196

REFERENCES   198

APPENDIXES

A Enhancing the Assessment of Reading   219
B Research About Student Learning as a Basis for Developing
   Assessment Materials: An Example from Science   231
C A Sample Family of Items Based on Number Patterns at Grade 4   237
D Exploring New Models for Achievement-Level Setting   256
E Biographical Sketches   262

INDEX   267

GRADING THE NATION'S REPORT CARD

Executive Summary

The National Assessment of Educational Progress (NAEP) is the only continuing measure of the achievement of the nation's students in key subject areas. Also known as "the nation's report card," NAEP has provided periodic data regarding what American students know and can do for nearly 30 years. Throughout that time, NAEP results have been increasingly used by policy makers, educators, and the public as indicators of the nation's educational health. The NAEP program is sponsored by the U.S. Department of Education and administered by the National Center of Education Statistics (NCES). Since 1989, NAEP policy has been determined by the nonpartisan, independent National Assessment Governing Board (NAGB).

When NAEP was first administered in the late 1960s, and through the early 1980s, results were presented on a question-by-question basis; reports indicated the percentages of students who were able to answer each question correctly. Results were presented for the nation, for regions of the country, and for major demographic subgroups. Progress (or the lack thereof) was monitored by tracking changes over time in the percentages of students who correctly answered each question.

In the early 1980s, partly in response to the growing national concern about the quality and international competitiveness of the nation's educational system, reflected in such reports as the 1983 *A Nation at Risk*, NAEP was redesigned. As a result of the implementation of innovative design and analysis strategies, the program began reporting results based on performance on the entire assessment, rather than on a question-by-question basis. Results were presented as numerical

1

scores (on a scale, for example, of 0 to 500) that summarized student achievement across a subject area for the nation, for demographic subgroups, and over time.

The utility of NAEP summary scores that answer questions such as "How well are American fourth graders achieving in mathematics?" and "How much has the science achievement of female students improved over time?" was recognized by the Alexander-James Panel in 1987 when it recommended that the NAEP program begin collecting and reporting state-level results. This enabled states to evaluate their students' achievement relative to the nation and to each other and to track their own progress in state-level education reform.

The congressional legislation that established the state NAEP program also mandated standards-based reporting of NAEP results; it stated that NAEP results should be presented both as overall scores and in terms of percentages of students who meet established standards for performance. Thus, in the 1990s, most NAEP assessments have reported summary scores and the percentages of students performing at or above basic, proficient, and advanced levels of performance. Recognizing the likely political ramifications of state-level and standards-based reporting, this same legislation established the National Assessment Governing Board, the independent body charged with determining policy for the NAEP program and overseeing standard-setting and the development of the frameworks that delineate what will be assessed in each of NAEP's subject areas.

These events in NAEP's history are evidence of the perceived utility of NAEP as a measure of student achievement. Indeed, through the 1990s, pressures on NAEP to do more and more beyond its established purposes have risen. Various educators and policy makers have suggested, for example, that NAEP be used as a lever for education reform, as an anchor for other assessments, as an accountability tool, and as an international assessment tool. In response to the many varied and competing demands on NAEP, NAGB and NCES currently are implementing a second redesign of NAEP intended to focus its purposes, streamline its design, and enhance its utility to its constituents.

It is against this backdrop of change and pressure on NAEP that the National Research Council's Committee on the Evaluation of National and State Assessments of Educational Progress conducted its congressionally mandated evaluation of the program. The committee examined NAEP's mission and measurement objectives; sampling, design, and analysis strategies; framework and assessment development and achievement-level-setting processes; and the reporting and utility of NAEP's results.

The committee focused its efforts on improving the utility of NAEP assessment results. It is clear that Americans want the kinds of information about the achievement of the nations' students currently provided by NAEP summary scores and achievement-level results. However, users of NAEP not only want to know about the overall achievement of students and their performance in relation to established standards for achievement; they also want and need information that helps them know what actions to take in response to NAEP results. In this report the committee provides a series of conclusions and recommendations, which focus on enabling the U.S. Department of Education, NCES, NAGB, and the NAEP program to provide more useful information about student achievement and the nation's educational systems to the community of educators, policy makers, and the public who can have an impact on education.

The primary messages of the report are highlighted below. Each is presented as a summary conclusion based on the committee's observations and analyses of the current National Assessment of Educational Progress, accompanied by a summary recommendation for action that can contribute to a satisfactory resolution of some of the issues facing the current assessment program. If implemented, these recommendations will greatly enhance the utility and information value of the NAEP assessments; if left unaddressed, NAEP's effectiveness and future prospects for success will be undermined.

CREATING A COORDINATED SYSTEM OF INFORMATION TO ASSESS EDUCATIONAL PROGRESS

Summary Conclusion 1. **The current NAEP assessment has served as an important but limited monitor of academic performance in U.S. schools. Neither NAEP nor any other large-scale assessment can adequately measure all aspects of student achievement. Furthermore, measures of student achievement alone cannot meet the many and varied needs for information about the progress of American education.**

In an attempt to satisfy the multiple needs of diverse users, the NAEP program has adopted varied, and often conflicting, objectives without changing its basic features. As a result, NAEP now has a complex and costly design and operational structure. This proliferation of users and uses is indicative of NAEP's perceived value as a social indicator and, in some sense, suggests that the NAEP program has been weighed down by its success.

In general, successful indicator systems not only perform a monitoring function, but also help users understand results. Indeed, an examination and analysis of the purposes ascribed to NAEP is consistent with this observation; users want NAEP to:

• Provide descriptive or "barometer" information. Stakeholders want NAEP to serve as a monitor of American students' academic performance and progress.

• Serve an evaluative function by helping NAEP users know whether students' performance is "good enough." The establishment of performance standards in NAEP potentially allows policy makers and others to judge whether observed performance measures up to externally defined goals.

- Provide interpretive information to help NAEP's users better understand achievement results and begin to investigate their policy implications.

Both historically and currently, NAEP serves as a good barometer of student achievement. However, the interpretive and evaluative functions are currently not well achieved by NAEP. The question is how to accomplish these functions without further burdening NAEP. A solution for enhancing the interpretive function lies in a broader conceptualization of progress in American education.

Summary Recommendation 1. The nation's educational progress should be portrayed by a broad array of education indicators that includes but goes beyond NAEP's achievement results. The U.S. Department of Education should integrate and supplement the current collections of data about education inputs, practices, and outcomes to provide a more comprehensive picture of education in America. In this system, the measurement of student achievement should be reconfigured so that large-scale surveys are but one of several methods used to collect information about student achievement.

STREAMLINING NAEP'S DESIGN

Summary Conclusion 2. Many of NAEP's current sampling and design features provide important, innovative models for large-scale assessments. However, the proliferation of multiple independent data collections—national NAEP, state NAEP, and trend NAEP—is confusing, burdensome, and inefficient, and it sometimes produces conflicting results.

NAEP has many strong features. Its frameworks and sample assessment materials have the potential to stimulate national debate about teaching and learning. The assessment items and tasks have served as important guides and benchmarks for state and local assessment development efforts. NAEP's sampling, scaling, and analysis procedures serve as important models for the measurement community.

However, several factors suggest that NAEP's design should be simplified: recent discrepancies between results from trend NAEP and main NAEP assessments; the burden on states and schools that is created by participating in multiple data collection efforts; and the inherent inefficiencies associated with the ongoing administration of assessments for every trend line that the NAEP program supports. Exploration and implementation of methods to merge the trend NAEP and main NAEP assessments, and to streamline the data collections for the national and state components of main NAEP, are clearly warranted.

Summary Recommendation 2. NAEP should reduce the number of independent large-scale data collections while maintaining trend lines, periodically updating frameworks, and providing accurate national and state-level estimates of academic achievement.

IMPROVING PARTICIPATION AND ASSESSMENT OF ALL STUDENTS IN NAEP

Summary Conclusion 3. NAEP has the goal of reporting results that reflect the achievement of all students in the nation. However, many students with disabilities and English-language learners have been excluded from the assessments. Some steps have been taken recently to expand the participation of these students in NAEP, but their performance remains largely invisible.

Historically, the NAEP program has done little to understand the special testing needs and achievements of students who have disabilities or for whom English is a second language. Although some successful steps to enhance the participation of these students in NAEP assessments have been implemented, the performance of many of them is not included in NAEP's overall results. In addition, inconsistent criteria for identifying these students and for including them in the assessments potentially influences overall results in unknown ways.

Summary Recommendation 3. NAEP should enhance the participation, appropriate assessment, and meaningful interpretation of data for students with disabilities and English-language learners. NAEP and the proposed system for education indicators should include measures that improve understanding of the performance and educational needs of these populations.

PROVIDING MORE COMPLETE AND INFORMATIVE PORTRAYALS OF STUDENT ACHIEVEMENT

Summary Conclusion 4. The current assessment development process for main NAEP, from framework development through reporting, is designed to provide broad coverage of subject areas in a large-scale survey format. However, the frameworks and assessment materials do not capitalize on contemporary research, theory, and practice in ways that would support in-depth interpretations of student knowledge and understanding. Large-scale survey instruments alone cannot reflect the scope of current frameworks or of more comprehensive goals for schooling.

As NAEP's frameworks and assessments have evolved and changed, so has scientific understanding of the nature of student learning as well as understanding of the complex nature of curriculum. Unfortunately, many of the changes in NAEP instrumentation over the last 30 years reflect only minimally the changes in certain critical areas of scientific knowledge. In fact, the core assumptions related to cognition and curriculum that underlie NAEP's assessment design have remained relatively unchanged while research and theory in these areas has advanced substantially. NAEP's consensus-based frameworks and the assessments based on those frameworks focus on covering the breadth of a subject-area content. However, they do not fully capitalize on current research and theory about what it means to understand concepts and procedures, and they are not structured to capture critical differences in students' levels of understanding. Thus, they do not lead to portrayals of student performance that deeply and accurately reflect student achievement.

The development of such portrayals will require the use of multiple methods for measuring achievement that go beyond current large-scale assessment formats. The NAEP program has been a leader among large-scale testing initiatives with respect to developing and applying innovative procedures to assess more complex aspects of achievement, but it is clear that large-scale survey methods alone are not adequate for assessing complex aspects of achievement described in current frameworks. Nor are they adequate for assessing broader conceptualizations of achievement that are consonant with the more comprehensive goals for schooling that will be prominent in the 21st century.

Summary Recommendation 4. **The entire assessment development process should be guided by a coherent vision of student learning and by the kinds of inferences and conclusions about student performance that are desired in reports of NAEP results. In this assessment development process, multiple conditions need to be met: (a) NAEP frameworks and assessments should reflect subject-matter knowledge; research, theory, and practice regarding what students should understand and how they learn; and more comprehensive goals for schooling; (b) assessment instruments and scoring criteria should be designed to capture important differences in the levels and types of students' knowledge and understanding both through large-scale surveys and multiple alternative assessment methods; and (c) NAEP reports should provide descriptions of student performance that enhance the interpretation and usefulness of summary scores.**

SETTING REASONABLE AND USEFUL
ACHIEVEMENT STANDARDS

Summary Conclusion 5. **Standards-based reporting is intended to be useful in communicating student results, but the current process for setting NAEP achievement levels is fundamentally flawed.**

Although reporting student achievement in relation to clearly defined performance standards fulfills a highly desired evaluative role for NAEP, the current achievement levels have not yet realized their potential impact on the education community. This committee, as well as the U.S. General Accounting Office, the National Academy of Education, and other evaluators, have judged the current achievement-level-setting model and results to be flawed. It is clear that the current processes are too cognitively complex for the raters, and there are notable inconsistencies in the judgment data by item type. Furthermore, NAEP achievement-level results do not appear to be reasonable compared with other external information about students' achievement.

Summary Recommendation 5. **The current process for setting achievement levels should be replaced. New models for setting achievement levels should be developed in which the judgmental process and data are made clearer to NAEP's users.**

The implementation of these recommendations, and more specific recommendations described in the body of the report, will require changes in the design and operations of the NAEP program and many other data collections of NCES. Most notably, the successful implementation of these recommendations will require that the design of NAEP's measures of student achievement adhere much more closely to the principle that assessment design should closely match the intended purpose of the assessment. It should not be assumed that large-scale assessments are the primary means by which the achievements of the nation's students are measured; the use of multiple alternative types of surveys and assessments will be required.

Large-scale assessments should remain as important components of the NAEP program; we recommend that the core subjects of reading, mathematics, science, and writing continue to be assessed in part using large-scale survey methods and that the measurement of trends continue in these subject areas. But we also recommend that multiple assessment strategies become a much more prominent component of the NAEP program and be used to measure, for example: achievement in subject areas not assessed frequently enough to establish trend lines; subject areas (or portions of subject areas) in which not all students receive instruction (e.g., fine arts, advanced mathematics); aspects of student achievement not well addressed by large-scale survey methods (e.g., scientific investigation and problem-solving strategies); and the accomplishments of students with disabilities and English-language learners. NAEP *Report Cards* should include results from the array of methods used to assess achievement in a subject area.

The development of an improved NAEP within a coordinated system of indicators is a major task and has cost implications. Streamlining NAEP's design may result in cost savings. The costs of implementing the coordinated system of indicators are likely to be substantial, as are the costs for improving the participation and assessment of English-language learners and students with disabilities. Use of multiple methods to assess student achievement in NAEP's subject areas will require reallocation of funds currently devoted to the development of the current large-scale survey assessments. However, substantial efforts to these ends will result in better descriptive, evaluative, and interpretive information about American students' academic achievement and educational progress broadly conceived.

Introduction

CHANGING SOCIOPOLITICAL CONTEXT OF NAEP

Since its establishment in the late 1960s, the National Assessment of Educational Progress (NAEP) has become a very significant part of America's educational landscape. NAEP has earned a reputation as the nation's best measure of student achievement in key subject areas over time, and, increasingly, its results get the attention of the press, the public, and policy makers as indicators of the nation's educational health. However, over its 30-year history, the sociopolitical context in which NAEP exists has changed significantly. Partly in response to this changed context, many major changes have been made in NAEP; it has become an exceedingly complex entity, reflecting the desires and needs of multiple constituencies.

Perhaps the most critical feature of the changing context has been a deep and increasingly public concern about the quality of education in the United States. Concern about the condition of U.S. schools and levels of students' achievement began in 1957 with the launching of Sputnik and has been amplified by numerous documents and reports, such as *A Nation at Risk* (National Commission on Excellence in Education, 1983), a watershed publication in promoting public awareness of the shortcomings of American education. Public concern has led to increased investment in education at all levels.

The world has changed substantially over the last three decades, witnessing the fall of the Iron Curtain, the "triumph" of capitalism over communism, and the shift to a highly competitive global economy. Discussions of workforce readiness, especially the international competitiveness of America's workforce, permeate the media. The increasingly intense focus on the results of large-scale assessments, including those from programs such as NAEP, reflects the desire to know how the United States stands in comparison to past performance and, most especially, in comparison to international competitors. Such comparisons have become a routine part of America's economic, social, and political rhetoric. And comparisons are not limited to contrasts between the United States and other industrialized countries; they include comparisons of states with each other and with international benchmarks. Increasingly, states want indicators of the quality of their education systems, partly to evaluate the return on investments made to support education reform since the mid-1980s.

Today, a key focus of the concern is a debate on questions of accountability. Citizens, educators, and policy makers—at levels from local school districts to the federal bureaucracy—want to know whether the substantial investments that have been made in education are reaping rewards. Accountability has become the goal of educational policy makers, the business community, and the public; this focus on accountability is closely tied to burgeoning awareness of the changing nature of commerce and the emergence of internationalism. Large-scale, high-stakes assessment programs have become the proposed means to that end.

The focus on U.S. academic achievement was further heightened by the promulgation of national education goals during the early 1990s. Objectives such as "being first in the world in mathematics and science by the year 2000" (P.L. 103-227, Goals 2000: Educate America Act, 1994), regardless of how unrealistic they may be, have served to raise the political ante. The national education goals, together with the development of national standards in multiple curriculum areas, have been a dominant force in shaping American educational policy during this decade. For example, various federal policies and legislation have been enacted promulgating a top-down strategy for systemic reform. Examples include legislation that requires states to adopt more rigorous standards for curriculum and student achievement in order to obtain federal funds (P.L. 103-328, Improving America's Schools Act, Title 1, 1994). Although states are free to set their own standards, federal review of those standards requires that they must be rigorous and aligned with various national standards, such as the *Curriculum and Evaluation Standards for School Mathematics* (National Council of Teachers of Mathematics, 1989) and the *National Science Education Standards* (National Research Council, 1996a).

Several changes in the NAEP program, including the introduction of a state assessment program and standards-based reporting, are a direct outgrowth of this confluence of forces, and there is little doubt that NAEP has been exceedingly responsive at both the federal and state levels. As a result, it has achieved prominence as the country's primary vehicle for monitoring levels of educational achievement. In fact, many groups want more NAEP—more often, more subjects, and with faster reporting—albeit at less cost. The popularity of the nation's national assessment program is a blessing, but also a curse: much of NAEP's current complexity is a product of these pressures, and its capacity for change may be limited by its prominence.

COMMITTEE CHARGE

It is in this context of the sociopolitical and educational changes of the past 30 years, and of the challenges NAEP faces as a result of those changes, that this committee has conducted an evaluation of NAEP. Our charge, levied by Congress, includes evaluation of the national assessment, the state program, the student performance standards, and the extent to which the results are reasonable, valid, and informative to the public (P.L. 103-382). It is also with a congressional mandate for ongoing evaluation of NAEP that we conduct this work.

In many important ways, our evaluation research builds on the work of previous evaluators. The National Academy of Education reviewed the NAEP administrations in 1990, 1992, and 1994 (National Academy of Education, 1992, 1993, 1996). The Technical Review Panel for NAEP conducted evaluation and other research during this same period. Some of the work of the NAEP Validity Studies Panel also is evaluative in nature. In addition, analysts from NAEP's sponsoring and cooperating agencies, contractors, and advisers conduct research on an ongoing basis on the psychometric properties of NAEP, its use, and the value of its results.

We build on this broad base of information in this report. We reiterate and synthesize the results of prior evaluators and researchers. We discuss earlier findings and recommendations as a conceptual foundation for what we hope is a unique and important contribution to the reconceptualization of NAEP's measures of student achievement and to a broadening of the definition of "the assessment of educational progress." We rely on earlier work and on our own research to provide a unifying vision for assessing educational progress and charting NAEP's future.

We began this work in 1996 with an analysis of the policy directives of the National Assessment Governing Board (NAGB) for future NAEP assessments; we reviewed the May 1996 draft of NAGB's policy statement, entitled *Policy Statement on Redesigning the National Assessment of Educational Progress* (National Assessment Governing Board, 1996) in an earlier committee report (National Research Council, 1996b). We deliberated about and prepared a volume on standard setting (*Applied Measurement in Education,* 1998). We commissioned a series of papers on NAEP's mission and measurement objectives and on varied sampling, data collection, and analysis issues (National Research Council, 1999). Our evaluation culminates in this report and with suggestions for advancing the agenda it lays out.

HISTORY AND CURRENT STATUS OF NAEP

In 1963 Francis Keppel, then U.S. Commissioner of Education, appointed a committee to explore options for assessing the condition and progress of American education. The committee's chair, Ralph Tyler, described the need for a base of information to help public officials make decisions about education (Tyler, 1966:95):

> [D]ependable information about the progress of education is essential. . . . Yet we do not have the necessary comprehensive and dependable data; instead, personal views, distorted reports, and journalistic impressions are the sources of public opinion. This situation will be corrected only by a careful, consistent effort to obtain data to provide sound evidence about the progress of American Education.

In 1966 the Keppel committee recommended that a battery of tests be developed to the highest psychometric standards and with the consensus of those who would use it. NAEP was conceived to provide that information base and to monitor the progress of American education (National Center for Education Statistics, 1974; Office of Technology Assessment, 1992).

NAEP's Original Design

A number of key features were recommended in the original design of the assessment (Jones, 1996). With respect to matters of content, each assessment cycle was supposed to target one or more broadly defined subject areas that corresponded to familiar components of school curricula, such as mathematics. Although the subjects to be assessed were defined by the structure of school curricula, NAEP was intended to assess knowledge and skills that were not necessarily restricted to school learning. For each subject area, panels of citizens would be asked to form consensus groups about appropriate learning objectives at each target age for that particular subject area. Test questions or items were then to be developed bearing a one-to-one correspondence to particular learning objectives. Thus, from NAEP's beginning, there were heavy demands for content validity as a part of the entire development process.

There were also a number of interesting technical design features proposed for the assessment program. For example, multiple-choice item formats were to be discouraged in favor of short-answer items and those that asked students to perform tasks, features that would further support the content validity of the assessment.[1] Some items and tasks would need to be administered individually, whereas others could be administered to small groups. All test items, whether

---

[1]Despite this proposed design feature, throughout the 1970s and 1980s multiple-choice items were predominant in all NAEP subject-area assessments except for writing.

administered individually or in group formats, would be presented by trained personnel rather than by local school personnel in order to maintain uniformly high standards of administration.

Of special note was the proposal for using a matrix-sampling design, a design that distributes large numbers of items broadly across school buildings, districts, and states but limits the number of items given to individual examinees. In essence, the assessment would be designed to glean information from hundreds of items, several related to each of many testing objectives, while restricting the amount of time that any student would have to spend responding to the assessment. The target period was proposed to be approximately 50 minutes per examinee.

For each assessment cycle, test booklets would include items for each subject assessed in that cycle, with a distribution of easy, moderately difficult, and hard test items. The latter feature was intended to ensure that all respondents would have a probability of succeeding on some, but not necessarily all, of the items that they were given. Items and tasks not only would be presented in printed form but also would be read aloud by tape recording to permit even poor readers to demonstrate what they knew in subjects other than reading. This was also intended as a mechanism to pace performance so that all students would have sufficient time to work through every test item. At all ages, the multiple-choice items would include the response choice, "I don't know," to discourage guessing and nonresponse.

The populations of interest for NAEP were to be all U.S. residents at ages 9, 13, and 17, as well as young adults. This would require the selection of private and public schools into the testing sample, as well as selection of examinees at each target age who were not in school. Results would then be tabulated and presented by age and by demographic groups within age—but never by state, state subunit, school district, school, or individual. Assessment results would be reported to show the estimated percentage of the population or subpopulation that answered each item and task correctly. And finally, only a subset of the items would be released with each NAEP report. The unreleased items would remain secure, to be administered at a later testing for determining performance changes over time, thereby providing the basis for determining trends in achievement.

The agenda laid out for NAEP in the mid-1960s reflected the political and social realities of the time (National Assessment Governing Board, no date). Prominent among these was the resistance of state and local policy makers to a national curriculum; state and local leaders feared federal erosion of their autonomy and voiced concern about pressure for accountability. The designers responded by defining testing objectives for NAEP that were too expansive to be incorporated into any single curriculum. They specified that results be reported for specific test items, not in relation to broad knowledge and skill domains. Tests were developed for and administered to 9-, 13-, and 17-year-olds rather than to students at specific grade levels. These features thwarted perceptions of the program as a federal testing initiative addressing a nationally prescribed curriculum. Indeed, NAEP's design provided nationally and regionally representative data on the educational condition of American schools while avoiding any implicit federal standards or state, district, and school comparisons. NAEP was coined the "nation's educational barometer."

Redesign of the Original Plan

As NAEP's design emerged, however, the educational landscape changed. There was a dramatic increase in the racial and ethnic diversity of the school-age population and a heightened commitment to educational opportunity for all. Schools across the United States developed new programs to respond to various federally sponsored education initiatives. The Elementary and Secondary Education Act of 1965 established mechanisms through which schools could address the learning needs of economically disadvantaged students. In the ensuing years, federal support expanded to provide additional resources for English-language learners and students with disabilities. As federal initiatives expanded educational opportunities, they fostered an administrative imperative for assessment data to help gauge the effect of these opportunities on the nation's education system.

NAEP's original design could not accommodate the increasing demands for data about these educationally important populations and issues. Age-level (rather than grade-level) testing made it difficult to link NAEP results to state and local education policies and school practices. Furthermore, its reporting scheme allowed for measurement of change on individual items, but not on the broad subject areas; monitoring the educational experiences of students in varied racial and ethnic, language, and economic groups was difficult without summary scores. Increasingly, NAEP was asked to provide more information so that government and education officials would have a stronger basis for making judgments about the adequacy of education services; NAEP's constituents were seeking information that, in many respects, conflicted with the basic design of the program.

The first major redesign of NAEP took place in 1984, when responsibility for its development and administration was moved from the Education Commission of the States to the Educational Testing Service. The design for NAEP's second generation (Messick et al., 1983) changed the sampling, objective-setting, item development, data collection, and analysis. Tests were administered by age and grade groupings; summary scores were provided for each subject area. These and other changes afforded the program much greater flexibility in responding to policy demands as they evolved.

Almost concurrently, however, the earlier mentioned report, *A Nation at Risk* (National Commission on Excellence in Education, 1983), was issued. It warned that America's schools and its students were performing poorly. The report's publication spawned a wave of state-level education reforms. As states invested more and more in their education systems, they sought information about the effectiveness of their efforts. State-level policy makers looked to NAEP for guidance on the effectiveness of alternative practices. The National Governors' Association issued a call for state-comparable achievement data, and a new report, *The Nation's Report Card* (Alexander and James, 1987), recommended that the NAEP program be expanded to provide state-level results. This set of recommendations departed dramatically from the political sensitivities that guided NAEP's inception.

As the program retooled to accommodate this change, participants in a 1989 education summit in Charlottesville, Virginia set out to expand NAEP even further. At the summit, President George Bush and the nation's governors challenged the prevailing assumptions about national expectations for achievement in American schools. They established six national goals for education and specified the subjects and grades in which progress should be measured with respect to national and international frames of reference (Alexander, 1991). By design, these subjects and grades paralleled NAEP's structure. The governors called on educators to hold students to "world-class" standards of knowledge and skill. The governors' commitment to high academic standards included a call for the reporting of NAEP results in relation to rigorous performance standards. They challenged NAEP to describe not only what students currently know and can do, but also what young people *should* know and be able to do as participants in an education system that holds its students to high standards.

Current NAEP

The program that resulted is the NAEP we know today. It is a large and complex program. Current NAEP includes two distinct assessment programs with different instrumentation, sampling, administration, and reporting practices. The two assessments are referred to as *trend NAEP* and *main NAEP*.

Trend NAEP is a collection of test items in reading, writing, mathematics, and science that have been administered many times over the last three decades. As the name implies, trend NAEP is designed to document changes in academic performance over time. During the current decade, trend NAEP will have been administered in 1990, 1992, 1994, 1996, and 1999. Trend NAEP is administered to nationally representative samples of 9-, 13- and 17-year-olds.

Main NAEP consists of test items that reflect current thinking about what students know and can do in the NAEP subject areas. They are based on recently developed content and skill outlines in reading, writing, mathematics, science, U.S. history, world history, geography, civics, the arts, and foreign languages. Typically, two subjects are tested at each biennial administration. Main NAEP has two components, *national NAEP* and *state NAEP*.

National NAEP typically tests nationally representative samples of students in grades 4, 8, and 12. The object is to measure achievement in NAEP subject areas in relation to current thinking about curriculum and instruction. In most but not all subjects, NAEP is administered two, three, or four times during a 12-year period, which makes it possible to examine changes in performance over a decade.

National NAEP also occasionally includes assessment studies that do not rely exclusively on large-scale assessments; these are referred to as *special studies*. Special studies are designed to gather information on important aspects of achievement not well addressed by large-scale assessment methods; for example, recent studies focused on oral reading fluency and extended writing performance. The data from these studies are not used to measure trends in performance, and they usually include a wide range of data on curriculum and instruction in tested subjects.

State NAEP assessments are administered to state-representative samples of students in states that elect to participate in the state assessment program. State NAEP uses the same large-scale assessment materials that are used in national NAEP. State NAEP is administered in grades 4 and 8 (not in high school) and in reading, writing, mathematics, and science (although not always in both grades in each of these subjects).

To recapitulate, current NAEP consists of two assessments, trend NAEP and main NAEP. Main NAEP includes both national and state-level administrations. Figure I-1 depicts the components of the current NAEP assessments, and Table I-1 summarizes the features of each of these components. Table I-2 provides a schedule of NAEP administrations from 1990 through 2002.

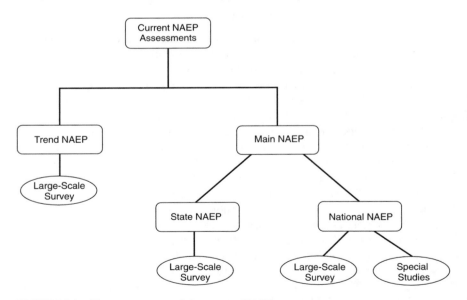

FIGURE I-1   The components of the current NAEP assessments.

TABLE I-1 Components and Features of Current NAEP

Component	Purpose	Sample	Assessment Design
Main NAEP			
National NAEP	Measure national-level achievement in 9 subject areas specified in national education goals; measure short-term trends	Grades 4, 8, and 12[a]	Assessments based on recently developed frameworks
State NAEP	Measure state-level achievement in reading, writing, mathematics, science; measure short-term trends	Grades 4 and 8[b]	Same assessments as national NAEP
Trend NAEP	Measure long-term trends in student achievement in reading, writing, mathematics, and science	9-, 13-, and 17-year-olds in reading, mathematics, and science; grades 4, 8, and 11 in writing	Assessment is based on collections of items that have been administered many times over the past 20-30 years

[a]All three grades are assessed in most, but not all, subject areas.
[b]Both grades have not always been assessed in each subject area.

Current Governance

NAEP's complex design is mirrored by an increasingly complex governance structure. In 1988, amendments to the authorizing statute for NAEP established the current management and governance structure. Under this structure, the commissioner of education statistics, who leads the National Center for Education Statistics (NCES) in the U.S. Department of Education, retains responsibility for NAEP operations and technical quality control. NCES procures test development and administration services from cooperating private companies; currently, these are the Educational Testing Service and WESTAT.

The program is governed by the National Assessment Governing Board, appointed by the secretary of education but independent of the department. The board, authorized to set policy for NAEP, is designed to be broadly representative of NAEP's varied audiences. It selects the subject areas to be assessed and ensures that the content and skill outlines, or NAEP frameworks, that specify goals for assessment are produced through a national consensus process. During the 1990s, NAGB contracted with the Council of Chief State School Officers for this consensus development. In addition, NAGB establishes performance standards for each subject and grade tested, in consultation with its contractor for this

TABLE I-2 Administration Schedule for Current NAEP Assessments, 1990-2002

Year	National NAEP[a]	State NAEP[b]	Trend NAEP[c]
1990	Reading Mathematics Science	Mathematics (8)	Reading Writing Mathematics Science
1992	Reading Writing Mathematics	Reading (4) Mathematics (4, 8)	Reading Writing Mathematics Science
1994	Reading U.S. History Geography	Reading (4)	Reading Writing Mathematics Science
1996	Mathematics Science	Mathematics (4, 8) Science (8)	Reading Writing Mathematics Science
1997	Arts (grade 8 only)	—	—
1998	Reading Writing Civics	Reading (4, 8) Writing (8)	—
1999	—	—	Reading Writing Mathematics Science
2000	Mathematics Science	Mathematics (4, 8) Science (4, 8)	—
2001	U.S. History Geography	—	—
2002	Reading Writing	Reading (4, 8) Writing (4, 8)	—

[a]All national NAEP assessments are administered at grades 4, 8, and 12, unless otherwise indicated.

[b]Grades at which state NAEP is administered are indicated in parentheses.

[c]Trend NAEP assessments are administered at ages 9, 13, and 17 in reading, mathematics, and science, and in writing at grades 4, 8, and 11.

SOURCE: Data from National Assessment Governing Board.

task, the American College Testing Program. NAGB also develops guidelines for NAEP reporting.

CURRENT CONTEXT AND DEMANDS

As previously noted, NAEP was envisioned in the 1960s as a fairly straightforward indicator, a barometer of academic achievement for the nation, large geographic regions, and major demographic subgroups. Since that time, several related changes in the sociopolitical and educational landscape have occurred.

First, as noted above, there has been increased federal, state, and local funding of education and growing public attention to education and demands for accountability, followed by an expansion of state involvement in education with increased responsibility for the disbursement of state (and often federal) funds. Second, there has been a marked increase in the racial and ethnic diversity of the school-age population and strong national commitment to providing educational opportunities to all children, including English-language learners and students with disabilities. Third, there has been the emergence of new knowledge, primarily through research on cognition, about how students learn and what they understand in various disciplines. And fourth, there has been the emergence of standards-based education reform and the need for measures of progress against stringent educational goals. We discuss these changes in turn below and in the chapters that follow.

*   *Educational indicators and data sources.* The increased demands for accountability have led to a proliferation of educational indicators (e.g., of student achievement, school resources, teacher preparation), both within and beyond NCES, that are often disconnected from each other. Also, in addition to national-level data, many policy makers want indicator information at the state and local levels. Such demands are also frequently accompanied by the expectation that the indicators be tied to information that helps provide context for and even explains the indicator results. For NAEP, this has led to increased desires that it be used as a source of information to help explain why achievement results are what they are.
*   *Participation.* The increased diversity of the student population and the national commitment to participation have led to pressures on the NAEP program to take steps to include all students in the assessment, including students with disabilities and English-language learners, and to provide modes of assessment that capture the knowledge and skills of all members of this increasingly diverse U.S. student population.
*   *Cognitive theory and curriculum.* NAEP's original purpose as an indicator of what students know and can do in key subject areas led to assessments that were highly content- and curriculum-based—that is, they test students' knowledge in a discipline but reveal little about how they think and learn. The program

is increasingly called on to incorporate current findings from disciplinary research and cognitive and developmental research in NAEP assessments so as to
reflect broader conceptualizations of achievement at the same time that it is asked
to provide measures of progress over time—measures that require some level of
constancy in assessment content.

  • *Standards.* Finally, NAEP is expected to reflect both current curriculum
and practice and the goals of standards-based educational reform. For example,
NAEP is expected to determine and measure what students know, as well as what
students should know to meet the nation's far-reaching educational goals.

These major changes have combined to produce an audience for the program
that is much more diverse than that envisioned by NAEP's originators. This
audience now includes policy makers at national, state, and local levels, reform-
ers, parents, teachers, and researchers, all seeking to use NAEP for many, varied,
and often conflicting purposes. The response to the pressures brought on by these
multiple users has led the program to add more and more components. The result
is that the NAEP assessment program faces difficult decisions about trade-offs
between purposes and uses of the assessment, assessment design, and available
program funds, which must be addressed and resolved in any future (re)design.

OVERVIEW OF THE REPORT

In the remaining chapters of the report, we examine current NAEP and make
recommendations for action that can contribute to a satisfactory resolution of
some of these issues. In several instances, it is the committee's view that current
problems and issues, if left unaddressed, are likely to undermine NAEP's effectiveness and future prospects for success.

Chapter 1 examines the information needs of NAEP's users and looks at the
extent to which the program does and does not satisfy the many and varied needs
for data and judgments about the progress of American education. In Chapter 1,
we also propose a coordinated system of indicators for assessing educational
progress and for providing context for improved understanding of NAEP's student achievement results. We discuss the implementation of such a system
within NCES.

Chapters 2 through 5 focus on NAEP's assessments of student achievement.
Chapter 2 discusses NAEP's sampling, data collection, analysis, and reporting
designs. Chapter 3 documents and evaluates NAEP's efforts to include and
meaningfully assess students with disabilities and English-language learners.
Chapter 4 evaluates NAEP's frameworks and assessment materials and the extent
to which they lead to data that support clear and useful inferences about the
academic capabilities of the school-age population. And Chapter 5 documents
recent efforts to set reasonable and useful performance standards for NAEP.
Each of these chapters provides background information and evidence that the

committee considered during its evaluation, as well as specific conclusions and recommendations related to the chapter's broader topic. Chapter 6 provides suggestions for timelines, strategies, and priorities for implementing recommendations presented in Chapters 2 through 5.

1

Creating a Coordinated System of Education Indicators

Summary Conclusion 1. **The current NAEP assessment has served as an important but limited monitor of academic performance in U.S. schools. Neither NAEP nor any other large-scale assessment can adequately measure all aspects of student achievement. Furthermore, measures of student achievement alone cannot meet the many and varied needs for information about the progress of American education.**

Summary Recommendation 1. **The nation's educational progress should be portrayed by a broad array of education indicators that includes but goes beyond NAEP's achievement results. The U.S. Department of Education should integrate and supplement the current collections of data about education inputs, practices, and outcomes to provide a more comprehensive picture of education in America. In this system, the measurement of student achievement should be reconfigured so that large-scale surveys are but one of several methods used to collect information about student achievement.**

INTRODUCTION

NAEP has chronicled academic achievement for over a quarter of a century. It has been a valued source of information about the academic proficiency of students in the United States, providing among the best available trend data on the academic performance of elementary, middle, and secondary students in key subject areas. The program has set an innovative agenda for conventional and performance-based testing and, in doing so, has become a leader in American achievement testing.

NAEP's prominence, however, has made it a victim of its own success. In the introductory chapter, we reviewed the demographic and sociopolitical conditions that have pushed the NAEP program in varied and, in some cases, conflicting directions. Recent demands for accountability at many levels of the educational system, the increasing diversity of America's school-age population, policy concerns about equal educational opportunity, and the emergence of standards-based reform have had demonstrable effects on the program. Policy makers, educators, researchers, and others with legitimate interest in the status of U.S. education have asked NAEP to do more and more beyond its central purpose (National Assessment Governing Board, 1996). Without changing its basic design, structural features have been added to NAEP and others changed in response to the growing constituency for assessment in schools. The state testing program, the introduction of performance standards, and the increased numbers of hands-on and other open-response tasks have made NAEP exceedingly complex (National Research Council, 1996).

In this chapter, we advance the following arguments:

• NAEP cannot and should not attempt to meet all the diverse needs of the program's multiple constituencies. However, a key need that should be addressed by the U.S. Department of Education is providing an interpretive context for NAEP results—helping policy makers, educators, and the public better understand student performance on NAEP and better investigate the policy implications of the results.

• The nation needs a new definition of educational progress, one that goes beyond NAEP's student achievement results and provides a more comprehensive picture of education in America. NAEP should be only one component of a more comprehensive integrated system on teaching and learning in America's schools. Data on curriculum and instructional practice, academic standards, technology use, financial allocations, and other indicators of educational inputs, practices, and outcomes should be included in a coordinated system.

• Educational performance and progress should be portrayed by a coordinated and comprehensive system of education indicators. The U.S. Department of Education should exploit synergies among its existing data collections and add components as necessary to build a coordinated system. The system should include a broad array of data collected using appropriate methods.

• Measures of student achievement necessarily remain important components of the assessment of educational progress. However, the current NAEP achievement surveys fail to capitalize on contemporary research, theory, and practice in the disciplines in ways that support in-depth interpretations of student knowledge and understanding. The surveys should be structured to support analyses within and across NAEP items and tasks to better portray students' strengths and weaknesses.

• NAEP's student achievement measures should reach beyond the capacities of large-scale survey methods. The current assessments do not test portions of the current NAEP frameworks well and are ill-suited to conceptions of achievement that address more complex skills. Student achievement should be more broadly defined by NAEP frameworks and measured using methods that are matched to the subjects, skills, and populations of interest.

We begin our discussion in this chapter by reviewing information that led to our conclusion that the U.S. Department of Education must address educators' and policy makers' key need for an interpretive context for NAEP's results. We provide examples of the types of inferences—some supportable and some not—that NAEP's constituents draw from the results. We describe the purposes these interpretations suggest, noting those that are poorly served by the current program. To better serve the needs suggested by these data interpretations, we build the case for better measures of student achievement in NAEP and for the development of a broader indicator system on American education. In doing so, we describe the characteristics of successful social indicator systems and discuss possible features of a coordinated system of indicators for assessing educational progress.

NAEP'S CURRENT MISSION

In the most recent reauthorization of the NAEP program (P.L. 103-384, Improving America's Schools Act of 1994), Congress mandated that NAEP should:

provide a fair and accurate presentation of educational achievement in reading, writing, and other subjects included in the third National Education Goal, regarding student achievement and citizenship.

To implement this charge, the National Assessment Governing Board (NAGB) adopted three objectives for NAEP (National Assessment Governing Board, 1996:3):

• To measure national and state progress toward the third National Education Goal and provide timely, fair, and accurate data about student achievement at the national level, among states, and in comparison to other nations;

• To develop, through a national consensus, sound assessments to measure what students know and can do as well as what they should know and be able to do; and

• To help states and others link their assessments to the National Assessment and use National Assessment data to improve education performance.

NAGB's three objectives call for the collection of data that support descriptions of student achievement, evaluation of student performance levels, and the use of NAEP results in educational improvement. These policy goals presage our discussion of the diverse needs of NAEP's users. This ambitious agenda for NAEP is the crux of the problem we described in 1996 (National Research Council, 1996), that we address in this report, and on which others have commented (National Academy of Education, 1996, 1997; KPMG Peat Marwick LLP, and Mathtech, Inc., 1996; Forsyth et al., 1996; National Assessment Governing Board, 1996). Indeed, the National Academy of Education panel that authored *Assessment in Transition: Monitoring the Nation's Educational Progress*, (National Academy of Education, 1997) began their report by affirming that, since its beginning, NAEP has accurately and usefully monitored and described the achievement of the nation's youth. However, it stated (pp. vi-vii):

> [I]n less than 10 years, NAEP has expanded the number of assessed students approximately four-fold; has undergone substantial changes in content, design, and administration; and has drawn to itself veritable legions of stakeholders and observers. Taken singly, each of these changes represents a notable advancement for NAEP. Taken together, however, they have produced conflicting demands, strained resources, and technical complexities that potentially threaten the long-term viability of the entire program. . . . NAEP is at a point where critical choices must be made about its future.

VIEWS OF NAEP'S PURPOSE AND USE
FROM PRIOR EVALUATORS

As stated in the introductory chapter, recent education summits, national and local reform efforts, the inception of state NAEP, and the introduction of performance standards have taken NAEP from a simple monitor of student achievement trends—free from political influence and notice—into the public spotlight. The speeches of President Clinton, the nation's governors, and state superintendents are punctuated with data on educational outcomes, much of which relies on NAEP results. Newspapers, news magazines, education weeklies, and education journals often carry data collected by NAEP.

In 1994 the Panel on the Evaluation of the NAEP Trial State Assessment of the National Academy of Education (NAE) identified criteria for the successful reporting of NAEP results (National Academy of Education, 1996). Among them was the likelihood that results would be interpreted correctly by NAEP's users. The panel applied this criterion to an examination of the interpretation of NAEP results by policy makers and the press after the 1990, 1992, and 1994

NAEP administrations. In their most recent review, the NAE panel examined NAEP-related articles in 50 high-volume newspapers across the United States.

The panel reported significant coverage of NAEP results, particularly for states that performed poorly in comparison to other states or in relation to past results. In poorly performing states, discussion emphasized the lackluster performance of students and schools and often went well beyond the capabilities of the data and NAEP's design to attribute blame to various school, home, and demographic variables. The panel's review revealed that many commentators drew unwarranted inferences from the data in attempts to explain the achievement results. For example, in California, where student performance was particularly disappointing, policy makers and reporters claimed that results were evidence of a myriad of sins, including overcrowded classrooms and the state's whole-language reading curriculum. When scores were released, the governor's education adviser declared (National Academy of Education, 1996:120):

> California made a horrendous mistake in taking out the phonics and the basic decoding skills from our reading programs, and when you do that, kids aren't going to learn to read anywhere well enough, if at all.

South Carolina's poor showing was attributed to low expectations for student performance; local newspapers reported (National Academy of Education, 1996:122):

> South Carolina students ranked near the bottom in a national test of reading skills, as more than half failed to achieve even basic reading levels. . . . State education superintendent Barbara Nielsen said that the scores come as no surprise. "I know we need to raise our standards, and we will raise our scores," she said. "When children are expected to do more, they will do more."

Elsewhere, poor performance was ascribed to large proportions of English-language learners and transient students, too much television, meager education funding, parents' lack of involvement in children's education, and parents' inability or unwillingness to read to their sons and daughters. In their analysis, the NAE panel observed that some of the variables targeted as sources of poor student performance were absent from the variables measured by NAEP. In other cases, interpretations went beyond the data to bolster commentators' preconceived notions or already established political agendas.

The NAE panel noted that many accounts of the data included suggestions for educational improvement. From the 1994 NAEP data, reporters and policy makers made a variety of suggestions (National Academy of Education, 1996; Hartka and Stancavage, 1997; Barron and Koretz, in press). They called for ambitious education reform, more rigorous teacher training and certification, more stringent academic standards, increased education funding, better identification of student weaknesses, increased resources for early education, and the use of alternative assessments—all inferences that exceed NAEP's design. The NAE panel concluded their analysis by commenting on users' clear need to identify the reasons for both good and poor achievement and to try to use this information in the service of educational improvement.

FINDINGS FROM OUR EVALUATION: USES OF NAEP

Building on this work, we examined the use of NAEP data following the 1996 release of the mathematics and science assessments. Our analysis relied on reports in the popular and professional press, NAEP publications, and various letters, memoranda, and other unpublished documents gathered during the course of the evaluation. We sought to determine and document the kinds of arguments users made with the most recent NAEP results.

Our analysis of the large body of reports on the 1996 mathematics and science assessments revealed that NAEP data were used by varied audiences to make descriptive statements, to serve evaluative purposes, and to meet interpretive ends. Our observations about these numerous uses of NAEP results parallel those of McDonnell (1994) in her research on state policy makers' use of assessment results, and of Barron and Koretz (in press) in their recent examination of the interpretation of state NAEP results. Specifically, we saw that 1996 results were used to:

- describe the status of the education system,
- describe the performance of students in different demographic groups,
- identify the knowledge and skills over which students have (or do not have) mastery,
- support judgments about the adequacy of observed performance,
- argue the success or failure of instructional content and strategies,
- discuss relationships among achievement and school and family variables,
- reinforce the call for high academic standards and education reform, and
- argue for system and school accountability.

Table 1-1 illustrates our findings. These illustrations come from the popular press, but they exemplify uses made of NAEP data in the varied publications we examined. Although the source data for some of the statements in Table 1-1 are unclear, what is clear is that the 1996 data were used to support descriptive, evaluative, and interpretive statements about student achievement in mathematics and science. The first column of the table identifies the sources of the reports. The second column includes statements that describe how well American students, subgroups of students, or states performed on 1996 NAEP. In describing the results, column 2 shows that users often drew comparisons—to the past, across states, across population groups—to bring more meaning to the data. The descriptive statements in these and the other reports we reviewed were generally consistent with NAEP's design. The third column gives examples of evaluative

TABLE 1-1 Excerpts from Newspaper Reports on 1996 Main NAEP Science and Mathematics Results

Newspaper, Date	Descriptive	Evaluative	Interpretive
Los Angeles Times, 2/28/97	"The nation's schools received an upbeat report card in mathematics, but the bad news continued for California as its fourth-graders lagged behind their peers in 40 states and came out ahead of only those in Mississippi. California eighth-graders performed somewhat better but still ranged behind students in 32 states in the 1996 NAEP. . . . California's poor students in the fourth grade ranked last compared to similar pupils elsewhere, the state's higher-income students, represented by those whose parents graduated from college, did slightly better but were still 35th out of 43 states."	"[O]nly one in 10 of the state's fourth-graders and one in six of the older students are considered 'proficient' in math, a skill level higher than merely measuring the basics. . . . Governor Pete Wilson (said) the results were deplorable and intolerable."	"The test found that 54% of California's fourth-graders are not mastering essential basic skills such as measuring something longer than a ruler. . . . Those findings are likely to fuel criticism that math 'reform' efforts of recent years have not produced gains. . . . Governor Pete Wilson . . . said results . . . point up the need now more than ever to teach basic computational math skills in the classroom'. . . . State Superintendent Delaine Eastin responded to the poor showing by renewing her call for academic standards that would be both demanding and mandatory, as well as statewide tests to monitor student performance on a system of rewards and sanctions."

San Francisco Chronicle, 2/28/97	"Nationally, scores rose four points on a 500-point scale for fourth-graders and 12th-graders, and five points for eighth graders. . . . California math scores improved over 1992 for fourth-graders by one point . . . . Eighth-graders improved by two points, beating out eight states. . . . In the 1994 reading test, California fourth-graders tied with Louisiana for worst state but did outperform Guam."	"The good news is California has stopped the downward spiral," (Superintendent) Eastin said. The bad news is we stopped it in the basement."	"The fact that our students are the worst in the nation on average mathematics proficiency should be a wake-up call for every educator, parent, and elected official in our state that the math programs we are currently using just aren't working."
Washington Post, 10/22/97	"Maryland and Virginia finished slightly above the national average . . . while the District was much lower."	"A rigorous new test of what American students know in science has revealed that many of them are not demonstrating even basic competence in the subject in certain grades. More than 40 percent of high school seniors across the country who took the science exam, and more than one-third of fourth- and eight-graders, could not meet the minimum academic expectations set."	"Education officials said the latest test results presented stark new evidence of a problem in how science is being taught. Too many schools, they contend, still emphasize rote memorization of facts instead of creative exercises that would arouse more curiosity in science and make the subject more relevant to students."

Continued on next page

TABLE 1-1 Continued

Newspaper, Date	Descriptive	Evaluative	Interpretive
Washington Times, 2/28/97	"Commenting on the 'intriguing patterns' in the test results, William T. Randall, chairman of the National Assessment Governing Board, observed, 'The public schools in D.C. have the lowest-scoring group of black students in the nation and the highest-scoring group of whites.'"	"[N]early 40 percent of eighth graders still can't perform at a good, solid proficient standard of achievement."	"[The report is] more troubling for what it says about the condition of urban schools . . . [in that] four out of five eighth graders . . . performed worse than six years ago on the 1996 NAEP test of mathematical ability. . . . Eighth graders who can't function at the basic level have difficulty with whole numbers, decimals, fractions, percentages, diagrams, graphs, charts and fundamental algebraic and geometric concepts. . . . The states with the biggest gains all participated in an initiative funded by the National Science Foundation that allowed them, among other things to focus on the math curriculum and push algebra for all eight graders."

statements about student performance in 1996 that primarily relied on NAEP achievement-level results. These accounts speak to the adequacy of students' performance in 1996. (We discuss the validity and utility of the achievement levels in Chapter 5.) The final column of Table 1-1 shows users' attempts to provide an interpretive context for NAEP data. These statements illustrate the need for clearer explication of the data and for possible explanations of the results. The statements in column 4 generally reach beyond the data and the design used to generate them to identify sources of good or poor performance.

In our view, the excerpts in Table 1-1 demonstrate how users hope and try to use NAEP results to inform thinking about the performance of the education system, schools, and student groups. As was observed for earlier administrations, some NAEP users accorded more meaning to the data than was warranted in laying out reasons for strong and weak performance. Others sought to better understand strengths and weaknesses in students' knowledge and skills.

To be sure, it is difficult to gauge and document the impact of statistical data on political and public discussion of education issues. We believe they can play an important role in stimulating and informing debate. Boruch and Boe (1994) argue that estimates of reliance on social science data in political discussion and decision making are biased downward. They say that normal filtering systems contribute to underestimates of the value and impact of statistical data in the policy arena. They explain (p. 27):

> National Longitudinal Studies and High School and Beyond data have been used in academic reports by manpower experts . . . . Those reports have been augmented through further data analysis by the Congressional Budget Office. The results of the Congressional Budget Office reports, in turn, are filtered and given serious attention that leads to decisions and perhaps recommendations by the National Academy of Sciences Committee on Youth Employment Programs (National Research Council, 1985). These recommendations may then lead to changes in law, agency regulations, or policy.

Even NAEP's stewards seek to use NAEP results to more tangible ends. During the May 1998 meeting of the National Assessment Governing Board, board members discussed the inadequacy of some of the current data presentations. NAGB asked NAEP's technical staff from the National Center for Education Statistics (NCES) and the Educational Testing Service to explore options for exploiting the policy relevance of NAEP's findings. At the meeting, members noted that current presentations of NAEP results by grade, demographic group, state, and a small number of additional variables do not point policy makers and educators to possible sources of disappointing or promising performance or to their possible policy implications.

To illustrate their concern, board members brought up the oft-cited finding that fourth graders who received more hours of direct reading instruction per week did less well on the 1992 NAEP reading assessment than students who spent fewer hours in direct reading instruction (Mullis et al., 1993:126-127). An analogous relationship was reported for fourth and eighth graders on the 1994 U.S. history assessment: students in classrooms with greater access to technology scored less well than students in classes with fewer computers (Beatty et al., 1996:47).

It probably is not the case that reading instruction depresses reading performance or that technology use depresses history knowledge. NAEP test takers with more hours of reading instruction may have received extra remedial instructional services, and students with more computers in the classroom may have attended schools in economically depressed areas where funding for technology may be easier to secure (and where, on average, students score less well on standardized tests). Board members pointed out that current data presentations may prompt faulty interpretations of results, in that the associations suggested by the paired-variable tables (e.g., summaries of NAEP scores by population group or by hours of instruction) may misrepresent complex relationships among related and, in many cases, unmeasured variables. Discussion of the reading and history results, for example, may have been informed by data on types of instructional services provided or the uses made of computers in the classroom. Although, on their own, survey data of the type NAEP collects cannot be used to test hypotheses and offer definitive statements about the relationships among teaching, learning, and achievement, they can fuel intelligent discussion of possible relationships, particularly in combination with corroborating evidence from other datasets. Most important, they can suggest hypotheses to be tested by research models that help reveal cause and effect relationships.

To reiterate, our analysis of press reports, NAEP publications, and other published and unpublished documents suggests that NAEP's constituents want the program to:

• *Provide descriptive information.* NAEP has served and continues to serve as an important and useful monitor of American students' academic performance and progress. NAEP is a useful barometer of student achievement.

• *Serve an evaluative function.* In this role, NAEP serves as an alarm bell for American schools. The establishment of performance levels for NAEP potentially allows policy makers and others to judge whether results are satisfactory or cause for alarm. They are meant to support inferences about the relationships among observed performance and externally defined performance goals.

• *Provide interpretive information to help them better understand student achievement results and begin to investigate their policy implications.* Policy makers and educators need an interpretive context for NAEP to support in-depth understanding of student achievement and to intelligently investigate the policy implications of NAEP results—particularly if performance is disappointing. In fact, as shown in Table 1-1 and elsewhere, in the absence of contextual data, some educators and policy makers go beyond the data and NAEP's design to lend their own interpretations to NAEP results.

Examination of the current NAEP program indicates that the program does a good job of meeting the descriptive needs of its users; NAEP performs the "barometer" function well. Currently, however, the evaluative and interpretive purposes are not well achieved by NAEP.

In speaking of the evaluative role for NAEP in 1989, past NAGB chairman Chester Finn (1989) explained that "NAEP has long had the potential not only to be descriptive but to say how good is good enough." Finn asserted that NAEP can serve an evaluative purpose. From their introduction, however, NAEP's standard-setting methods and results were roundly criticized (Stufflebeam et al., 1991; U.S. General Accounting Office, 1993; Koretz and Deibert, 1995/1996; Burstein et al., 1996; National Academy of Education, 1996; Linn, 1998). For a variety of reasons, evaluators have characterized NAEP standards as seriously flawed. Despite this, we note that the popularity of performance levels—and the evaluative judgments they support—is undeniable. Many policy makers and educators remain hopeful that NAEP standards will provide a useful external referent for observed student performance and signal the need to celebrate or revamp educational efforts. As others have, we encourage NAGB to continue improving their recently assumed evaluative activities, so that NAEP can make reasonable and useful statements about the adequacy of U.S. students' performance. In Chapter 5, we discuss the evaluative function in detail and make recommendations for improving the way that NAEP performance standards are set.

Also not well met are the interpretive functions users ascribe to NAEP. Improvement of NAEP's interpretive uses can occur at two levels, one internal to NAEP's assessments of achievement and the other external to the overall NAEP program:

• Interpretive information about strengths and weaknesses in the knowledge and skills tested by NAEP can be obtained from more in-depth analyses of student responses within and across NAEP items and tasks than presently occurs. There appears to be considerable room for improvement in NAEP in supporting this level of interpretive activity. In Chapter 4 we discuss ways that framework and assessment development and reporting can evolve to provide interpretive information that supports better understanding of student achievement.

• Interpretive information about the system-, school-, and student-level factors that relate to student achievement can be provided by including NAEP in a broader, well-integrated system of education data collections. Within the context of NCES' data collections, there appears to be considerable need for improvement in data coordination to support this level of interpretive activity.

We devote the remainder of this chapter to a proposal for building and using a broader system of indicators to address many of the interpretive needs of NAEP's users. We argue for the availability of contextual data to help users better understand NAEP results and focus their thinking about potentially useful or informative next steps. Historically, NAEP has attempted to fulfill this need for contextual information by collecting data using student, teacher, and school background questionnaires on factors thought to be related to student achievement. However, as we have already discussed, these data generally are presented in paired-variable tables. In recent years, the length of the background questionnaires gradually has been reduced, in part because they have failed to capture policy makers' and educators' attention. We contend that the current NAEP student, teacher, and school background questionnaire results should not be the principal source of data to meet NAEP users' interpretive needs. We seek, therefore, to accomplish this second type of interpretive function without further burdening NAEP.

To this end, we next develop a conceptual and structural basis for a coordinated system of indicators for assessing educational progress, housed within NCES and including NAEP and other currently discrete, large-scale data collections. We argue for a system that (1) expands the conception of educational progress to include educational outcomes that go beyond academic achievement, (2) informs educational debate by raising awareness of the complexity of the educational system, and (3) provides a basis for hypothesis generation about the relationships among academic achievement and school, demographic, and family variables that can be tested by appropriate research models. For ease of reference in this chapter and throughout the report, we call the proposed system CSEI: (the coordinated system of education indicators). We are not recommending this nomenclature for operational use by NCES but adopt it here for clarity and to streamline the text.

We foreshadow our discussion of the system by noting that much of the data we seek on student characteristics, teaching, learning, and assessment already reside at the U.S. Department of Education. The feasibility of the effort we propose relies on the department's ability to capitalize on potentially powerful synergies among current efforts in ways that enhance the usefulness of NAEP results and contribute to the knowledge base about American educational progress. Several of the current data collections could serve as important sources of contextual information about student achievement and signify educational progress in their own right. Among them are NCES's Schools and Staffing Survey, the Common Core of Data, the National Education Longitudinal Study, and upcoming longitudinal studies. Collectively, these surveys gather a wide range of data on students and schools, including demographic characteristics, enrollments, staffing levels, school revenues and expenditures, school organization and management, teacher preparation and qualifications, working conditions, teacher satisfaction, teacher quality, instructional practice, curriculum and instruction, parental involvement, and school safety.

Each year NCES compiles recent data on many of these variables from across several separate surveys and publishes them in a compendium, *The Condition of Education* (e.g., Smith et al., 1997). This volume serves as a valued source of information on education indicators (with approximately 60 indicators selected for inclusion in each volume). Our recommendation for creating a coordinated system of indicators was instigated in part by imagining the enhanced value of these indicators if the data collections from which they were drawn were coordinated so that cross-connections between datasets could be realized. For example, if in CSEI, collection of data on public elementary and secondary expenditures (currently collected in the Common Core of Data) and high school course-taking patterns (currently collected in High School Transcript Studies) were coordinated with collections of data on student achievement (such as NAEP), relationships among these (and other) variables could be explored and presented in future reports. A more comprehensive view of the inputs, processes, and outputs of American education would be the result.

Table 1-2 shows many of the current NCES data collections and notes their elements. The table suggests important commonality among the datasets; these correspondences among data elements, units of observation, and populations of inference should facilitate CSEI's development. We return to the discussion of these specific data collections later in the chapter.

PURPOSE AND USE OF INDICATOR SYSTEMS

It is difficult to conceive of a system of education indicators that does not assign a key role to measures of student achievement in informing the public about how well schools are fulfilling their role in a democratic society. NAEP must serve as a key indicator in the coordinated system of education indicators that we are recommending. In fact, much of this report is devoted to commentary on aspects of NAEP that are important to its becoming integral to a larger system of indicators of progress in American education.

Bryk and Hermanson (1993:455) warn, however, of the danger of focusing exclusively on "academic achievement and the processes instrumentally linked to it—while ignoring everything else." They say that such thinking implies unrealistic "segmentation in the organization of schools, their operations and their effects." As we do, they advocate for an indicator system that reflects the different, interrelated aims of schooling.

In 1988 the Hawkins-Stafford Elementary and Secondary School Improvement Amendment (P.L. 100-297) authorized the U.S. Department of Education, through NCES, to establish the Special Study Panel on Education Indicators. The panel called for the development of a system of education indicators that "respect[s] the complexity of the educational process and the internal operations

TABLE 1-2 Overview of Current NCES Data Collections

Data and Design Elements	NAEP	NELS	ELS	ECLS	TIMSS	CCD	PSUS	SASS	NHES
Data Elements									
Student achievement	✓	✓	✓	✓	✓				
Student background characteristics	✓	✓	✓	✓	✓	✓	✓	✓	✓
Home and community support for learning	✓	✓		✓	✓				
Standards and curricula	✓	✓		✓	✓				
Instructional practice and learning resources	✓	✓		✓	✓				
School organization/governance	✓	✓			✓	✓	✓	✓	
Teacher education and professional development	✓				✓	✓	✓	✓	
Financial resources				✓	✓	✓	✓	✓	
School climate	✓	✓			✓			✓	✓

Design Elements

Design Element									
Type of design (CS=cross-sectional; L=longitudinal)	CS, L	L	L	L	CS	L	L	CS, L	CS
Periodicity (TBD=to be determined)	2, 4, or 6 yrs.	2-6 yrs.	TBD	TBD	TBD	Annual	Biennial	2-5 yrs.	2-3 yrs.
Unit of observation (S=students, T=teachers, A=administrators, P=parents, SC=schools, D=district, ST=states, H=households)	S, T, A	S, T, A	S, A, P	S, T, A, P	S, T, A, P	SC, D, ST	SC	T, A, SC	H
Data collection method (S=survey, R=record analysis, I=interview, V=video, C=case study, O=other)	S, R	S, R	S, O	S, O	S, R, V, C	S, R	S	S	I
Population of inference (N=national, S=state, G=demographic group)	N, S, G	N, G	N, G	N, G	N	N, S, G	N	N, S, G	N, G

NELS: National Education Longitudinal Study of 1988
ELS: Educational Longitudinal Study of 2002
ECLS: Early Childhood Longitudinal Study
TIMSS: Third International Mathematics and Science Study

CCD: Common Core of Data
PSUS: Private School Universe Survey
SASS: Schools and Staffing Survey
NHES: National Household Education Survey

of schools" (Special Study Panel on Education Indicators, 1991:21). During the course of its work, the panel proposed such a system; it included academic achievement and other learner outcomes, the quality of educational opportunity, and support for learning variables. At the culmination of its work, the group issued a report entitled *Education Counts* (Special Study Panel on Education Indicators, 1991). This report documents the panel's thinking about the development of an education indicator system and makes recommendations for improved federal collection of education data. In the report, the panel provided a conceptual framework for a system that includes, but goes beyond student achievement data, identified relevant extant data sources, and cited gaps in currently available data and information. Their work provides important grounding for the efforts we propose here.

Functions of Social Indicator Systems

In an essay called "Historical and Political Considerations in Developing a National Indicator System," Shavelson (1987) explains that, in their typical conceptions, indicator systems chart the degree to which a system is meeting its goals; they are generally structured to be policy relevant and problem oriented. Shavelson observes that indicator systems historically have been heralded as a cure for many ills. Social indicator systems have been variously proposed as vehicles for setting goals and priorities (Council of Chief State School Officers, 1989), for evaluating educational initiatives (Porter, 1991), for developing balance sheets to gauge the cost-effectiveness of educational programs (Rivlin, 1973), for managing and holding schools accountable (Richards, 1988), and for suggesting policy levers that decision makers "can pull in order to improve student performance" (Odden, 1990:24).

Shavelson goes on to describe how enthusiasm for indicator systems has waxed and waned over time. Linn and Baker (1998) recently wrote about renewed attention to educational indicators and described how interest in their uses is rising. They explain that current proposals describe indicator systems as vehicles for communicating to parents, students, teachers, policy makers, and the public about the course of educational progress in hopes that the educational community can "work together to improve the impact of educational services for our students" (p. 1).

Shavelson (1987) and others remind us to be cautious, however. Shavelson asserts that social indicator systems are properly used to (1) provide a broad picture of the health of a system, (2) improve public policy making by giving social problems visibility and by making informed judgments possible, and (3) provide insight into changes in outcomes over time and possibly suggesting policy options. Sheldon and Parke (1975) argue that social indicators can best be used to improve "our ability to state problems in a productive fashion, obtain clues as to promising lines of endeavor, and ask good questions." They and de Neufville (1975) state that social indicators contribute to policy making by providing decision makers with information about the inputs, processes, and outputs of the system and raising awareness of the complexity of the system and the interrelationships among components.

The earlier-mentioned Special Study Panel on Education Indicators (1991:13) observed that "indicators cannot, by themselves, identify causes or solutions and should not be used to draw conclusions without other evidence." That panel and others contend that indicator systems can help identify school outcomes, student groups, and relationships among achievement and other variables that deserve closer attention and stimulate initial discussions about possible solutions (Bryk and Hermanson, 1993; Burstein, 1980; National Research Council, 1993).

We agree. We seek a system that suggests relationships among student, school, and achievement variables and that stimulates democratic discussion and debate about American education. We believe that NAEP is currently too "decoupled from important research and policy issues" (Bohrnstedt, 1997:2) and that, housed in broader system of education indicators, NAEP results can help drive and increase NAEP's relevance to policy research. Like Bohrnstedt (1997:10), we believe that a coordinated system will "provide a very fertile basis for hypothesis generation and the preliminary exploration of ideas about what works and doesn't in American education." It is our position that providing associative data about issues of concern to educators, policy makers, and the public will prompt more deliberate exploration and explanation of the interrelationships among achievement and educational variables. It is our hope that the system's products would be used to pose hypotheses about student achievement and test them, moving beyond observational to experimental research methods and using longitudinal designs.

We began this chapter by discussing interpretations of NAEP results by policy makers and others that exceed NAEP's data and the design used to generate them. We recognize that the system and products we propose here are likely to meet with similar treatment. We predict that some policy makers will use associative data from CSEI to tout their own initiatives, to argue for new educational practice, and to develop education policy. Our CSEI proposal is not intended as an argument for weak social science research or unwarranted inference. However, we start from the position that education policy based on imperfect empirical data is better than education policy with no empirical base. We believe that the benefits of documenting interrelationships among achievement and educational variables in ways that respect the complexity of the educational enterprise will outweigh its disadvantages.

Example Conceptions of Integrated Data Collections

It is beyond our purview to recommend a conceptual model for CSEI, but Figure 1-1 shows a set of possible indicators that might be included within such

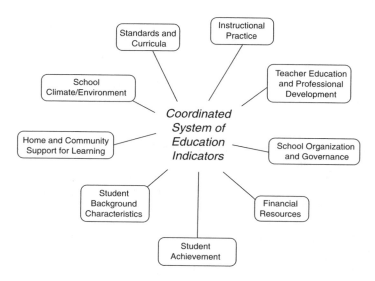

FIGURE 1-1   Possible elements in the proposed coordinated system of education indicators.

a system. The indicators are motivated by previous and current research and draw on the work of the Third International Mathematics and Science Study (Peak, 1996), the Reform Up Close project (Porter et al., 1993), RAND/UCLA's Validating National Curriculum Indicators project (Burstein et al., 1995), and the Council of Chief State School Officers' State Collaboratives on Assessment and Standards Project, as well as from the earlier-discussed Special Study Panel on Education Indicators (1991). The National Research Council and Institute of Medicine's work on *Integrating Federal Statistics on Children* (1995) and NCES's *From Data to Information* (Hoachlander et al., 1996) project also help suggest a framework for CSEI.

For example, in his ongoing examination of schooling, Porter (1996) is studying learning and its correlates by focusing on achievement measures, teacher background variables, student background variables, instructional practice indicators, and school climate variables. Porter and his colleagues are finding positive relationships between reform-relevant instructional practice and student achievement. Porter's earlier work with the Reform Up Close project (Porter et al., 1993) examined student work in relation to curriculum, instructional practices, and learning resources (technology, text, manipulatives, and other instructional equipment) and found that educational input and process indicators provided a useful context for understanding student achievement and helped to support policy-relevant statements about schooling.

As earlier noted, the NCES Special Study Panel on Education Indicators proposed an indicator system that focuses on issues of "enduring educational importance" (1991:9). They described a system that includes learner outcomes, including academic achievement measurable by traditional and alternative measures, attitudes, and dispositions; the quality of educational opportunity, including learning opportunities, teacher preparedness, school organization and governance, and other school resources; and support for learning variables, including family support, community support, and financial investments.

In 1995 NCES convened a workshop and later published a proceedings volume entitled *From Data to Information* (Hoachlander et al., 1996). The volume title serves as a mantra for NCES's long-range planning. Conference organizers sought to (p. 3):

> stimulate dialogue about future developments in the fields of education, statistical methodology, and technology, as well as to explore the implications of such developments for the nation's education statistics program . . . and continue as a key player in providing information to the American public, policy makers, education researchers, and educators nationwide.

Participants provided suggestions for tracking educational reform to the year 2010; measuring opportunity to learn, teacher education, and staff development; enhancing survey and experimental designs to include video and other qualitative designs; and effecting linkages to administrative records for research. The work of NCES staff and workshop participants provides important leads for designing CSEI.

Currently, within NCES itself as part of the Schools and Staffing Survey Program, researchers propose to track what is happening in the nation's schools around issues of school reform by collecting information on teacher capacity, school capacity, and system supports (National Center for Education Statistics, 1997). They will examine teacher capacity by documenting teacher quality, teacher career paths, teacher professional development, and teacher instructional practices. They will address school capacity by examining school organization and management, curriculum, and instruction—to include data on course offerings, instructional support, instructional organization and practices, school resources, parental involvement, and school safety and discipline. At this writing, NCES staff are considering the inclusion of student achievement data in the system, thus creating an initial version of a coordinated system of indicators, one function of which would be to better understand factors that influence patterns of student achievement.

With these efforts as a guide and to illustrate, but not prescribe, a conceptual model for CSEI, we refer to Figure 1-2, which shows possible elements of the system and shows the role of student achievement measures in CSEI. Figure 1-2 suggests the types and range of indicators that might be included in a coordinated system.

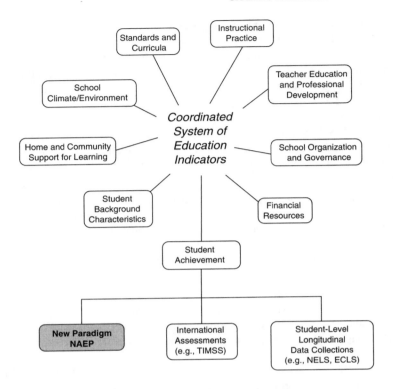

FIGURE 1-2 Measures of student achievement within the proposed coordinated system.
NOTE: TIMSS = Third International Mathematics and Science Study; NELS = National
Education Longitudinal Study; ECLS = Early Childhood Longitudinal Study.

POTENTIAL VALUE OF A COORDINATED
SYSTEM OF INDICATORS

Two studies illustrate the value of embedding measures of student achievement within a broader range of educational measures: the Third International
Mathematics and Science Study (TIMSS; Peak, 1996) and the secondary data
analysis of David Grissmer and Ann Flanagan (1997).

TIMSS

TIMMS is one example of a data system that provides information on student achievement and educational variables (Peak, 1996). It was designed to
describe student performance in mathematics and science and to promote understanding of the educational context in which learning and achievement take place.

The TIMSS dataset for grade 8 includes a wide variety of data about student achievement, curriculum and instruction, education policy, and teachers' and students' lives. The grade 8 study examined multiple levels of the education system using mixed methods of data collection. TIMSS researchers collected and analyzed data from student tests, student and teacher questionnaires, curriculum and textbook analyses, videotapes of classroom instruction, and case studies on policy topics.

TIMSS researchers posed a series of questions and then designed data collections to obtain the information needed to help answer those questions. TIMSS researchers designed the study to learn:

- how well students in the United States perform in mathematics and science,
- how U.S. curricula and expectations for student learning compare with those of other nations,
- how the quality of classroom instruction in the United States compares with that in other countries,
- how the level of support for U.S. teachers' efforts compares with that received by their colleagues in other nations, and
- how students in the United States approach their studies as compared with their international counterparts.

TIMSS results indicated that U.S. students are not among the top nations of the world in mathematics and science (Peak, 1996). At the eighth-grade level, the U.S. performance was somewhat below the international average in mathematics and slightly above it in science. Furthermore, there appeared to be little improvement in U.S. students' international standing in mathematics and science over the past 30 years.

Classroom-, school-, and system-level data collections enabled TIMSS researchers to suggest a number of factors potentially associated with American students' lackluster performance that bear further investigation. The content of U.S. eighth-grade mathematics classes was found to be less challenging than that of other countries. Topic coverage was found to be less focused in U.S. eighth-grade mathematics classes than in classrooms of other nations. Although most U.S. teachers report familiarity with recommendations for reform of the discipline, only a few apply the key tenets in their teaching.

The TIMSS research examined education policy and practice broadly and used this information to describe American education and students' achievement and to frame hypotheses about strong and weak academic performance. This work has important implications for NAEP and CSEI, since it illustrates how different and complementary research methods and data can be brought to bear on important education policy questions.

Recent heated debate about the meaning of the disappointing performance of high school students on TIMSS stands in contrast to earlier discussion of the eighth-grade data. Many explanations have been offered for the poor showing of American twelfth graders: some analysts have attributed results to shallow and variable curricula, others to inadequate teacher education and professional development, others to students' insufficient motivation to perform, and still others to the large numbers of nonnative English-speaking students in America's schools. In the absence of the data collected for the eighth-grade study, users have few leads about the meaning of the high school data and face few constraints in assigning blame for disappointing results. The eighth-grade study provides an important precedent for the design, development, and operation of a coordinated system, albeit a smaller-scale system, than the one we envision.

Linkages of NAEP and Other Data Sources

Another study that suggests the value of coordinated data systems was conducted by David Grissmer and Ann Flanagan (1997) at RAND. They combined information from several federal databases to help explore student performance data, define problem areas for closer examination, and stimulate discussion of possible solutions.

Grissmer and Flanagan probed oft-cited NAEP data about the improved academic performance of U.S. minority students from 1971 through 1990. Data from trend NAEP showed that achievement gains for black and Hispanic students were greater than those for non-Hispanic white students through the 1970s and 1980s. Policy makers, the press, and researchers attributed these gains to various sources, including expansion of social welfare programs, increased public investment in education, increased allocations to schools in economically disadvantaged communities, and changes in family characteristics (e.g., poverty levels, number of adults in the home, employment status of mothers, family size, language dominance).

Grissmer and Flanagan investigated potential sources of improved performance by combining NAEP information with census data, information from the National Longitudinal Survey of Youth, and from the National Education Longitudinal Study. They studied academic gains in relation to data on changing family characteristics, changed education and social policies, and increased investment. Like other analysts, Grissmer and Flanagan found a strong relationship between family variables and academic performance. Most important, however, they found that class size and student/teacher ratio variables bore a lesser but still strong relationship to academic performance, a finding that ran counter to earlier, much publicized research. The smaller class sizes were funded by compensatory education monies available to minority students and schools during the time periods studied.

By creating links between NAEP and other data sources, Grissmer and

Flanagan were able to suggest issues that need to be further probed by researchers, perhaps through natural experiments or randomized studies. Findings from research on possible manipulable sources of differences in achievement on NAEP (i.e., class size) would make an important contribution to education policy.

DESIGNING AND SUPPORTING A COORDINATED SYSTEM

The pressures to satisfy many audiences and many purposes are not unique to NAEP but characterize the work of the U.S. Department of Education and, in particular, the National Center for Education Statistics. Over the last 15 years, the department and NCES have responded positively and aggressively to requests for better information about the condition of education. NCES has designed and conducted data collections on curriculum and instruction, school organization and governance, student achievement, school finance, and other aspects of schooling.

Historically and currently, however, the data collections exist as discrete entities, ignoring opportunities to reduce resource and response burden and enhance value and usefulness through coordinated sampling, instrumentation, database development, and analysis. In fact, these data collections could serve as important sources of contextual and associative data for NAEP and provide more telling information about educational performance. CSEI, the coordinated system of education indicators we envision, should:

- address multiple levels of the education system, with data collected at the system, school and student levels,
- include measures of student achievement as a critical component,
- rely on mixed methods, including surveys, interviews, observations, logs, and samples of teacher and student work, and
- forge links between existing data collections to increase efficiency.

We discuss each of these features in turn.

Addressing Multiple Levels of the Education System

CSEI should include sampling, data collection, analysis, and reporting for multiple levels of the education system, including:

- *System level.* We envision a data system that produces national and state profiles of student achievement and other educational inputs, practices, and outcomes on a trend and cross-sectional basis. Data on school finance and governance, academic standards and curriculum, learning resources, enrollment and inclusion patterns, teacher professional development, and other schooling and student population variables would help describe American education and reveal general trends and associations. Many of these data are already resident at NCES.

• *School level.* We envision a system that supports closer examination of the school and classroom practices that covary with learning or signify educational progress in their own right. This should be a multifaceted program that can take advantage of ideas and instrumentation already developed by NCES and the Office of Education Research and Improvement. Work in this area would span the range of existing NCES data collections to more innovative data collections that use emerging technologies to describe schools and classrooms dynamically. Components of TIMSS and of several earlier-mentioned initiatives (e.g., the RAND/UCLA Validating National Curriculum Indicators project, Burstein et al., 1995; Council of Chief State School Officers' SCASS project, Porter, 1996), including video samples and analyses of data extracted from naturally occurring student and teacher work, also suggest possibilities for this investigation.

• *Student level.* We envision a program of longitudinal data collection efforts that support inferences about developmental patterns of achievement and learning variables. Examples of current NCES efforts include the High School and Beyond Survey and the National Education Longitudinal Study. NCES recently explored links between NAEP and the longitudinal studies, but links are not yet in place. The longitudinal designs provide better support for inferences about sources of achievement gains and decrements. Because longitudinal designs follow individual students over time, they provide a better—although not unambiguous—basis for tracing cause and effect.

Integrating Measures of Student Achievement

Measures of student achievement should be a critical and integral component of CSEI. As we view the system, the measures of student achievement should include:

• *International assessments,* such as TIMSS. These capture natural variation in schooling practices and support for learning outside the school, thus providing a comparative base for U.S. performance and making the associative data more informative.

• *Longitudinal measures,* such as the National Education Longitudinal Study and the new Early Childhood Longitudinal Study. These collect information from individual students over time and, again, support stronger inferences about the relationship between education and achievement.

• *New paradigm NAEP.* In CSEI, we conceptualize NAEP as a suite of national and state-level student achievement measures. We propose that NAEP's student achievement measures be reconfigured in some significant ways. In our view, the NAEP process of assessment development should be based on a new paradigm, one that does not assume that all (or most) of the measures of achievement should be configured as large-scale assessments and in which the assessment method is selected to match both the knowledge and skills of interest and the testing purpose. In this new paradigm NAEP, we envision assessment frameworks that define broader achievement domains than those described in the current main NAEP frameworks. This broader conceptualization of achievement would include the kinds of disciplinary and cross-disciplinary knowledge, skills, and understanding that are increasingly expected to be outcomes of schooling, such as solving complex problems in a subject area, using technological tools to solve a multidisciplinary problem, and planning and carrying out tasks in a group situation. We discuss this conceptualization of student achievement in more detail in Chapter 4.

This new paradigm NAEP would continue to rely, in part, on large-scale survey assessments for the subjects assessed frequently enough to establish trend lines. Throughout this report we refer to this trend component of new paradigm NAEP as *core NAEP*. Our conception of core NAEP in CSEI is consistent with many features of the current main NAEP program—based on subject-area frameworks, measured by large-scale survey methods, and reported in relation to performance standards. We discuss core NAEP more fully in Chapter 2 and elsewhere in the report.

New paradigm NAEP would also address other aspects of achievement, using assessment methods tightly matched to assessment purpose. For example, in order to measure achievement in NAEP subjects for which only some students have had instruction, such as economics, smaller-scale surveys targeted only to those students who have had specified levels of instruction would be administered. For assessing aspects of the subject-area frameworks that are not well assessed by large-scale survey assessments, such as performing investigations in science and assessing the broader, cross-disciplinary aspects of achievement described above, collections of students' classroom work or videotapes of students' performances could be analyzed. Throughout this report, we refer to NAEP designs that go beyond large-scale survey assessments to targeted samples and differing methods as *multiple-methods NAEP*. Multiple-methods NAEP is described in more detail in Chapter 4.

The major components of the measures of student achievement within CSEI are presented in Figure 1-3. The rationale and more detailed descriptions of new paradigm NAEP—both core NAEP and multiple-methods NAEP—are addressed in subsequent chapters of this report.

Relying on Mixed Methods of Data Collection

Student achievement measures should rely on survey and other measurement methods; the same is true for schooling variables. There are important system-, school-, and classroom-level factors not measurable by large-scale survey meth-

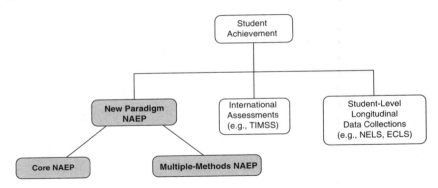

FIGURE 1-3   Measures of student achievement, including new paradigm NAEP. NOTE: TIMSS = Third International Mathematics and Science Study; NELS = National Education Longitudinal Study; ECLS = Early Childhood Longitudinal Study.

ods. Like the TIMSS researchers, we contend that the methods used to generate data for CSEI should be well suited to what one intends to measure and to the units of observation; in addition to survey data collections, the system's architecture should rely on interviews, videotaped observations, logs, and other samples of teacher and student work. If used to examine student performance and to document school and classroom practices, we believe nonsurvey methods can help illuminate student achievement results and portray education more comprehensively. Next, we provide examples of relevant variables and varied methods to help illustrate our view.

Teacher logs, checklists, or weekly reports, for instance, might be used to gather data on the knowledge and skills that are presented to students in the classroom. These methods could be used to examine topic coverage, the time and emphasis given to individual topics, targeted mastery levels, prior knowledge, and teacher expertise. Logs also could be used to document instructional practices and learning resources. Information about presentation formats, student activities, homework, and the use of technology and other instructional aids could be gathered and used to describe classroom practice as an end in itself and to better explore student performance results.

Observations, whether recorded by primary observation reports or on videotape, also could provide important information about school and classroom practice. These could be used to examine many of the same areas addressed by teacher logs. The resulting data would differ in that they would represent actual practice, rather than teachers' perceptions of it. As intimated earlier, videotaped observation methods were successfully used in TIMSS (Peak, 1996). TIMSS researchers developed schema for coding and analyzing observational data (Stigler and Hiebert, 1997). These strategies provide important models for CSEI.

Samples of student and teacher work or classroom artifacts could also be collected to examine and enrich the portrayal of lesson content and student activity. Analyses of textbooks, curriculum guides, lesson plans, assignments, tests, and student projects and portfolios could be conducted to cross-check content and obtain a clearer picture of students' classroom experiences. Sampling intervals would need to be determined; coding schemes would be needed. Classroom artifacts might be collected in conjunction with observations or interviews.

Interviews of administrators, teachers, and students could be used to collect information about teaching and learning and improve understanding of student achievement results. Again, interviews could be used to gather data about curriculum, instructional practice, educational resources, school organization and governance, teacher professional development, and student performance. Interviews are helpful in learning about topics for which there is widely differing terminology and to further probe ideas and gather illustrations in ways not possible using forced-choice formats.

In the volume of research papers that accompanies this report James Stigler and Michelle Perry (1999) discuss these methods and describe their advantages and disadvantages, logistical hurdles and costs, and strategies for integrating nonsurvey-based methods into a coordinated indicator system.

Making System Design Efficient

As we noted earlier, the design of an efficient and informative system of indicators will rely on the U.S. Department of Education's ability to capitalize on potentially powerful synergies among its discrete data collection efforts. Several recent NCES initiatives provide a good foundation for the coordinated system. Some were previously mentioned, including the appointment of the NCES Special Study Panel on Education Indicators (1991), work on the Third International Mathematics and Science Study (1995-1998), and the NCES-sponsored workshop entitled *From Data to Information* (Hoachlander et al., 1996).

From Data to Information provides important direction for the system we propose. Conference organizers sought to "consider more careful strategies that will permit integrated analysis of the interrelationships among education inputs, processes, and outcomes" (Hoachlander et al., 1996:1-3). They noted that, although existing surveys do an admirable job of providing nationally representative data on important education issues, they do not support analyses that "might increase knowledge about what works and why" (p. 1-3). Participants laid out three objectives; they said NCES should "(1) expand the amount and type of data it collects, (2) adopt a wider range of data collection and analytic methods, and (3) function within the tight resource constraints that are certain to affect almost all federal agencies" (p. 1-3). During the conference, speakers and NCES staff provided suggestions for tracking educational reform to the year 2010; measuring opportunity to learn, teacher education, and staff development; enhancing survey and experimental design to include video and other qualitative designs; and making linkages to administrative records for research. They challenged NCES to transform "quantitative facts about education into knowledge useful to policy makers, researchers, practitioners, and the general public" (p. 1-24).

Building on this and other NCES efforts, several analysts have discussed the integration of education datasets and documented factors that will help or inhibit data combination in the U.S. Department of Education; here, we describe the work of Hilton (1992) and Boruch and Terhanian (1999). These analysts detailed the purposes of varied data collections, the methods employed, sampling strategies used, the units of observation and data collection, the levels of analysis and inference supported by the datasets, the time of data collections during the school year, the periodicity of the efforts, and types of designs (cross-sectional or longitudinal) employed.

In 1992 Hilton conducted research for the National Science Foundation that examined the feasibility of combining different sources of statistical information to produce a "comprehensive, unified database" of science indicators for the United States. His goal was to capitalize on extant data on the education of scientists, mathematicians, and engineers. Hilton reviewed 24 education statistics databases. Early in his work, he determined that eight databases potentially could be combined to characterize the nature and quality of scientific training; these included NCES's National Education Longitudinal Study (NELS) of 1972 and 1988, the Equality of Opportunity Surveys, cross-sectional data on tests like the SAT, and NAEP.

Hilton eventually decided that links could not be forged to create a comprehensive science database. Factors preventing data combination, he stated, were a paucity of common variables across datasets; differences between surveys in the way variables like socioeconomic status and race and ethnicity are operationally defined; differences in sampling designs, measurement methods, and survey administration procedures; and inattention to the use of comparable conventions across datasets to enable linking.

Starting with Hilton's analyses, Robert Boruch and George Terhanian, in a paper in the volume that accompanies this report entitled "Putting Datasets Together: Linking NCES Surveys to One Another and to Data Sets from Other Sources" (Boruch and Terhanian, 1999), examined past linking efforts and suggested a hierarchical model for effecting future links. They laid out a conceptual framework for data combination that calls for designation of a primary dataset and making intended links by augmenting the primary data.

Boruch and Terhanian prompt designers to consider respondents from the primary data collection to be the primary sample and to consider samples from the same population, but from other data collections, as augmentations to the main sample. Similarly, they suggest that variables from secondary datasets should augment those from the primary data collection; they cite information derived from students' high school transcripts as an example of augmentation data. They discuss appending additional time panels for the primary sample, adding data from relatives of primary sample members, adding data from different levels (aggregate or nested) of the education system, enriching the primary dataset with data from different measurement modes (video surveys, for example), adding a new population to the dataset, and replicating the primary sample dataset with a sample of different or the same population using identical measures.

The authors also discuss four NCES datasets that are likely candidates for linkage: the Schools and Staffing Survey (SASS), the National Education Longitudinal Study of 1988 (NELS:88), the Common Core of Data (CCD), and NAEP. They begin by stating that SASS, NELS:88, CCD, and NAEP should be linkable at the district level; and that SASS, NELS:88, and CCD are linkable at the school level. They conclude their examination, however, by stating that, although not incompatible, the surveys do not fit together nicely like pieces of an interesting "education puzzle." They state that, in some cases, for example, elements from one dataset have to be combined to match elements in another; in others, missing data in one dataset limit the number of cases matching to a second. They also cite as an impediment to linking the length of time taken to compile and make available individual NCES datasets.

Boruch and Terhanian suggest that a mapping of variables (and operational definitions) be developed across datasets to make possible linkages obvious and to suggest potentially useful standardization for future data collections. They suggest that NCES adopt a survey design strategy that fosters linkages and calls for pilot studies to test useful strategies.

We extend their call for pilot studies by suggesting that studies focus on the ways that the sampling schemes, construct definitions, instrumentation, database structures, and reporting mechanisms of individual databases can capitalize on the strengths of the other data collections. Once developed, CSEI should change so that its structure, links, and components are informed and improved by experience and the system's findings over time. Better understanding and analysis of the data that are collected also should lead to improved measurement and database design. Domain and construct definitions, sampling constraints, data collection designs, instrumentation, accommodations, analysis procedures, and reporting models also should improve as information from the field and from large-scale survey data collections suggest questions of interest for small-scale observational or experimental studies; knowledge derived from the smaller studies should be funneled back into the large-scale data collections.

PLANNING AND MANAGING THE SYSTEM

The development and implementation of CSEI calls for careful consideration of alternatives and careful planning. At a minimum, development of the system's conceptual and structural framework calls for:

- the conduct of a feasibility study to determine likely costs for develop-

ment, implementation, maintenance, and management of the coordinated system,
- development of a conceptual framework for the system that delineates issue areas and specifies the levels of the education system and educational performance that should be characterized,
- specification of key variables that should be tracked,
- identification of data elements already resident at NCES and the U.S. Department of Education,
- for these elements, analysis of factors that aid or complicate linking, including similarities and differences in data collection objectives, sample definition, variable definitions, measurement methods, periodicity, confidentiality conventions, and design,
- identification of data elements not collected by NCES or the U.S. Department of Education and determination of other data sources (other government statistical agencies or new data collections) with development of domain definitions for relevant variables not already measured,
- specification of (and, if necessary, research about) measurement methods for the new schooling variables,
- development of a plan for effecting the links,
- development of a plan for organizing and housing the data,
- specification of timelines for data linking and data availability,
- development of a plan for reporting the data, and
- design of mechanisms for revisiting, reviewing, and strengthening the system.

The organizational responsibility for planning and conducting this work should be accorded to NCES. This effort is consistent with their congressional charter, which calls for the collection and reporting of "statistics and information showing the condition and progress of education in the United States and other nations in order to promote and accelerate the improvement of American education" (National Education Statistics Act of 1994, 20 U.S.C. 9001 Section 402b).

In conducting this work, NCES should seek advice from several research and practitioner groups, including the :

- Institute on Student Achievement, Curriculum, and Assessment,
- National Center for Research on Evaluation, Standards, and Student Testing,
- National Center for Improving Student Learning and Achievement in Mathematics and Science,
- National Center for the Improvement of Early Reading Achievement,
- National Research and Development Center on English Learning and Achievement,
- National Center for History in the Schools,
- national disciplinary organizations, such as the National Council of Teach-

ers of Mathematics, the International Reading Association, the National Science Teachers Association, the National Council of Teachers of English, and the National Council for the Social Studies,
- Institute on Educational Governance, Finance, Policy Making, and Management,
- National Center for Research on the Organization and Restructuring of Schools,
- National Center for the Study of Teaching and Policy,
- National Center on Increasing the Effectiveness of State and Local Education Reform Efforts,
- National Association of State Test Directors, the Council of Chief State School Officers, and the Council of the Great City Schools, and
- NAEP's subject-area standing committees and NCES's Advisory Council on Education Statistics.

The development and implementation of CSEI will be challenging. These research and practitioner groups can help expand deliberation about the conceptual and structural framework of the system. They can help evaluate and refine system plans and operations.

Commendably, the U.S. Department of Education and NCES already have paved the way for a more efficient indicator system. Previous efforts and those currently under way provide important building blocks for the activity we propose. Much of the groundwork for CSEI has been laid. Unfortunately, despite the number of researchers, panels, and conferences that have issued calls for development of a coordinated system of education indicators, none provided cost and time estimates for developing, managing, and refining the system, nor did we uncover sufficiently parallel work in other statistical agencies to support estimation. Thus, the cost of implications of changing from NCES's current structure to the proposed coordinated system are not well understood, and they would undoubtedly be highly dependent on the design of the new system. We surmise that the costs of integrating the existing NCES data collections would be considerable and that this work would require funding in addition to NCES's current congressional budget authorization. It seems reasonable to conjecture that the cost of maintaining the system, once in place, may not differ significantly from current costs, since the system may not require significant new data collections. And it is possible that economies would result as currently separate data collections are combined and instrumentation, procedures, and data collections merge. With these economies, we would anticipate increases in the quality and utility of the systems' products. We therefore believe that consideration of costs and the source of any necessary new funding should be an integral part of further discussions about the proposed system. A feasibility study to determine possible designs and likely costs for development, implementation, maintenance, and management of the coordinated system should be conducted. The U.S. Department of

Education and the National Center for Education Statistics should quickly begin this study.

SUMMARY

In this chapter, the committee has made the case that:

• The NAEP program cannot and should not attempt to meet all the diverse needs of its multiple constituencies; however, a key need that should be addressed by the U.S. Department of Education is providing an interpretive context for NAEP results. NAEP's measures of student achievement should be reconceptualized to help policy makers, educators, and the public better understand strengths and weaknesses in student knowledge and skills.

• A more comprehensive picture of American education and educational progress is needed. Examinations of educational performance and progress should be based on a broad array of indicators that includes, but goes beyond, measures of student achievement. Other indicators of educational inputs, practices, and outcomes should be included in a coordinated system of education indicators. Data on curriculum and instructional practice, academic standards, technology use, financial allocations, and other important variables should be gathered using mixed methods of data collection.

• The system's student achievement measures should reach beyond test-based indicators. Large-scale assessment methods ignore portions of the current NAEP frameworks and are ill-suited to conceptions of achievement that address more complex skills. Academic achievement should be more broadly defined and measured using methods that are matched to the subjects, skills, and populations of interest.

• NAEP's current instruments fail to capitalize on contemporary research, theory, and practice in the achievement areas in ways that support in-depth interpretations of students' capabilities. Instrumentation should be restructured to support analyses within and across NAEP items and tasks to better portray student performance.

• The U.S. Department of Education should undertake efforts to build a coordinated system. The system could inform educational debate by raising awareness of the complexity of the system and providing a basis for hypothesis generation about educational success and related school, demographic, and family variables.

After data are reported, educators, policy makers, and other public figures will discuss and debate the meaning of the data and their potential policy implications; this public deliberation will be evaluative; and it will speak to the quality and utility of the effort. It will yield information that should be fed back into the system. The system's structure, links, and components should be informed and improved by experience, public debate over results, and the system's findings over time.

The subsequent chapters of this report demonstrate how the descriptive, evaluative, and interpretive purposes of NAEP's users would be met under our proposal for new paradigm NAEP and its inclusion in a coordinated system of education indicators.

2

Streamlining the Design of NAEP

Summary Conclusion 2. **Many of NAEP's current sampling and design features provide important, innovative models for large-scale assessments. However, the proliferation of multiple independent data collections—national NAEP, state NAEP, and trend NAEP—is confusing, burdensome, and inefficient, and it sometimes produces conflicting results.**

Summary Recommendation 2. **NAEP should reduce the number of independent large-scale data collections while maintaining trend lines, periodically updating frameworks, and providing accurate national and state-level estimates of academic achievement.**

INTRODUCTION

NAEP provides important information about the academic achievement of America's youth, and the assessment has many strong design features. For example, NAEP's sampling, scaling, and analysis procedures serve as important models for the measurement community. The frameworks and innovative assessment materials serve as guides for state and local standards and assessment programs, and state NAEP results provide a useful backdrop for state and local assessment data.

In this chapter, we describe and evaluate NAEP's current sampling, data collection, analysis, and reporting methods. As background, we review the current NAEP assessments, the sampling designs and analysis methods used, and the reports generated. We then briefly review the findings of previous evaluations and provide our own evaluation of the strengths and weaknesses of the current design. Our conclusions lead us to recommend strengthening NAEP's design and increasing its usefulness. We argue for reducing the number of independent large-scale data collections currently carried out. We discuss and provide proposals for:

- Combining the trend NAEP and main NAEP designs in core subjects to preserve measurement of trends and allow updating of frameworks;
- Using more efficient sampling procedures for national NAEP and state NAEP in order to reduce the burden on states and schools, decrease costs, and potentially improve participation rates;
- Using multiple assessment methods to assess subject areas for which testing frequency generally prohibits the establishment of trend lines;
- Exploring alternatives to the current assessment of twelfth graders by NAEP with the goal of minimizing bias associated with differential dropout rates and the differing course-taking patterns of older students, encouraging student effort, and expanding assessment domains to include problem solving and other complex skills critical to the transition to higher education, the workplace, and the military; and
- Improving NAEP reports by providing (1) descriptive information about student achievement, (2) evaluative information to support judgments about the adequacy of student performance, and (3) contextual, interpretive information to help users understand students' strengths and weaknesses and better investigate the policy implications of NAEP results.

OVERVIEW OF NAEP'S CURRENT SAMPLING, DATA COLLECTION, ANALYSIS, AND REPORTING PROCEDURES

The National Assessment of Educational Progress is mandated by Congress to survey the academic accomplishments of U.S. students and to monitor changes in those accomplishments over time. Originally, NAEP surveyed academic achievement and progress with a single assessment; it has evolved into a collection of assessments that now includes the trend NAEP and main NAEP assessments. Main NAEP has both the national and state components. National NAEP includes the large-scale survey assessments and a series of special studies that are not necessarily survey-based. Special studies generally focus on specific portions of NAEP's subject domains and on the associated teaching and learning data. Current NAEP is described in the Introduction; Figure I-1 shows the components of the current program.

Components of Current NAEP

The primary objective of trend NAEP is to provide trend lines of educational achievement for the U.S. population and major population subgroups over extended time periods. To avoid disruptions in trend lines caused by differences in NAEP administration or content, administration procedures and assessment items for trend NAEP are held as constant as possible over time.

Main NAEP is a larger assessment program than trend NAEP; it provides more precise estimates of educational achievement in population subgroups, includes more contextual variables, and is based on frameworks that are updated on a regular basis to reflect changes in curriculum and pedagogical thought. Again, main NAEP includes both national and state components. The state data collections are structured to provide estimates with adequate degrees of precision for individual states.

Tables 2-1 through 2-3 summarize the administrations of current NAEP since 1984, with assessments based on the same frameworks indicated by the same symbol and joined by lines to indicate whether trend estimation is feasible. Note that, in addition to the trend lines established using trend NAEP, short-term trend lines for main NAEP have been established in reading in national NAEP (grades 4, 8, and 12) and state NAEP (grade 4) from 1992 to 1998. Short-term trend lines from 1990 to 1996 have also been established in mathematics in national NAEP (grades 4, 8, and 12) and state NAEP (grade 8; and for 1992-1996, grade 4). However, as noted previously, the short-term trend lines of national NAEP and state NAEP reflect different assessment materials and student samples than does trend NAEP.

NAEP's multiple assessment programs evolved to preserve trend lines, at the same time allowing for updating of NAEP frameworks, and to obtain state-level NAEP estimates in main NAEP. The distinct programs allow the objectives of each component to be achieved without compromising the aims of the others. However, it may be unnecessary to have separate assessment programs with such similar objectives. Later in this chapter, we consider whether there is a compelling need for distinct assessment programs or whether these activities could be merged.

Sampling Designs for Current NAEP

The NAEP program differs fundamentally from other testing programs in that its objective is to obtain accurate measures of academic achievement for populations of students rather than for individuals. This goal is achieved using innovative sampling, scaling, and analysis procedures. We discuss these procedures next. Note that their description and evaluation is reliant on technical terminology that is difficult to translate into nontechnical terms. Technical lan-

TABLE 2-1 NAEP Frameworks, Designs, and Samples by Discipline and Year Tested: Reading and Writing

Designs and Samples	Grades	1984	1986	1988	1990	1992	1994	1996	1998
Reading									
National NAEP	4, 8, 11	Y							
	3, 7, 11								
	4, 8, 12			O	O	Z	Z		Z
State NAEP	4					Z	Z		Z
	8								Z
Trend NAEP	Ages 9, 13, 17	X[a]	[b]	X	X	X	X	X	
Writing									
National NAEP	4, 8, 11	X[c]							
	3, 7, 11								
	4, 8, 12			O		Z			V
State NAEP	8								V
Trend NAEP	4, 8, 11	Y[a]		X	X	X	X	X	

NOTES: Lines indicate comparability between tests (i.e., assessments based on the same or similar frameworks and equated via bridge studies). Contents of cells (i.e., X, O, and Z) indicate different frameworks within a period of time (e.g., reading frameworks: 1984, 1988-1990, 1992-1998).

[a] Trend line extends back to 1969-1970 (writing) and 1971 (reading).

[b] No results reported.

[c] Basis for 1988-1996 trend assessments.

TABLE 2-2 NAEP Frameworks, Designs, and Samples by Discipline and Year Tested: Science and Mathematics

Designs and Samples	Grades	1984	1986	1988	1990	1992	1994	1996	1998
Science									
National NAEP	4, 8, 11		Y^a						
	3, 7, 11							Z	
	4, 8, 12								
State NAEP	8				O			Z	
Trend NAEP	Ages 9, 13, 17		X^b		X	X	X	X	
Mathematics									
National NAEP	4, 8, 11		Y^a						
	3, 7, 11								
	4, 8, 12				O	O		O	
State NAEP	4					O		O	
	8				O	O			
Trend NAEP	Ages 9, 13, 17		x^b		X	X	X	X	

NOTES: Lines indicate comparability between tests (i.e., assessments based on the same or similar frameworks and equated via bridge studies). Contents of cells (i.e., X, O, and Z) indicate different frameworks within a period of time (e.g., reading frameworks: 1984, 1988-1990, 1992-1998).
^{a}No results for overall proficiency reported; test objectives were enhanced versions of trend objectives.
^{b}Trend line extends back to 1969-1970 (science) and 1973 (mathematics).

TABLE 2-3 NAEP Frameworks, Designs, and Samples by Discipline and Year Tested: Geography, History, and Civics

Designs and Samples	Grades	1984	1986	1988	1990	1992	1994	1996	1998
Geography									
National NAEP	4, 8, 11								
	3, 7, 11								
	4, 8, 12				X[a]			O	
Trend NAEP	Ages 9, 13, 17								
History									
National NAEP	4, 8, 11								
	3, 7, 11								
	4, 8, 12			X ———	X[b]				
Trend NAEP	Ages 9, 13, 17				O			Z	
Civics									
National NAEP	4, 8, 11								
	3, 7, 11								
	4, 8, 12				X				O
Trend NAEP	Ages 9, 13, 17				X[c]				

NOTES: Lines indicate comparability between tests (i.e., assessments based on the same or similar frameworks and equated via bridge studies).
Contents of cells (i.e., X, O, and Z) indicate different frameworks within a period of time (e.g., reading frameworks: 1984, 1988-1990, 1992-1998).
[a] 12th graders tested only.
[b] 11th graders tested only; no results for overall proficiency reported.
[c] 13- and 17-year-olds tested only; trend line extends back to assessments administered in 1976 and 1982.

guage is used in this chapter in a way that is atypical of the remainder of this report.

NAEP tests a relatively small proportion of the student population of interest using probability sampling methods. Constraining the number of students tested allows resources to be devoted to ensuring the quality of the test itself and its administration, resulting in considerably better estimates than would be obtained if all students were tested under less controlled conditions. The use of sampling greatly reduces the burden placed on students, states, and localities in comparison to a national testing program that tests a substantial fraction of the nation's children.

The national samples for main NAEP are selected using stratified multistage sampling designs with three stages of selection. The samples since 1986 include 96 primary sampling units consisting of metropolitan statistical areas (MSAs), a single non-MSA county, or a group of contiguous non-MSA counties. About a third of the primary sampling units are sampled with certainty, and the remainder are stratified and one selected from each stratum with the probability proportional to size. The second stage of selection consists of public and nonpublic schools within the selected primary sampling units. For the elementary, middle, and secondary samples, independent samples of schools are selected with probability proportional to measures of size. In the final stage, 25 to 30 eligible students are sampled systematically with probabilities designed to make the overall selection probabilities approximately constant, except that more students are selected from small subpopulations, such as private schools and schools with high proportions of black or Hispanic students, to allow estimates with acceptable precision for these subgroups. In 1996 nearly 150,000 students were tested from just over 2,000 participating schools (Allen et al., 1998a).

The sampling design for state NAEP has only two stages of selection— schools and students within schools—since clustering of the schools within states is not necessary for economic efficiency (Allen et al., 1998b). In 1996 for each state, approximately 2,000 students in 100 schools were assessed for each grade. Special procedures were used in states with many small schools for reasons of logistical feasibility.

The national and state designs limit students to one hour of testing time, since longer test times are thought to impose an excessive burden on students and schools. This understandable constraint limits the ability to ask sufficient questions in the NAEP subject areas to yield accurate assessments of ability for individual students or subareas in a discipline. Time limits and NAEP's expansive subject-area frameworks have led to students receiving different but overlapping sets of NAEP items, using a form of matrix subsampling known as balanced incomplete block spiraling. The data matrix of students by test questions formed by this design is incomplete, yielding complications for the analysis. The analysis is currently accomplished by assuming an item response theory model for the items and drawing multiple plausible values of the ability parameters for sampled students from their predictive distribution given the observed data (Allen et al., 1998a).

The school and student sampling plan for trend NAEP is similar to the design for national NAEP. Schools are selected on the basis of a stratified, three-stage sampling plan with counties or groups of contiguous counties defined by region and community type and selected with probabilities proportional to size. Public and nonpublic schools are then selected. In stage three, students within schools are randomly selected for participation. Within schools, students are randomly assigned to either mathematics/science or reading/writing assessment sessions, with item blocks assigned using a balanced, incomplete design. In 1996, between 3,500 and 5,500 students were tested in mathematics and science and between 4,500 and 5,500 in reading and writing (Campbell et al., 1997).

Analysis Methods for Current NAEP

Standard educational tests generally involve a large enough set of items to allow an individual student's proficiency on a tested topic to be captured with minor error from a simple summary, such as a total score or average test score. Since everyone takes the same test (or if different versions are used, the alternatives are carefully designed to be parallel), scores from different students can be compared directly and distributions of ability estimated. It was found that these simple approaches to analysis did not work well for the NAEP assessments since the tests are short, and they contain relatively heterogeneous items so that, in combination, multiple test forms capture NAEP subject areas adequately. As a result, simple summary scores for NAEP have sizable measurement error, and scores from different students can vary significantly because of differences in the items appearing on individual test forms.

The analysis for main NAEP and trend NAEP needs a glue in order to patch together results from heterogeneous forms assigned to heterogeneous students into clear pictures of educational proficiency. The glue of current NAEP analysis is supplied by item response theory modeling (IRT), which captures heterogeneity in items through item parameters and heterogeneity between students through individual student proficiency parameters. The basic forms of IRT used are the three-parameter logistic model (Mislevy et al., 1992) for multiple-choice or other right/wrong items and the generalized partial credit model of Muraki (1992) for items for which more than one score point is possible. Parameters are estimated for sets of homogeneous items by the statistical principle of maximum likelihood using the NAEP bilog/parscale program, which accommodates data in the form of the matrix samples collected (Allen et al., 1998a). A variety of diagnostic checks of these models are carried out, including checks of the homogeneity of the items (unidimensionality), goodness of fit of the models to individual items, and checks of cultural bias suggested by residual subgroup differences for students with similar estimated proficiencies.

The IRT models relate main NAEP and trend NAEP items to a set of K scales of unobserved proficiencies (Allen et al., 1998a). Each sample individual j is assumed to have a latent $(K \times 1)$ vector of unobserved proficiencies Θ_j, the values of which determine the deterministic component of responses to items related to each scale. Given the estimates of item parameters, the predictive distribution of each individual student's Θ_j can be estimated based on the observed performance on the items. This predictive distribution is multivariate and conditioned on the values of fixed background variables characterizing the student. For each student j, five sets of plausible values $(\Theta_{j1},...,\Theta_{j5})$ are drawn from this predictive distribution. Five sets are drawn to allow the uncertainty about the latent proficiencies, given the limited set of test questions, to be reflected in the analysis. This step is an application of Rubin's (1987) multiple imputation method for handling missing data and is called the plausible values methodology in the NAEP context (Mislevy, 1985). Once plausible values are imputed for each individual student on a common scale, inferences can be drawn about the distribution of proficiencies, and proficiencies can be compared between subgroups and over time. For main NAEP, cutscores along the proficiency scales can also be determined to reflect levels of performance that are judged to represent basic, proficient, and advanced achievement.

Statistics of interest, such as proficiency distributions for the current NAEP samples and for subgroups defined by demographic characteristics, can be regarded as functions of aggregates of predicted latent proficiencies and student characteristics $g(\Theta_j, y_j)$ for each student j. As in the analysis of many probability surveys, sampled individuals who contribute to the aggregate statistics are weighted to allow for differential inclusion probabilities arising from sample selection, unit nonresponse adjustments, and poststratification. The sampling variance of estimates, initially ignoring uncertainty in the Θ_j, is computed by jackknife repeated replication, an established method for computing sampling errors from surveys that take into account the stratification, clustering, and weighting of the complex sample design (Kish and Frankel, 1974). The uncertainty in the Θ_j is then incorporated by adding to the average jackknife sampling variance of the statistic computed for each set of plausible values $\{\Theta_{(j,k):k = 1,...,j}\}$, a component of imputation variance based on the variability of the estimates computed from each set of plausible values. This computation is an application of Rubin's (1987) multiple imputation method.

NAEP Reporting

From the program's inception, NAEP has had the goal of reporting results in formats that are accessible to potential users, promote valid interpretations, and are useful to NAEP's varied constituencies. The NAEP program currently produces an impressive array of reports, including:

- *Report Cards.* These are the primary reports of the results of main NAEP. Results are presented for the nation, for states (if applicable), for major demographic groups, and in relation to key context variables (e.g., for public and private schools).
- *State Reports.* These report results from main NAEP, with a report tailored specifically for each participating state.
- *Focus on NAEP/NAEP Facts.* These are two- or four-page mini-reports that summarize NAEP frameworks, assessment results, and address topics of current and special interest.
- *Instructional Reports.* These show performance data in relation to instructional background variables; they are issued 6 to 12 months after the *Report Cards.*
- *Focused Reports.* These contain NAEP results from the special studies component of main NAEP (e.g., on the performance of English-language learners and students with disabilities or on special features of the assessments). These are also issued 6 to 12 months after the *Report Cards.*
- *Trends in Academic Progress.* This is the primary report of the results of trend NAEP.

This differentiated product line is intended to serve a variety of audiences, with differing information needs, interest in findings, and sophistication in interpreting results.

SELECTED FINDINGS FROM PREVIOUS NAEP EVALUATIONS

Components of Current NAEP

Again, main NAEP and trend NAEP test different student populations and use distinct assessment exercises and administration procedures. The national and state components of main NAEP also use different administration procedures. There is a good deal of sympathy among policy makers, testing experts, and NAEP's evaluators for the need to streamline NAEP's designs (National Academy of Education, 1996, 1997; Forsyth et al., 1996).

NAEP's policy board, the National Assessment Governing Board (NAGB), has expressed concern over the inefficiency of maintaining main NAEP and trend NAEP; they recently announced plans to investigate more efficient design options. They said "[it] may be impractical and unnecessary to operate two separate assessment programs." They have called for a "carefully planned transition . . . to enable the main National Assessment to become the primary way to measure trends in reading, writing, mathematics, and science in the National Assessment program" (National Assessment Governing Board, 1996:10). NAGB also registered concern about the inefficiency and burden imposed on states by separate state and national NAEP data collections. To address this concern for future assessments, NAGB has said that "where possible, changes in national and state sampling procedures shall be made that will reduce burden on states, increase efficiency, and save costs" (National Assessment Governing Board, 1996:7).

Sampling Designs for Current NAEP

As we do later in this chapter, the National Academy of Education (NAE; 1992, 1993, 1996), KPMG Peat Marwick LLP and Mathtech (1996), the Design/Feasibility Team (Forsyth et al., 1996), and others have examined the sampling designs for NAEP. The NAE panel focused on the conduct and results of the state component of main NAEP in 1990, 1992, and 1994, reviewing sampling and administration practices for the state assessments. KPMG Peat Marwick and the Design/Feasibility Team examined both the national and state programs.

The National Academy of Education panel found that sampling procedures for the state assessment program were consistent with best practice for surveys of this kind and concluded that sampling and administration were done well for the state program (National Academy of Education, 1996). They expressed concern, however, about declining school participation rates as the program progressed and recommended that the National Assessment Governing Board (NAGB) and the National Center for Education Statistics (NCES) consider design changes to decrease sample size requirements or otherwise reduce the burden on states, particularly small states. They warned that heavy program requirements might threaten school and state participation rates, particularly in years when multiple subjects and grades are tested. The panel cautioned that diminished participation in the state program might have deleterious effects on national NAEP.

They and others have reviewed school and student sampling for national NAEP and concluded that the national samples are drawn by experienced staff using well-established scientific, multistage stratified probability sampling designs (KPMG Peat Marwick LLP and Mathtech, 1996). As noted earlier, the sampling design for trend NAEP parallels that for national NAEP.

As explained above, NAEP's inclusive frameworks require that a balanced incomplete block design be used for test administration. Although reviewers applaud the ingenuity of the design, some worry about the complexity and fragility of the analytic machinery the design necessitates (National Academy of Education, 1996). The NAEP program has been urged to explore alternatives for simplifying the design. The NAE panel warned that the frameworks for main NAEP push the limits of form design and may strain current methods, particularly in light of recent pressure to hasten scaling, analysis, and reporting. Reviewers point to anomalies in NAEP findings as indicators of design stress and call for research to develop a more streamlined design for the assessment (U.S. General Accounting Office, 1993; National Academy of Education, 1993; Hedges and Venesky, 1997).

Analysis Methods for Current NAEP

Continuing in this vein, reviewers observe that the complex models that allow NAEP to maximize information while minimizing testing burden for examinees are beginning to fray (National Academy of Education, 1996). They note that programmatic changes have burdened the already complex statistical design, citing the introduction of innovative assessment tasks that call for mathematical models suited to multicategory scoring and violations of local item independence; the need to repeat scoring, scaling, and analysis for each state participating in the state testing program; and increased pressure for innovation in assessment design and technology. After the 1994 administration, the NAE panel called for studies to validate the current analysis and scaling models. They asked for research to test the strength of the models used and their robustness to violations of assumptions (National Academy of Education, 1996). They also sought mechanisms for checking the integrity of NAEP data prior to their release.

NAEP Reporting

In past reviews of the NAEP program, the National Academy of Education defined four criteria for successful reporting (1996); in laying criteria out, they praised the program's steady work in making progress toward these ends. The NAE panel examined the: (1) accuracy of results, (2) likelihood results would be interpreted correctly by the intended audience(s), (3) extent to which the results are accessible and adequately disseminated, and (4) timeliness with which results were made available.

The NAE panel made many positive statements about NAEP reports. They praised NAEP's innovative graphic formats for conveying the statistical significance of differences between states and over time; they applauded the map graphics, the more prevalent use of charts, simplified data tables, and shorter reports. They commented favorably on the introduction of *Focused* reports and on the summary reports for states.

However, the NAE panel and others have been critical of the length of time it takes to issue NAEP reports. The 1992 *Report Card* in reading followed test administration by more than 2 years; this time lag between administration and reporting was the longest ever experienced. The NAEP program has been strongly encouraged to press for more timely reporting.

Other reviewers join the NAE panel in making suggestions for the improvement of NAEP reports (Hambleton, 1997; Hambleton and Slater, 1996; Jaeger, 1992, 1996, 1997; Wainer, 1997; Silver and Kenney, 1997; Barron, 1999; Widmeyer Group, 1993). These analysts have encouraged NAEP's sponsors to:

• continue ongoing efforts to search for data displays and report formats that are more comprehensible to the lay reader and more likely to yield correct interpretations, including enlisting media representatives to help identify the most comprehensible methods for displaying results;

- produce more focused research reports for various audiences, including reports that draw on other research to corroborate and inform relationships observed in NAEP data;
- provide more examples of assessment tasks and student responses; and
- explore ways to support states in generating their own reports of NAEP findings.

THE COMMITTEE'S EVALUATION

We begin our own analysis of NAEP's design with a discussion of sampling, analysis, and reporting issues. From there, we turn to discussion of NAEP's multiple data collections. Again, this discussion relies on technical terminology to a greater extent than other chapters.

Sampling Designs for Current NAEP

The role of probability sampling is crucial for current NAEP, since it minimizes selection biases in making inferences from the sample to the population. As with any sample survey, NAEP is equipped to provide estimates at high levels of aggregation (national, state, gender), but it is not sufficiently fine-grained to provide estimates for low levels of aggregation, such as for schools or school districts. We, too, judge that the NAEP samples are selected using well-established stratified probability sampling designs by highly experienced contractors.

We share the concerns of other evaluators, NAGB, and NCES, however, about the testing burden NAEP imposes on small and low-density states and large school districts. In fact, we note that for the 1998 administration, the participation rate dropped to 40 states from 44 in 1996 for mathematics; 43 states participated in 1996 for science. We discuss these concerns further in conjunction with our recommendations for streamlining NAEP's design.

Furthermore, although we question the analytical complexity that marks main NAEP's matrix sampling design, we note that the design, whereby examinees receive only a subset of items, seems an inescapable feature of NAEP. The alternative approach of limiting students to a narrow subject matter area does not permit broad assessment and the measurement of associations between achievement in different areas of knowledge within a particular subject.

Analysis Methods for Current NAEP

The analysis of NAEP is perhaps uniquely complex among national probability surveys, bringing together modern ideas in survey sampling, incomplete data analysis, and item response theory to yield inferences on a diverse set of topics. The complexity of the enterprise has led to appeals to simplify the procedure and yield results that are more stable, less time-consuming to produce, more easily understood by nontechnical audiences, and more easily used by secondary analysts. In a paper that appears in the volume that accompanies this report, Barron (1999) describes the analytic difficulties currently faced by secondary users of NAEP data.

On one hand, both internal (Forsyth et al., 1996) and external (KPMG Peat Marwick LLP and Mathtech, 1996) reviews of the technical details of the NAEP analysis process suggest that much of the intricacy of the analysis methods appears justified. Alternative analysis approaches for the existing design may involve a sacrifice of statistical efficiency, and major modifications of the design to simplify the analysis would involve sacrifices in the depth and value of the surveys. On the other hand, the statistical machinery of current NAEP is thought to be fragile, and our evaluation points us to questions about simplifying the analysis methods. We discuss a number of these issues here.

Standard Error Calculation

An important feature of the jackknife method of computing standard errors is that it incorporates features of the sample design, such as clustering, stratification, and weighting; evidence suggests that standard errors computed using simple random sampling assumptions for NAEP would be seriously underestimated (Allen et al., 1996, 1998a). One approximation involved in the process of computing standard errors is worthy of mention and further study.

Item parameters are fixed at their estimated values when plausible values of the latent proficiencies are drawn. This approach does not allow uncertainty in the item parameter estimates to be reflected in the plausible values. Rubin (1987) calls this form of multiple imputation improper. Although the estimates based on improper multiple imputation are valid, standard errors tend to be underestimated, particularly when the fraction of missing information is large. One possible fix is to include the entire process of fitting the item response models and creating the plausible values in the jackknife standard error calculation. This option was considered by NAEP analysts, but it imposes an added computational burden to a process that already involves a lot of computing. A less burdensome option is to estimate the IRT models on a different jackknifed sample prior to imputing each set of plausible values (Heitjan and Little, 1991). This approach incorporates uncertainty in the estimated item parameters in the plausible values at the expense of requiring five fits of each IRT model rather than just one. Studies to assess the impact of these refinements on standard errors appear worthwhile.

Dimensionality

The dimensionality of the data is central to the scaling, analysis, and reporting of NAEP's large-scale assessment results. The current analytical approach is quite strongly tied to the assumptions of the IRT models used in the analysis. NAEP analysts spend some time assessing the fits of individual items to the models and checking by differential item functioning analysis that group differences do not remain after accounting for the estimates of proficiency that the items are intended to reflect. This model-checking activity is important and useful, but options for modifying the analysis based on its results appear limited to rejecting suspect items from the analysis. The sensitivity of answers to more wide-ranging modifications of the basic models, including models with higher dimensionality, appear worth exploring, to increase confidence that results are not unduly tied to unrealistic model assumptions. Studies that assess the dimensionality of NAEP data (Carlson, 1996; Zhang, 1997; Yu and Nandakumar, 1996; Sireci et al., 1999) do not appear to have uncovered major departures from unidimensionality, but the impact of potential violations on the final NAEP inferences is largely unknown.

Content Coverage

Reviews of the analysis process for main NAEP (KPMG Peat Marwick LLP and Mathtech, 1996) have concluded that simplifications of the analysis would limit the usefulness of results unless the underlying NAEP design is significantly modified. One possible alternative design would limit tests of individual students to relatively narrow content areas, with sufficient numbers of questions given to yield relatively precise estimates of proficiency in these areas from simple summaries such as total scores. The distributions of performance in each of these narrow areas of proficiency could then be easily computed as empirical score distributions, with standard errors computed using jackknife repeated replication. Summary measures such as means of proficiencies aggregated over the narrow areas would also be easy to derive, but distributions of the aggregate summaries would not be available, since there would be no information on how each student performs on areas other than the one tested. Thus, results from this simplified design and analysis would appear to be much more limited. Furthermore, the information obtained from each student would be proscribed by focusing on the relatively precise measurement of a particular skill, rather than less precise measurement of proficiencies for a wider range of skills.

NAEP Reporting

Much attention has focused on improving NAEP reports, and progress recently has been made in more quickly issuing the primary reports. However, in our view, the clarity of NAEP's main messages, the presentation of tables, graphs, and statistical data, and the general utility of the reports still can be much improved. In addition, we note that states continue to ask for a shorter timetable for releasing state results.

Specifically, our analysis of reporting for current NAEP and its timeliness, clarity, and utility suggests the following.

Timeliness

As we have noted, a major effort of the NAEP program has been to produce reports, especially the *Report Cards*, in a more timely manner. Earlier in the program, national results were issued 18 to 24 months after administration, and trend reports were published as long as 24 to 30 months after the data collection. The 1996 NAEP mathematics and science *Report Cards* (Reese et al., 1997; O'Sullivan et al., 1997) were published 11 and 13 months, respectively, after the administration. The 1996 trend report was issued in August 1997 (Campbell et al., 1997), approximately 15 months after the administration was completed. We find these time lines impressive.

Clarity

Despite recent improvements in reporting student achievement results for the nation, states, and major demographic groups, NAEP reports still are frequently viewed as being overly complex. We believe the complexity of reports is partly a function of the complexity of the program. As we have noted, the design and analysis of NAEP data are complex and hard to understand, even for relatively sophisticated users.

The development of clear and comprehensible reports for nontechnical readers is and should continue to be a high priority for the program. The committee believes that it is possible to present results in clear and comprehensible ways to nontechnical readers. The development of clear methods of presentation should continue to be a high priority for NAEP analysts; the limitations of the data should be deliberately and fully communicated in the reports. Specific efforts to enhance report clarity might include:

- providing examples of assessment tasks to aid with interpretation,
- field-testing all tables and displays prior to release,
- developing and including a glossary of terms with reports,
- developing summary reports that present NAEP findings in a concise format, and
- developing and providing states with a protocol of state assessment media press packages complete with appropriate and inappropriate test interpretations.

We make other suggestions for increasing the clarity of reports below and in Chapter 4.

Reporting Metrics

An obstacle to understanding NAEP data comes with the fact that results are reported on a proficiency scale that is indirectly tied to performance on specific questions. As noted by the NAGB Design/Feasibility Team (Forsyth et al., 1996), a more promising approach may be to work harder to present results in a more intuitive and easily understood metric. The Design/Feasibility Team describes an approach that relates proficiencies to performance on a broad-ranging collection or market basket of items, rather than to the latent proficiency scales that emerge directly from the IRT models. They explained that plausible value predictions of performance on a standard market basket of items could be created and summary results presented in terms of these predictions. The underlying IRT models still would provide the glue for calibrating across items and individuals, but the analysis would be in terms of a more understandable metric. The item collection would be published so that users could review the items students attempted. We urge NAGB and NCES to conduct research on the market basket and other reporting metrics with potential to simplify the interpretation of results by NAEP's users. Research on improved reporting metrics should receive as much attention as research on NAEP's psychometrics.

We also encourage the NAEP program to reexamine the way that scale score and achievement-level results are reported in NAEP documents. When presenting descriptive and evaluative results in the *Report Cards*, the data should not be presented in disassociated chapters or separate reports written by different authors. The findings should be discussed in an integrated way and accompanied by a description of the relationship between the two portrayals. Reports should indicate how well students performed and how well that performance stacked up against expectations.

Utility

Despite the variety of reports, many users do not yet feel that NAEP reports serve them as well as they could. The concerns voiced by various current and potential audiences for NAEP reports were identified and summarized for NAGB in 1993 in a review by the Widmeyer Group. In general, policy makers, teachers, administrators, and parents said that achievement data are important but that NAEP results and reports do not point them to potential implications for policy and practice. We contend that the NAEP program should report descriptive (scale score/proficiency), evaluative (achievement levels), and contextual, interpretive information in a well integrated report series. Users would thus have on hand (1) information about levels of student performance, (2) an evaluation of how well student achievement measures up to performance standards, and (3) information that helps them better understand student strengths and weaknesses and guides them in thinking about what to do in response to the findings.

It will be challenging to present this comprehensive set of information in ways that make clear the interrelationships between the portrayals and the unique contributions of each report. NAEP *Report Cards* have and should include the descriptive and achievement-level results in the same reports. By necessity, reports that provide interpretive information internal to the test—that is, based on in-depth analyses of students' responses to individual items or sets of items—would follow initial reports. Generation of reports that draw on data from the coordinated system to help interpret NAEP results also would follow in a secondary reporting stage.

The release of second-stage reports should be guided by a dissemination strategy that seeks to garner as much, if not more, attention from the press, the public, and policy makers as the initial reports. The associations between reports and their unique objectives and contributions should be clearly and prominently articulated.

We extend this idea to the reporting of trend and main NAEP data. If mechanisms for integrating trend NAEP and main NAEP are implemented, the initial *Report Cards* should present current and trend results in tandem (not in separate reports or separate sections of the same report), since the trend information provides an important context for interpreting current results.

TOWARD A MORE UNIFIED DESIGN FOR NAEP

Like NAGB and NCES, the committee contends that NAEP's designs should be streamlined. There are a number of arguments for seeking to combine the data collection efforts. Several already have been mentioned; others are discussed next.

Rationale for Combining Designs

Inconsistent Findings

The existence of multiple assessments is potentially confusing to NAEP's constituencies; for example, it can and has led to situations in which the trend in results in two successive national NAEPs are in the opposite direction from trends in successive trend NAEPs over the same time period. Figures 2-1 through 2-6 show NAEP results for reading and mathematics by grade for the national NAEP and the trend NAEP designs. The potential for confusion is illustrated in Figure 2-1, which plots summary results from grade 4 reading. For example, mean NAEP reading scores for grade 4 went up between 1988 and 1990 for national NAEP and down for trend NAEP over the same period. Indeed, for the

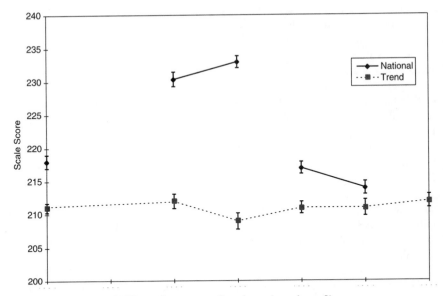

FIGURE 2-1 Mean NAEP reading scores (fourth grade and age 9).

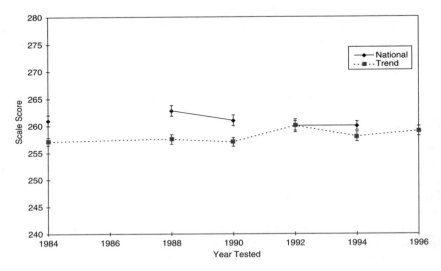

FIGURE 2-2 Mean NAEP reading scores (eighth grade and age 13).

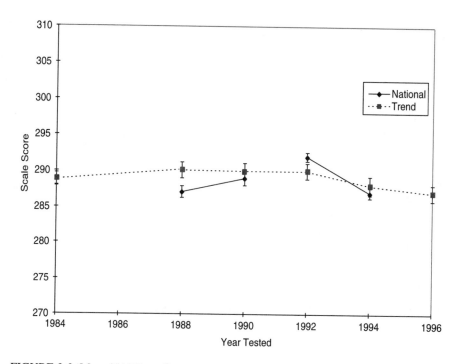

FIGURE 2-3 Mean NAEP reading scores (twelfth grade and age 17).

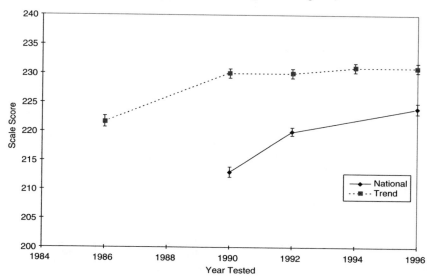

FIGURE 2-4 Mean NAEP mathematics scores (fourth grade and age 9).

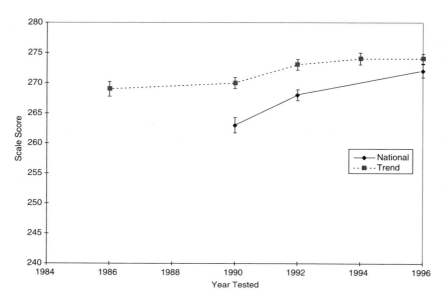

FIGURE 2-5 Mean NAEP mathematics scores (eighth grade and age 13).

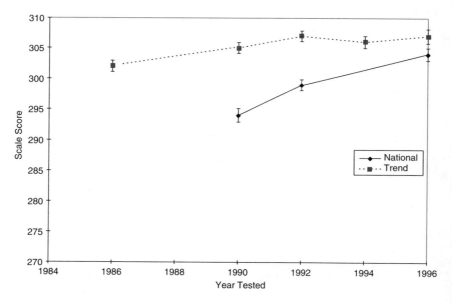

FIGURE 2-6 Mean NAEP mathematics scores (twelfth grade and age 17).

12 most obvious data comparisons across grades and disciplines (the three grades and four time periods from 1990 to 1992 and from 1992 to 1996 in mathematics and from 1988 to 1990 and from 1992 to 1994 in reading), four periods show similar results on national NAEP and trend NAEP and eight show dissimilar results.[1] Replication is useful for uncovering methodological inconsistencies, but it is not obvious what conclusions can be drawn from discordant results across somewhat different designs.

Meaningfulness of Trend Frameworks

Trend NAEP is designed to keep changes in design, administration, and questions to a minimum. The anomalies in the reading results for 1986 and 1994 NAEP (Zwick, 1991; Hedges and Venesky, 1997) demonstrated that very modest changes in data collection and assessment procedures can have unexpectedly large effects on assessment results. Analyses of the 1986 incident, including a set of randomized experiments built into the subsequent (1988) assessment, led measurement specialists to conclude that if you want to measure change, don't change the measure.

Despite the obvious wisdom of this approach in the short run, it may have some drawbacks over longer periods of time. It is not inconceivable that, held constant for long periods of time, frameworks become increasingly irrelevant by failing to reflect changes in curricula and instructional practice. An increasing gap between assessment and practice could make estimated trends from assessments built to old frameworks potentially misleading.

We examined this assertion in an attempt to push our thinking about design alternatives. We commissioned research to assess the relevance of NAEP trend items to current standards and instructional practice (Zieleskiewicz, 1999). Middle school teachers and disciplinary specialists were asked to examine a set of trend NAEP materials and main NAEP items to determine their relevance to current curriculum and instruction in mathematics and science. Respondents were asked about the extent to which students currently have opportunities to master the knowledge and skills addressed by the items. They also relayed their perceptions of the relevance of the trend NAEP and main NAEP items to national disciplinary standards. Zieleskiewicz sought the views of teachers in states on the vanguard of standards-based reform and in a randomly selected group of states. She also surveyed disciplinary specialists active in mathematics and science reform at the national level.

The resulting data are described and summarized in a volume of papers commissioned to inform our evaluation (National Research Council, 1999). The

---

[1]Two of the inconsistencies in national NAEP and trend NAEP data may be attributable to anomalies in the 1994 reading results for grades 4 and 12.

data show that teachers and disciplinary specialists rated trend NAEP and main NAEP items similarly on students' opportunity to learn tested knowledge and skills and on their relevance to current curricula and national standards. That is, in this trial and on these dimensions, disciplinary specialists and middle school mathematics and science faculty did not distinguish between trend items and items written to current frameworks. We do not know whether similar data would result for the other grade levels in mathematics or science or for other subject areas, but for this grade and these subjects, the data showed that trend and main NAEP items are similarly aligned with current practice and standards. The findings run counter to the common presumption that trend instrumentation is dated and bolster arguments for developing and maintaining a single trend line for current NAEP. The data are consistent with arguments for streamlining trend assessment for current NAEP.

Costliness and Burden

As we have said, the current NAEP designs involve separate samples, tests, and data collection procedures. This practice is costly, since it constitutes essentially three different data collection programs. Past evaluators have discussed direct costs and attempted to estimate indirect costs for the state and national designs (KPMG Peat Marwick LLP and Mathtech, 1996). Currently, assessment of two subjects and two grades by state NAEP is nearly as expensive as testing two subjects at three grades by national NAEP. In addition, the separate data collections place a burden on small and low-population states and large districts that may have had a deleterious effect on participation. Additional inefficiencies are associated with ongoing administration of assessments for every trend line the NAEP program supports. As currently configured, every cycle of trend NAEP administration, analysis, and reporting adds $4,000,000 to NAEP program costs.

Merging the Main NAEP and Trend NAEP Designs

Many assert that maintaining a statistical series is the most important thing NAEP does (Forsyth et al., 1996), and we agree that this should remain a major priority in the future. However, the current means for achieving this goal are inefficient and not without problems, as discussed above. It is the committee's judgment that trend and main NAEP should be reconfigured to allow accurate and efficient estimation of trends. Our conception of a combined design would accord main NAEP the more stable characteristics of trend NAEP in repeated administrations over 10-to-20 year time spans. The main objective would be to minimize the design flux that has characterized main NAEP, with the goal that it reliably assess not only current level but also trends in core subject areas. This proposal is consistent with the ideas about NAEP's redesign offered by NAGB (National Assessment Governing Board, 1997), the NAGB Design/Feasibility

Team (Forsyth et al., 1996), and the NAE panel (National Academy of Education, 1997).

In a paper published in a volume that accompanies this report, Michael Kolen (1999a) offered a number of suggestions for phasing out the current trend data collection and continuing with main NAEP while maintaining a long-term trend line. As background for his proposals, Kolen discussed differences between the assessments, including variation in content, operational procedures, examinee subgroup definitions, analysis procedures, and results.

In cataloguing differences between the two designs, Kolen explained that the content specifications for trend NAEP were developed and have been stable since 1983/1984 for reading and writing and 1985/1986 for mathematics and science, whereas the frameworks for main NAEP have evolved. He noted that trend NAEP has a higher proportion of multiple-choice than constructed-response items in comparison to main NAEP. In main NAEP, he said, students are given test items in a single subject area, and in trend NAEP students test in more than one subject area.

Kolen also explained that main NAEP oversamples minority students to permit subgroup comparisons, but trend NAEP does not. Subgroup definitions also differ for the two designs. Main NAEP identifies students' race and ethnicity information from multiple sources, giving priority to student-reported information. Trend NAEP uses administrators' observations to designate students' race. Kolen noted the differences between grade-based sampling for main NAEP and age-based sampling and reporting for trend NAEP.

After recounting differences between the two assessments, Kolen presented five designs for estimating long-term trends with NAEP and laid out the statistical assumptions, linking studies, and research required to develop and support the designs. In one design, Kolen proposed monitoring long-term trends with the main NAEP assessment and using overlapping NAEP assessments to initially link main NAEP to trend NAEP and then to link sequential assessments whenever assessment frameworks and/or designs are modified. He explained that implementation of this design relies on the conduct of research to estimate the effects of differences between subgroup and cohort definitions and administration conditions on main NAEP and trend NAEP. Research to examine the effects of content differences and differences in item types for trend NAEP, main NAEP, and successive assessments would also needed. Linking and scaling research would be needed initially to place main NAEP results on the trend scale or trend results on the main scale and, again, to continue the trend line as NAEP evolves. Because long-term trends would be assessed with main NAEP in this design, main NAEP must be more stable than it has been in the past, Kolen explained.

In another design, Kolen suggested allowing main NAEP to change to reflect current curricula and use a separate trend assessment, with occasional updating, to maintain a trend line. With this design, modest changes in the content of trend NAEP would be allowed to ensure its relevance, but the operational conditions of the assessment would remain constant. This design would allow for the replacement of some items in the trend instruments and alternate forms of the trend instruments would be equated. The design would continue to provide long-term trend estimates without an extensive research program, but it requires the continuation of both assessments. For Kolen's discussion of these and alternative models, see the volume of research papers that accompanies this report.

Assessing NAEP Disciplines

It is important to note that proposals for merging trend NAEP and main NAEP are limited to the large-scale assessments in reading, writing, mathematics, and science. We discuss this construction in greater detail below but, again, note that assessment of these disciplines using large-scale assessment methods is part of the core NAEP component of our proposal for new paradigm NAEP (see Chapter 1). If history, geography, or other disciplines are assessed frequently enough in the large-scale survey program to support trend estimation, these too would constitute core NAEP, but tracking trends back to the 1970s and 1980s would not be possible in these subjects.

As we stated in Chapter 1, NAEP should address those disciplines for which testing frequency generally prohibits the establishment of trend lines using multiple assessment methods, rather than as components of the NAEP large-scale assessment program. This approach has two possible advantages: (1) by reducing scale and releasing resources, it enables more in-depth treatment of these subject areas and the teaching and learning opportunities that define them and (2) it affords more frequent measurement and trend estimation for core disciplines and may allow more thorough reporting in these subjects. We include the assessment of noncore subjects in our proposal for multiple-methods NAEP. Chapter 4 provides further discussion of this and other components of multiple-methods NAEP.

High School Testing

A number of conditions point to insufficient clarity about the meaning of results for high school examinees under the current designs. First, test administrators observe that some high school examinees do not make a serious effort to answer NAEP questions, rendering their scores of questionable value. The administrators' observations are corroborated by the high omit and noncompletion rates of 17-year-olds on trend NAEP and seniors on national NAEP. The nonresponse rates are particularly high on the constructed-response items for national NAEP. Despite concerted effort to date, the NAEP program and stakeholders have been unable to identify workable incentives for high school students' participation and effort.

Second, the curricula of high school students are variable; course-taking patterns are sufficiently variable that it is difficult to render judgments about students' opportunity to learn tested content, particularly for older high school students. Finally, differential dropout rates muddy the interpretation of high school results across locales and over time. Differing school-leaving rates over time make the meaning of score changes unclear. The same logic applies to cross-state comparisons.

In the committee's judgment, NAGB and NCES should explore alternatives to the current assessment practices for twelfth graders. Testing high school students at an earlier grade (grade 10 or 11) or using longitudinal studies as the primary source of achievement data for high school students, with assessments still tied to NAEP frameworks, may bear consideration. In fact, NCES recently proposed a follow-up data collection on NAEP twelfth graders to study their postsecondary plans and opportunities. Following up on high school dropouts to include them in the NAEP samples also should be considered. Assessing high school students using multiple measurement methods—in smaller settings and perhaps with more engaging tasks—may moderate current motivation problems. Multiple-methods assessment may also permit collection of richer data on students' high school experiences and their plans for work, higher education, and the military. A shift to this strategy should occur in conjunction with the implementation of a new series of framework and assessments, otherwise the current main NAEP short-term trend lines for high school seniors would be disrupted.

Streamlining the National and State Designs

National NAEP and state NAEP use the same instrumentation but differ in the populations for which inferences are to be made. If NAEP was first being designed today, the idea of distinct samples and administration procedures for state and national estimates would no doubt be rapidly rejected in favor of a single design that attempts to address both population groups. Declining participation rates and earlier mentioned arguments about burden and inefficiency suggest the need to coordinate designs for national and state NAEP. In 1996 the NAE panel recommended that the scope and function of the state assessment program be reviewed in the context of an overall reevaluation of the NAEP program; at the same time, they noted that state NAEP is an important component of the NAEP program and recommended that it move beyond a developmental status. We agree with their assessment and recommend that the state component be accorded permanent status in the next congressional reauthorization of NAEP. As state NAEP moves from trial to permanent status, it makes sense to consider streamlining the national and state designs.

NAEP historically has been successful at garnering participation in the state assessment program. State commitment to the 1998 program, however, declined in relation to earlier assessments. Fewer states signed up for 1998 testing than participated in 1996. The NAEP program suspects the decrease is attributable to increasingly heavy state and local testing requirements. Without a mandate to participate in NAEP and without local feedback for NAEP testing, state and district testing directors may accord state NAEP lower priority than other assessments (Kelly Weddel, National Center for Education Statistics, personal communication, April 8, 1998).

Separate state and national testing is costly, since it requires that national NAEP and state NAEP are essentially two different data collection programs. Recall that the state program costs as much as the national assessment for testing at fewer grades. As discussed by Rust (1996), a more coordinated design for the two components was considered by the contractors for the 1996 assessment, but it was rejected because of operational concerns involving equating and the choice of subjects and grades assessed. Despite this, in our view it may be possible to combine these two programs into a single design.

Several differences between the current state and national designs merit attention in any discussion of their possible combination. State NAEP and national NAEP could be combined only if both assess the same grades and subjects. State NAEPs have assessed only fourth and eighth graders in mathematics, science, reading, and, in 1998, writing. And there appears to be little interest among the states in a state NAEP assessment of twelfth graders (DeVito, 1996). The coordination of state and national NAEP assessment cohorts and subjects is a solvable problem. For example, a combined program could assess reading, writing, mathematics, science, and any other subjects designated as core in grades four and eight. High school testing could continue with a national sample.

A second difference between current state and national NAEP is that the administration of national NAEP is carried out by a NAEP contractor, whereas the administration of state NAEP is carried out by school personnel, with training and monitoring (on a sampling basis) by a NAEP contractor. The use of school personnel for test administration is substantially less costly (at least in terms of direct costs to NAEP) than the use of a NAEP contractor for that purpose. However, the difference in procedures raises questions about the comparability of data derived from these two different data collection procedures. Differences may be attributable to the actions of the test administrators, or they may be due to the potentially greater motivation associated with a test that yields scores for a state, rather than for the nation.

Spencer (1997a) recently concluded that an equating adjustment may be necessary to bring estimates from data collected under state NAEP conditions into conformity with those from data collected under national NAEP conditions. He notes that comparisons of item responses in state and national NAEP showed that the scores were generally higher in state NAEP than in a subsample of national data comparable to the state data. The average differences were small enough to be attributable to sampling error (that is, reasonably consistent with the hypothesis of no true difference) in 1992, but not in 1990 or 1994 (Hartka and McLaughlin, 1994; Hartka et al., 1997a). For example, in 1994 the difference between state NAEP and a comparable subset of the national NAEP in percent correct on a common set of items was 3.1 percent (56.0 percent versus 52.9 percent), which is substantial. Furthermore, differences between the percent correct observed under state NAEP and national NAEP coordinators were not uniform across states.

This and other research suggests that sizable calibration samples may be needed to adjust or equate estimates derived from current state NAEP to make them comparable to those from national NAEP. It is unclear whether calibration samples would be necessary in every state in which main NAEP data would be derived from state NAEP administrations, or if calibration samples would be necessary in every state in which national NAEP data would be derived from state NAEP administrations. The need for calibration samples would reduce cost savings and sampling efficiencies from combining state and national NAEP. Hence, a goal of a coordinated design would be to avoid the need for calibration samples by minimizing differences in administration for the state and national NAEP samples. This design option seems preferable to analytical adjustments for the effects of differences in administration before data from different administration conditions are combined.

The third difference between state and national NAEP may be in levels of nonsampling errors. Nonsampling errors are, in general, difficult to analyze or even to detect. However, in the 1994 assessment, there appeared to be some differences in the rates of school nonparticipation on state and national NAEP in the fourth grade (Hartka et al., 1997b). The implications for bias, however, are unclear (Spencer, 1997a, 1997b). To some extent, they depend on how well the mechanisms used to adjust for the effects of nonparticipation (namely substitution and reweighting) function to eliminate bias. Some research suggests that these mechanisms have worked reasonably well in NAEP (Hartka et al., 1997b).

Specific suggestions for streamlining the national and state designs rely on additional research. More needs to be known about the effects of the differences in participation rates, administration, and other potential sources of bias. In a paper in the volume that accompanies this report, Kolen (1999b) recounted design alternatives proposed by Spencer (1997a) and Rust and Shaffer (1997). The alternatives vary in sampling approaches, administration procedures, and analytic adjustments. In proposing next steps, Kolen laid out research questions that must be answered in attempting to streamline NAEP designs:

• To what extent are the linking constants equal across states? Differences among states in ability, participation rates, and recruitment procedures should be investigated as variables that might influence linking constants.
• How large is the random error component in estimating the linking constants?
• To what extent does bias or systematic error influence the linking constants?

• Do the differences in administration and recruitment conditions affect the constructs that are being measured by the NAEP assessments?

These questions should be thoroughly addressed before any design for combining national and state NAEP samples is implemented under current recruitment and administration conditions.

SUMMARY OF PROPOSED DESIGN FEATURES

A number of characteristics distinguish our proposal for a new paradigm NAEP:

• Trends in reading, writing, mathematics, science, and other subjects for which there are sufficient resources would be estimated by core NAEP using large-scale assessment methods (separate testing for trend NAEP and main NAEP would be discontinued).
• National and state estimates would be reported by core NAEP, but efficiency in sampling and reduction in testing burden would be realized for the two designs.
• For subjects for which administration frequency generally prohibits the establishment of trend lines, testing would occur at the national level using multiple measurement methods. (Multiple-methods NAEP is described in Chapter 4.)

Figure 2-7 shows new paradigm NAEP as we have discussed it.

MAJOR CONCLUSIONS AND RECOMMENDATIONS

Conclusions

Conclusion 2A. **The existence of multiple NAEP assessments is confusing and creates problems of burden, costliness, and inconsistent findings.**

Conclusion 2B. **The current collection of meaningful NAEP data in the twelfth grade is problematic given the insufficient motivation of high school seniors and their highly variable curricula and dropout rates.**

Conclusion 2C. **Because of its complexity and the many demands of its constituents, NAEP has developed multiple, dissociated reporting metrics and types of reports.**

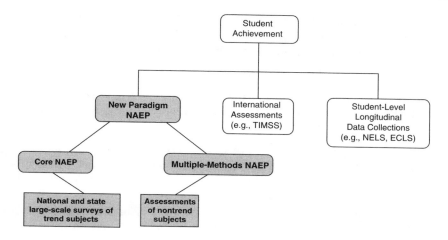

FIGURE 2-7 Measures of student achievement, including new paradigm NAEP. NOTE: TIMSS = Third International Mathematics and Science Study; NELS = National Education Longitudinal Study; ECLS = Early Childhood Longitudinal Study.

Recommendations

Recommendation 2A. **For reading, writing, mathematics, and science, combine main NAEP and trend NAEP into a single design that preserves the measurement of trends and allows periodic updating of frameworks. If resources allow, trends could be established in other subject areas.**

Recommendation 2B. **In those disciplines for which testing frequency generally prohibits the establishment of trend lines, assessment of student achievement should be accomplished using a variety of assessment methods and targeted student samples.**

Recommendation 2C. **Alternatives to current NAEP assessment practices for twelfth graders should be explored, including: testing at grades 10 or 11, following up on high school dropouts to include them in NAEP's samples, and gathering data on the achievement of high school students primarily through NCES's longitudinal surveys.**

Recommendation 2D. **Coordinate the sampling and administrative procedures for national and state NAEP in order to reduce burden and decrease costs.**

Recommendation 2E. **The development of clear, comprehensible, and well integrated reports of NAEP results should remain a high priority, and reports should be redesigned to reflect NAEP's streamlined designs.**

Recommendation 2F. **In order to accomplish the recommendations listed above, NAEP's research and development agenda should emphasize the following:**

- **Estimation of the effects of differences in sample definition, content, task types, and administration procedures for trend NAEP and main NAEP with subsequent derivation of links to support the use of a single trend line in each discipline,**
- **Estimation of the effects of the differences in participation rates, administration procedures, and bias for state and national NAEP with subsequent development of more efficient sampling procedures,**
- **Exploration of alternatives for obtaining meaningful data from high school students, and**
- **Development of clear, comprehensible reports and reporting metrics that provide descriptive, evaluative, and interpretive information in a carefully articulated and described report series.**

3

Enhancing the Participation and Meaningful Assessment of All Students in NAEP

Summary Conclusion 3. **NAEP has the goal of reporting results that reflect the achievement of all students in the nation. However, many students with disabilities and English-language learners have been excluded from the assessments. Some steps have been taken recently to expand the participation of these students in NAEP, but their performance remains largely invisible.**

Summary Recommendation 3. **NAEP should enhance the participation, appropriate assessment, and meaningful interpretation of data for students with disabilities and English-language learners. NAEP and the proposed system of education indicators should include measures that improve understanding of the performance and educational needs of these populations.**

INTRODUCTION

Over the past decade, national concern about and attention to the assessment of students with disabilities and English-language learners has intensified, paralleling the growth in numbers of students with limited English proficiency[1] and

---

[1]The most commonly used term to refer to students who come from language backgrounds other than English and whose English proficiency is not yet developed to the point at which they can profit fully from English-only instruction is limited English proficient (LEP). LEP is the term used in many national and state data collections, federal and state legislation, and court cases involving these students (National Research Council and Institute of Medicine, 1997). In this report, we refer to these students as English-language learners, which is a more positive term. We consider the terms "English-language learner" and "student with limited English proficiency" to be synonymous.

the numbers of students who are identified with physical, learning, or emotional disabilities. This concern and attention is also in large measure a response to several pieces of legislation passed by the United States Congress, which specifically required the participation of *all* students in assessments used to measure student performance.

Enacted by Congress in 1994, the Goals 2000: Educate America Act (P.L. 103-227) provided resources to implement systemic education reforms to help all students meet challenging academic standards; it specifically provided funds to support the participation and accommodation of students with disabilities and English-language learners in assessments. Similarly, the Perkins Act (P.L. 98-524), although primarily focusing on vocational and technical education, mandated the use of appropriate methodologies in testing both students with disabilities and English-language learners. Both Title I and Title VII of the Improving America's Schools Act of 1994 (P.L. 103-328) state the need to assess all children and to provide reasonable adaptations and accommodations for students with disabilities, as well as for children who are in the process of learning English. The Department of Education Organization Act of 1994 specifically states that the secretary must ensure that English-language learners are included in assessments in ways that are valid, reliable, and fair (National Research Council and Institute of Medicine, 1997:132-133). Other legislation, such as the Americans with Disabilities Act (1990) and the Individuals with Disabilities Education Act (as amended, 1997) specifically urges the participation and reasonable accommodation of students with disabilities.

The 1997 amendments to the Individuals with Disabilities Education Act (IDEA) include provisions intended to increase the participation of students with disabilities in state- and district-wide assessment programs, with appropriate accommodations when necessary. The individualized education plans (IEPs) of students with disabilities, which are required by law for each child with a disability, must include statements of any accommodations or other modifications needed by the student to participate in the state- and district-wide assessments. If the student's IEP team determines that the student cannot participate, the IEP plan must include a statement of why the student will not participate and describe how the student will be assessed. Alternate assessments for these students must be in place not later than July 1, 2000. Finally, states must ensure proper reporting of information regarding the performance of students with disabilities on large-scale assessments.

NAEP and other assessment programs thus have a clear federal mandate to enhance the participation and meaningful assessment of English-language learners and students with disabilities. This participation is especially important for NAEP. NAEP's mission, to serve as a key indicator of the academic achievement of the nation's students, can be satisfactorily accomplished only if the assessment results include and portray data gathered from *all* groups of students, including students with disabilities and English-language learners.

In this chapter we present an analysis of NAEP's progress, through the 1996 assessments, to enhance the participation and accommodation of students with disabilities and English-language learners. We begin by presenting population data that make clear why the participation of these students is needed to provide an accurate view of national-level achievement. We then review progress in participation and accommodation that has been made in large-scale assessment programs across the nation, recounting NAEP's efforts and accomplishments during the 1990s. We discuss the underlying challenge of accurate and consistent identification and classification of English-language learners and students with disabilities, and close the chapter by presenting a series of recommendations to guide NAEP's continuing efforts on this front.

ENGLISH-LANGUAGE LEARNERS AND STUDENTS WITH DISABILITIES

An examination of recent trends in the nation's student population provides pointed insight as to why better understanding of the educational achievements and experiences of students with disabilities and English-language learners are needed. Students with disabilities are approximately 12 percent of the kindergarten through grade 12 (K-12) student population (Olson and Goldstein, 1997:154). In recent years, the numbers of students participating in federal programs for students with disabilities have increased at a faster rate than total K-12 public school enrollment, at least in part because students with disabilities are increasingly better identified. Between 1977 and 1995, the number of students with disabilities increased by 47 percent and the total public school population decreased by 2 percent. During that same period, the percentage of children with specific learning disabilities increased from 1.8 to 5.7 percent of the total public K-12 enrollment, and those with speech and language impairments and mental retardation decreased slightly (Olson and Goldstein, 1997:154). Better understanding of the performance of these students and their place in the educational system is needed, because 25 percent of children ages 5 to 17 who have a disabling condition repeat at least one grade in school (Olson and Goldstein, 1997:54), and students with disabilities have higher dropout rates and lower graduation rates (Valdés et al., 1990; U.S. Department of Education, 1996).

In 1991, 2.3 million students—5.5 percent of the total K-12 student population—were classified as English-language learners (Fleischman and Hopstock, 1993:10). Nearly 1.7 million (73 percent) of these English-language learners are native speakers of Spanish. No other language is spoken by more than 4 percent of English-language learners (Fleischman and Hopstock, 1993:11). The percentage of English-language learners in the K-12 population decreases from 8.4 percent in kindergarten to 6.0 percent in grade 4, 4.2 percent in grade 8, and 3.2 percent in grade 12 (see Table 3-1; Fleischman and Hopstock, 1993:10).

English-language learners are concentrated in the West, in urban areas, and

TABLE 3-1 English-Language Learners in Each Grade Level

Grade Level	Number of English-Language Learners	Percentage of English-Language Learners in Grade Level	Total Students in U.S.	Percentage of English-Language Learners of Total Students
Kindergarten	277,914	12.1	3,305,619	8.4%
1st grade	279,257	12.1	3,554,274	7.9
2nd grade	246,979	10.7	3,359,193	7.4
3rd grade	221,936	9.6	3,333,285	6.7
4th grade	**197,211**	**8.6**	**3,312,443**	**6.0**
5th grade	177,412	7.7	3,268,381	5.4
6th grade	150,421	6.5	3,238,095	4.6
7th grade	134,907	5.9	3,180,120	4.2
8th grade	**125,849**	**5.5**	**3,019,826**	**4.2**
9th grade	159,208	6.9	3,310,290	4.8
10th grade	137,101	5.9	2,913,951	4.7
11th grade	103,337	4.5	2,642,554	3.9
12th grade	**75,423**	**3.3**	**2,390,329**	**3.2**
Ungraded	16,469	0.7	—	—
Total	2,303,424	100.0%	40,828,360	5.5%

NOTES: Data based on mail survey to school districts. Data for the grades at which main NAEP assessments are administered are highlighted in bold-faced type.
SOURCE: Fleischman and Hopstock (1993:10).

in large schools with 750 or more students. Schools with 20 percent or more minority students and 20 percent or more students receiving free or reduced-price lunches are also more likely to enroll larger proportions of English-language learners. A total of 42 percent of all public school teachers have at least one English-language learner in their classes; 7 percent of these teachers have classes in which over 50 percent of their students are identified as English-language learners (Olson and Goldstein, 1997).

This group of students warrants national attention because a large number of non-English-speaking children have both low levels of academic performance in English and high dropout rates. On average, English-language learners are classified as underachievers by their teachers and receive lower grades. They also score below their classmates on standardized mathematics and reading tests (Bradby, 1992).

In summary, students with disabilities and English-language learners comprise a significant proportion of the students in U.S. classrooms (12 percent and 5.5 percent, respectively). Their achievement must be reflected in NAEP results. A NAEP that does not include these students is a report card for only 85 to 90 percent of the nation's students.

EFFORTS TO ENHANCE PARTICIPATION IN NAEP
AND OTHER LARGE-SCALE ASSESSMENTS

In the last several years, a number of activities have focused on increasing the participation of students with disabilities and English-language learners in large-scale assessments from which they had previously been excluded. These activities have focused on approaches that can be used in developing and administering assessments in ways that are meaningful, challenging, and appropriate for all students. A number of interested offices within the U.S. Department of Education have strongly supported emerging efforts to increase the representation of these groups of students in NAEP and other large-scale assessments, including the Office of Educational Research and Improvement, the Office of Civil Rights, the Office of Bilingual Education and Minority Languages Affairs, the Office of Special Education and Rehabilitative Services, the Office of the General Counsel, and the National Center for Education Statistics. Outside the Department of Education, a number of organizations have also contributed to these efforts. These activities underscore the importance of the problem for various groups around the country, as well as the need to explore thoroughly the feasibility of developing valid and reliable procedures for including previously excluded students.

Two reports issued by the National Research Council in 1997 provide an important foundation from which strategies for enhancing participation and accommodation of students with disabilities and English-language learners can be built. *Educating One and All: Students with Disabilities and Standards-Based Reform* (National Research Council, 1997) provides a review and analysis of the current status of students with disabilities in assessment systems. The report presents two broad recommendations that provide guidance for program-specific efforts, such as those we describe later in this chapter for NAEP:

> Even if the individual needs of some students require alterations of the common standards and assessments, the committee strongly recommends that these students should be counted in a universal, public accountability system (pp. 9-10). Assessment accommodations should be provided, but they should be used only to offset the impact of disabilities unrelated to the knowledge and skills being measured. They should also be justified on a case-by-case basis, but individual decisions should be guided by a uniform set of criteria (p. 10).

The second report, *Improving Schooling for Language-Minority Children: A Research Agenda* (National Research Council and Institute of Medicine, 1997) summarizes the state of knowledge and key issues in the assessment of English-language proficiency and subject-matter knowledge for language-minority students. The report also provides a detailed agenda for research on both classroom-level and large-scale assessments. One recommendation in particular captures the key challenge for NAEP and other large-scale assessments:

Research is needed to develop assessments and assessment procedures that incorporate more English-language learners. Further, research is needed toward developing guidelines for determining when English-language learners are ready to take the same assessments as their English-proficient peers and when versions of the assessment other than the "standard" English version should be administered (p. 130).

To date, a number of different activities have taken place that parallel the directions recommended in these reports. Efforts to increase the participation of students with disabilities and English-language learners in both NAEP and other large-scale assessments have included a number of conferences, reports, commissioned working papers, and funded studies. Table 3-2 summarizes a number of efforts made in the past 15 years to increase the participation of students with disabilities in large-scale assessments. Table 3-3 summarizes similar efforts to increase the participation of English-language learners in large-scale assessments. For additional information in this area, a clear and thorough summary and analysis of recent progress is presented in the 1997 National Center for Education Statistics (NCES) report, *The Inclusion of Students with Disabilities and Limited English Proficient Students in Large-Scale Assessments: A Summary of Recent Progress* (Olson and Goldstein, 1997).

REVIEW OF PROGRESS THROUGH 1996

Prior to 1995, NAEP was administered in classroom-sized sessions as a timed assessment, exclusively in English, and without testing accommodations or adaptations. Schools had therefore been allowed to exclude students from NAEP if, in the judgment of knowledgeable school personnel, such students could not meaningfully participate in the assessment; NAEP personnel did provide specific criteria that schools were expected to use to inform their judgments about which students to exclude from the assessment. As a result of the implementation of these rules, 44 percent of students with disabilities and 41 percent of English-language learners were not included in the 1994 NAEP assessment (Mazzeo, 1997). It was also clear that the application of the criteria for excluding students varied widely across states, districts, and schools, affecting the state NAEP comparisons in unquantifiable ways.

For NAEP, the need to undertake efforts to enhance the participation of students with disabilities and English-language learners was stimulated in part by research from the National Academy of Education's evaluations of NAEP. These studies showed that large numbers of excluded students were capable of taking the NAEP assessment, some with various accommodations and others with no accommodations (National Academy of Education, 1993, 1996, 1997). Also, studies from the National Center on Educational Outcomes showed that up to 85 percent of traditionally excluded students were, in fact, capable of participating in large-scale assessments with appropriate accommodations (National Center on

TABLE 3-2 Efforts and Activities Directed at Increasing the Participation of Students with Disabilities in Large-Scale Assessments

Date	Title	Focus
Reports and Papers		
1980s	Testing Persons with Disabilities: A Report for ETS Programs and Their Constituents (ETS, n.d.)	Summarizes findings of a four-year study on accommodations and test scores.
1988	Testing Handicapped People (Willingham et al., 1988)	Reports on ETS studies conducted during the 1980s in the SAT and GRE testing programs.
1993	Testing Accommodations for Students with Disabilities: A Review of the Literature (NCEO SR4 1993)	Literature review. Recommends that guidelines be developed on both exclusion and inclusion, on accommodations and adaptations, and on score reporting.
1994	Making Decisions about the Inclusion of Students with Disabilities in Large-Scale Assessments: A Report on a Working Conference to Develop Guidelines on Inclusion and Accommodations (NCEO SR13 1994b)	Reports on the 1994 NCES conference listed below. Contains six main recommendations.
1994	Recommendations for Making Decisions about the Participation of Students with Disabilities in Statewide Assessment Programs (NCEO SR 15 1994a)	Includes recommendations for including and accommodating students with disabilities and for reporting results.
1995	A Compilation of States' Guidelines for Including Students with Disabilities in Assessments (NCEO SR17 1995b)	Survey of states' guidelines and policies.
1995	A Compilation of States' Guidelines for Accommodations in Assessments for Students with Disabilities (NCEO SR18 1995a)	Survey of states' guidelines and policies.
1995	Working Paper on Assessing Students with Disabilities and Limited English Proficiency (Houser, 1995)	NCES-commissioned paper. Discusses current NCES policies of exclusion of students with disabilities and LEP students.
1996	Statewide Assessment of Students with Disabilities (Bond, 1996)	Reports on data from the Association of State Assessment Programs. Thirty-seven states reported using special testing accommodations.

TABLE 3-2 Continued

Date	Title	Focus
1997	The Inclusion of Students with Disabilities and Limited English Proficient Students in Large-Scale Assessments: A Summary of Recent Progress (Olson and Goldstein, 1997)	NCES-commissioned report. Summarizes recent progress.

Conference

1994	Working Conference on Guidelines for Inclusion of Students with Disabilities and Accommodations in Large-Scale Assessment Programs	NCES-sponsored conference.

Studies and Projects

1997	Study of Exclusion and Assessability of Students with Disabilities in the 1994 Trial State Assessment of the National Assessment of Educational Progress (Stancavage et al., 1997b)	National Academy of Education-sponsored study. Examines exclusion and assessability of students in 1994 trial state assessment in reading. Findings suggested that 83 percent of fourth grade students with individualized education programs would have been assessable on the NAEP reading instrument based on their reading scores. Includes information about teachers' views on appropriate accommodations.
1997	Educating One and All: Students with Disabilities and Standards-based Reform (National Research Council, 1997)	Topics covered include accountability and assessment, assessment in standards-based reform, and implications of increased participation of students with disabilities in local and large-scale assessments.
On-going	Office of Educational Research and Improvement-funded projects designed to examine the exclusion/inclusion of students with disabilities in state assessments.	Projects funded in the following states: Delaware, Maryland, Minnesota, North Dakota, Oregon, Pennsylvania.
On-going	State Collaborative on Assessment and Student Standards (SCASS)	Involves consortium of 20 states with CCSSO coordinating work on inclusion of students with disabilities in state assessments. SCASS Consortium on Technical Guidelines for Performance Assessment sponsors research projects focusing on common issues.

TABLE 3-2 Continued

Date	Title	Focus
On-going	Investigating the Validity of the Accommodation of Oral Presentation (Weston, 1997)	Research proposal. Focuses on validating oral presentation as an accommodation used with students with disabilities in the category of learning-disabled.

CCSSO: Council of Chief State School Officers
NCEO: National Center for Educational Outcomes
SR: Summary Report

Educational Outcomes, 1994a). Over the past few years, NAEP has taken significant steps to implement enhanced inclusion and accommodations. These are summarized below; it is clear that these efforts have contributed much important information, but they have raised important questions as well (for a more detailed description of these efforts, see Olson and Goldstein, 1997).

The Puerto Rico Special Assessment

In 1994 a special project was carried out involving the development of a Spanish-language mathematics assessment instrument for use in Puerto Rico (the Puerto Rico Assessment of Educational Progress—PRAEP). NAEP assessment items and background questions were translated by staff in Puerto Rico into the Puerto Rican dialect of Spanish. Blocks of mathematics items used in previous assessments were adapted for use in PRAEP. All administration and data collection procedures used were similar to those used in NAEP. Extensive analyses of the data were conducted including examination of responses to background questions, as well as standard item analyses and differential item functioning analyses for the mathematics items. Item response theory (IRT) analyses were performed and results placed on a NAEP-like scale.

A number of problem areas were identified, including the finding that some items were found to have inappropriate translations or content that was not meaningful for students in Puerto Rico (Anderson and Olson, 1996). Researchers also concluded that "it was not possible to express the IRT results for PRAEP on the same scales as the NAEP results. In other words, the scales established for reporting Puerto Rico results were unique for that jurisdiction" (Olson and Goldstein, 1997:69).

TABLE 3-3 Efforts and Activities Directed at Increasing the Participation of English-Language Learners in Large-Scale Assessments

Date	Title	Focus
Reports and Papers		
1991	Summary of State Practices Concerning the Assessment of and the Data Collection about LEP Students (CCSSO, 1991)	CCSSO-sponsored report.
1994	The Feasibility of Collecting Comparable National Statistics about Students with Limited English Proficiency (Cheung et al., 1994)	CCSSO-sponsored report.
1994	Issues in the Development of Spanish-Language Versions of the National Assessment of Educational Progress (Secada, 1994)	National Academy of Education-sponsored. Recommends pilot study.
1994	A Study of Eligibility Exclusions and Sampling: 1992 Trial State Assessment (Spencer, 1994)	National Academy of Education-sponsored. Recommends examination of the cost-benefit analysis implicit in the exclusion of English-language learners.
1994	For All Students: Limited English Proficient Students and Goals 2000 (August et al., 1994)	Makes recommendations about assessments for English-language learners.
1995	Assessment Practices: Developing and Modifying Statewide Assessment for LEP Students (Hafner, 1995)	Paper presented at CCSSO conference.
1995	Working Paper on Assessing Students with Disabilities and Limited English Proficiency (Houser, 1995)	NCES-commissioned paper. Discusses current NCES policies of exclusion of students with disabilities and English-language learners.
1996	Quality and Utility: The 1994 Trial State Assessment in Reading (National Academy of Education, 1996)	Reports that a high proportion of English-language learners would have been assessable. States that most disturbing finding is the exclusion of students with four or more years in English-speaking schools.

TABLE 3-3 Continued

Date	Title	Focus
1996	Proceedings from the Conference on Inclusion Guidelines and Accommodations for Limited English Proficient Students in NAEP (August and McArthur, 1996)	Reports on the 1994 NCES conference listed below. Group cautioned on assessing students in their native language and voiced concern about translations.
1996	The Status Report of Assessment Programs in the United States: State Student Assessment Programs Database, School Year 1994-1995 (Bond et al., 1996)	Reports on data from the Association of State Assessment Programs. Thirty-seven states allowed for the exclusion of English-language learners. A smaller number of accommodations were provided than for students with disabilities. Only 4 states allowed the use of other languages.
1997	The Inclusion of Students with Disabilities and Limited English Proficient Students in Large-Scale Assessments: A Summary of Recent Progress (Olsen and Goldstein, 1977)	NCES-commissioned report. Summarizes recent progress.
1997	A Study Design to Evaluate Strategies for the Inclusion of LEP Students in the NAEP State Trial Assessment (Hakuta and Valdés, 1997)	Suggests general approaches for studying inclusion.

Conference

Date	Title	Focus
1994	NCES Conference on Inclusion Guidelines and Accommodations for Limited English Proficient Students	NCES-sponsored conference.

Studies and Projects

Date	Title	Focus
1997	The Impact of the Linguistic Features of the NAEP Test Items on Student's Performance in NAEP Assessments (Abedi et al., 1997)	Study sponsored by the National Center for Research on Evaluation, Standards, and Student Testing (CRESST). Concludes that the language of mathematics may disproportionately impact the scores of less language-proficient students.

TABLE 3-3 Continued

Date	Title	Focus
1997	Study of Exclusion and Assessability of Students with Limited English Proficiency in the 1994 Trial State Assessment of the National Assessment of Education Progress (Stancavage et al., 1997a)	National Academy of Education-sponsored study. Examines exclusion and assessability of students in 1994 trial state assessment of reading. Findings suggest that students enrolled in bilingual programs are more likely to be excluded from NAEP.
1997	Statewide Assessment Programs: Policies and Practices for the Inclusion of LEP Students	Center for Equity and Excellence (CEEE) sponsored study. Presents findings on state assessment policies.
1997	Accommodation Strategies for English Language Learners on Large-Scale Assessments: Student Characteristics and Other Considerations (Butler and Stevens, 1997)	CRESST-sponsored study.
1997	Improving Schooling for Language Minority Students: A Research Agenda (National Research Council and Institute of Medicine, 1997)	Topics covered include the measurement of English language proficiency, student assessment, and inclusion of students in large-scale assessments.
On-going	State Collaborative on Assessment and Student Standards (SCASS)	Involves consortium of 20 states with CCSSO coordinating work on inclusion of English-language learners in state assessments. SCASS Consortium on Technical Guidelines for Performance Assessment sponsors research projects focusing on common issues.

CCSSO: Council of Chief State School Officers

The 1995 Mathematics Field Test

As part of the 1995 mathematics field test for the 1996 national and state NAEP assessments, NAEP undertook efforts (1) to include more students in the assessment by providing a range of accommodations and (2) to increase the consistency with which decisions about inclusion were made. These efforts attempted to clearly define which students to include and to align these criteria more closely with those of state testing programs.

In order to achieve these goals, the inclusion criteria were modified, beginning with the 1995 NAEP field test. As Olson and Goldstein (1997:61) point out, prior to 1995, the procedures used by NAEP to determine who could participate in the assessment "were based on criteria for *excluding* students." Beginning with the 1995 field test, "the criteria were revised with the intention of making appropriate and consistent decisions about the *inclusion* of students with disabilities and LEP students" [emphasis added]. Schools were instructed to include all English-language learners and students with disabilities who, in the judgment of school staff, were capable of taking the assessment. They were also instructed to err on the side of inclusion. The old and new exclusion or inclusion rules for NAEP are summarized in Table 3-4.

In the 1995 field test, the following accommodations were provided if they were part of the students' normal testing procedure:

For students with disabilities:

- extra testing time,
- multiple sessions,
- individual or small group administrations,
- allowing a facilitator to read directions, items, and/or interpret diagrams or graphs,
- allowing students to give responses orally, using sign language, or point to the response option,
- allowing students to give answers using a special mechanical apparatus, (e.g., a tape recorder, braille typewriter, computer, etc.),
- large-print booklets and large-face calculators, and
- braille booklets and talking calculators.

For English-language learners:

- extra testing time,
- multiple sessions,
- individual or small group administrations,
- allowing a facilitator to read directions, items, and/or interpret diagrams or graphs,
- Spanish-English bilingual assessment booklets, with items in different languages printed on facing pages, and
- Spanish-only assessment booklets.

A number of these accommodations were offered simultaneously, for example, students assessed in bilingual sessions using Spanish-English bilingual assessment booklets could also be given extra time.

The results of the field test—involving both a study of English-language learners and a study of students with disabilities who had individual education plans (IEPs)—indicated that accommodation strategies and procedures could be

TABLE 3-4 Old and New Exclusion or Inclusion Rules for NAEP

Students	Old (1990-1994)	New (1995-1996)
	Exclude if:	Include if:
Students with Disabilities	—Student is mainstreamed less than 50 percent of the time in academic subjects and is judged incapable of participating meaningfully in the assessment, OR —IEP team or equivalent group determines that the student is incapable of participating meaningfully in the assessment.	—Student has an IEP, unless the IEP team or equivalent group determine that the student cannot participate, or if the student's cognitive functioning is so severely impaired that he or she cannot participate, even with accommodations.
English-Language Learners	—Student is native speaker of a language other than English, AND —Enrolled in an English-speaking school (not including bilingual education program) for less than two years, AND —Judged to be incapable of taking part in the assessment.	—Student has received academic instruction primarily in English for at least three years, OR —Student has received academic instruction in English for less than three years, if school staff determine that the student is capable of participating in the assessment in English, OR —Student, whose native language is Spanish, has received academic instruction in English for less than three years, if school staff determine that the student is capable of participating in the assessment in Spanish (if available).

IEP: Individualized education program.

SOURCE: Olson and Goldstein (1997:62).

implemented as part of the NAEP assessment and would allow for the participation of more students in the national assessment.

The study of English-language learners (Anderson et al., 1996) sought to examine the feasibility of using translated versions of NAEP instruments. The study included a close examination of the Spanish language characteristics of the items themselves in order to identify patterns of difficulty in producing equivalent items. The study also included a study of the degree to which it would be possible to scale data from a bilingual version or a Spanish-only version of the mathematics items to fit the NAEP reporting scale.

The issue of scalability was examined by scrutinizing item statistics (average item score and item-total correlation) and by comparing empirical item responses for English-language learners to the IRT functions of the respective English items. The results of the first analysis revealed that, for grade 4 study blocks (both bilingual and Spanish), 71 percent of the items were not parallel to the English version and, for grade 8, 76 percent of the items were not parallel to their English-language analogues. Andersen et al. (1996:31) concluded "[that] the translated versions of the assessment are not parallel in measurement properties to the English version and that scores are not comparable." More recent research (Abedi et al., 1997) has also revealed that simple grammatical translations of NAEP mathematics items to produce Spanish-language versions of the assessment are problematic, especially for linguistically complex items; lexical and semantic translations deserve further exploration as strategies for future accommodations for English-language learners are investigated.

The study of the field test results for students with disabilities (Anderson et al., 1996) provided limited information about psychometric issues because, for the group of students with disabilities, sample sizes were extremely small. The authors conclude that (p. 39):

> descriptive information provides evidence that students with disabilities are responding to many of the items differently than are students in the full sample. This does not indicate noncomparable measurement if the difference exists only due to the IEP group being of lower ability (and thus having lower percent corrects), but the differences in item-total correlations and omit rates indicated that many items may be measuring differently for students with disabilities than for full-sample groups.

The results of the 1995 NAEP field test in mathematics also indicated that use of the new inclusion criteria and the use of accommodations may affect the measurement of trends in student achievement in two ways, and the magnitude of these effects is difficult to evaluate. First, trends could be altered by the inclusion of students who previously would not have participated in NAEP but now appear in the national sample. Second, the availability of accommodations to students who previously would have participated in NAEP without them may have unknown impacts on their achievement.

The 1996 NAEP Assessment

Despite outstanding questions regarding the impact on constructs measured under alternative assessment conditions for English-language learners and students with disabilities, NAEP appropriately decided to move ahead with the new inclusion criteria and the testing accommodations for the 1996 mathematics and science assessments in a way that would both permit measurement of trends and further exploration of the effects of the new criteria and the accommodation procedures.

In 1996, national NAEP was administered to three subsamples. In Sample 1, as in previous NAEP administrations, old inclusion criteria were applied and no accommodations were provided (for trend measurement in mathematics); in Sample 2, the new inclusion criteria were applied, but no accommodations were provided (to measure the effect of the new criteria independent of the effect of providing accommodations); in Sample 3, the new inclusion criteria were applied *and* accommodations were provided (to measure the impact of accommodations above and beyond the new inclusion criteria). The numbers of students included and accommodated in the 1996 mathematics assessment are presented in Table 3-5.

For both students with disabilities and English-language learners and at all three grades, there were no significant differences between the percentages of students included in Sample 1 and Sample 2. Thus, the changes to the inclusion criteria did not have any impact on the rate of inclusion of these groups of students in the assessment. However, at grades 4 and 8, significantly greater percentages of both students with disabilities and English-language learners were included in Sample 3 as compared with Sample 2. Thus, the provision of an expanded array of accommodations positively affected participation in grades 4 and 8, although no similar increase occurred at grade 12 (Reese et al., 1997). Similar results were obtained for the 1996 NAEP science assessment (O'Sullivan et al., 1997). Providing accommodations moves NAEP solidly toward the goal of including *all* students; in Sample 3 at grade 4, only 4 percent of the national population was excluded from the assessment sample, and at grades 8 and 12, 3 percent were excluded.

The importance of enhanced participation through the provision of accommodations notwithstanding, it is important to note that nothing is known about how the accommodations affected students' performance on NAEP, compared with how they would have performed without accommodations. An analysis and discussion of the impact of accommodations on scaling and the actual and potential effects on the measurement of trends will be forthcoming from NCES (Mazzeo et al., 1998). However, the encouraging results presented here do appear to be laying a foundation for the operational use of accommodations and the accompanying enhanced participation of students with disabilities and English-language learners in future NAEP assessments.

PROBLEM OF CONSISTENT AND ACCURATE IDENTIFICATION

NAEP's efforts to date make clear that implementing enhanced inclusion and accommodation strategies for English-language learners and students with

TABLE 3-5 Percentage of Students with Disabilities and English-Language Learners in the National Population Included in the 1996 Main NAEP Mathematics Assessment, Public Schools Only

Students	SD			ELL		
	S1: Using Original Inclusion Criteria	S2: Using Revised Inclusion Criteria[a]	S3: Using Revised Criteria And Providing Accommodations/ Adaptions	S1: Using Original Inclusion Criteria	S2: Using Revised Inclusion Criteria[a]	S3: Using Revised Criteria and Providing Accommodations/ Adaptations
Grade 4						
Assessed under standard conditions	58	47	35[b,c]	61	41	47
Assessed with accommodation			37			30
Total assessed	58	47	72[b,c]	61	41	76[b]
Grade 8						
Assessed under standard conditions	55	58	46[b]	60	63	61
Assessed with accommodation			26			18
Total assessed	55	58	71[b,c]	60	63	78[b]
Grade 12						
Assessed under standard conditions	48	51	35[b]	84	73	81
Assessed with accommodation			19			6
Total assessed	48	51	54	84	73	87

[a]Differences between S1 and S2 results are not statistically significant.
[b]Indicates a significant difference between S2 and S3 results.
[c]Indicates a significant difference between S1 and S3 results.

SOURCE: Reese et al. (1997:72).

disabilities is not an easy task. They also show that the provision of accommodations can increase the rate of participation of both students with disabilities and English-language learners in the data collections on which national-level summaries are based. However, even with the availability of a broader array of accommodations, the appropriate participation of students in assessments and the appropriate analysis and reporting of results for these groups depend directly on accurate and consistent methods for identifying, classifying, and assigning accommodations to these students. Unfortunately, according to a number of scholars (e.g., National Center on Educational Outcomes, 1995b; Reschly, 1996; National Research Council, 1997; National Research Council and Institute of Medicine, 1997), existing methods for identifying and classifying students with disabilities and for identifying students with different levels of proficiency in English are highly variable and often unsatisfactory. This is an issue faced not only by NAEP, but also by all large-scale assessment programs.

According to recent work carried out on students with disabilities (for example, Lewit and Baker, 1996; Reschly, 1996), no single classification system for special education is used uniformly around the country. Students labeled "disabled" in one state may not be so labeled in another. Moreover, according to Reschly (1996:44), 78 percent of children ages 6 to 11 who are classified as disabled in schools are so classified because of mild learning disabilities and speech and language disorders; such disabilities are the most difficult to diagnose accurately and consistently.

For NAEP, the impact of this lack of uniformity is of particular concern when considering state comparisons, since state-to-state variations in identifying, classifying, and determining appropriate accommodations for students with disabilities are little understood and have unknown impacts on inclusion rates, state comparisons, and summary results.

The identification and classification of English-language learners is similarly problematic. According to a number of recently conducted surveys (Fleischman and Hopstock, 1993; Cheung et al., 1994; Rivera, 1995; August and Lara, 1996), both states and districts use a variety of methods to determine whether students can be classified as an English-language learner and placed in special language programs. These methods include surveys of language(s) used at home, observations, interviews, referrals, grades, and testing. According to Fleischman and Hopstock (1993), 83 percent of school districts use English-language-proficiency examinations to identify English-language learners.

A total of 74 percent of school districts also use these tests for monitoring student progress and for reclassifying English-language learners as fluent in speaking English. Unfortunately, as the recent study of English-language learners also pointed out (National Research Council and Institute of Medicine, 1997), English-language-proficiency instruments are highly flawed and focus on discrete language skills that are not well attuned to the language demands faced by students in schools and classrooms. The report concluded that "most measures used not only have been characterized by the measurement of decontextualized skills but also have set fairly low standards for language proficiency" (National Research Council and Institute of Medicine, 1997:118).

In addition, Valdés and Figueroa (1994) argue that a number of instruments currently used to assess the language proficiency of English-language learners tend to resemble paper-and-pencil tests administered orally. In spite of certain similarities, however, these instruments are quite different from each other and are based on often contradictory views about the nature of language competence. So different, indeed, are they that even the three instruments most widely used in California—i.e., the Bilingual Syntax Measure, the Basic Inventory of Natural Language, and the Language Assessment Scales classify very different proportions of students as non-English-speaking, limited-English-speaking, and fluent-English-speaking. All three of the measures, moreover, placed the very same students in different categories. So great were the discrepancies between the numbers of children included in the non-English-speaking and limited-English-speaking categories by different tests that cynical consultants often recommended (in jest) one "state-approved" instrument or another to school districts depending on whether administrators wanted to identify large or small numbers of English-language learners.

To date, the dilemmas described above have not been resolved. Children potentially in need of native language support are still being assessed at entry level using one of several instruments that many scholars have questioned, and some years later they are tested again using another of such instruments that is in no way comparable to the first. The field is no closer to developing means for assessing whether a child can or cannot function satisfactorily in an all-English program—or participate in all-English large-scale assessments—than it was in 1964.[2]

The problems associated with identifying and classifying students with disabilities and English-language learners reviewed here are not problems that the NAEP program can or should solve on its own. However, as a leader in the design and conduct of large-scale assessments, the NAEP program (and the National Center for Education Statistics and U.S. Department of Education) can act as a lever to push for improved accuracy and consistency of identification and classification methods. In the next section, we describe important next steps to enhance participation and accommodation in NAEP; however, it is important to keep in mind that improved identification and classification are a critical prerequisite if the goals of such enhancements are to be fully realized.

---

[2]Segments from the above discussion draw extensively from Valdés and Figueroa (1994).

GOALS FOR ENHANCING
PARTICIPATION AND ACCOMMODATION

In response to recent federal legislation that reflects a national commitment to the education of students with disabilities and English-language learners—and given the fact that these groups of students collectively comprise more than 15 percent of the nation's students—the goals for the participation of these students in NAEP and their representation in a coordinated system of indicators for assessing educational progress should be:

• to ensure that the national samples used in NAEP's standard large-scale surveys are as representative of the nation as possible, and thus that the overall proficiency scores that are reported include results from students with disabilities and English-language learners.

• to collect data on the achievement of these special populations and to be able to make interpretive statements about how these students are performing relative to the nation and relative to their educational opportunities and instructional experiences.

To accomplish these goals, the U.S. Department of Education and NCES should further strengthen the good efforts already begun in NAEP to increase the participation rates and the provision of accommodations to students with disabilities and English-language learners. As part of this commitment, NCES should play a central role in the ongoing effort to improve data collection on these populations of students. In particular, NCES should work with states and other jurisdictions to improve the consistency of the identification and classification of these students, given the current variability in definitions of English-language proficiency and of having a disability. NCES should also press for further steps to ensure the consistent application of inclusion criteria for students with disabilities and students with language needs across all jurisdictions that participate in NAEP.

NAEP's goals in relation to the assessment of these populations via large-scale surveys should be to produce summary results that include data from as many students with disabilities and English-language learners as possible, and to report reliable subgroup information for these two populations, so that their performance relative to the nation as a whole can be known.

When students cannot be included in NAEP's large-scale survey assessments, or when the impact of the accommodation raises serious questions about the validity of combining data for these students with overall NAEP data, then the use of alternative assessment methods should be explored, targeting the assessment method to the particular subgroup of students in question. These assessments would serve as vehicles for gathering information about the achievements of these students and provide a basis for *qualitative* reports of the results. Although such assessments and associated reports do not meet the same statistical standards as data from large-scale surveys and undoubtedly will be costly to develop and administer, these trade-offs are necessary in order to prevent the achievements of students not included in large-scale surveys from remaining invisible.

In addition to the current paucity of achievement data from students with disabilities and English-language learners, there is also a dearth of accompanying contextual data about these students' educational experiences that would allow educators and policy makers to better understand the performance and educational needs of these populations. An important focus of the integrated system of data collections that we propose in Chapter 1 is the reporting of information on the educational opportunities and instructional experiences of these students— designed to be linked to student achievement data from NAEP's large-scale survey assessments and the alternative assessments we have proposed.

Finally, NAEP's goals and plans for the participation, meaningful assessment, and reporting of results of students with disabilities and English-language learners should be clearly defined and broadly disseminated. NAEP's users should be made cognizant of the degree to which its national samples do or do not include these groups of students; in fact, a key measure in the assessment of educational progress should be the reporting of progress in the numbers of students with disabilities and English-language learners who participate in NAEP's large-scale surveys.

We recommend that (1) NAEP continue to strive to ensure that as many English-language learners and students with disabilities participate in NAEP's large-scale surveys as possible, (2) reliable subgroup results for these two groups be reported in conjunction with national *Report Card* results, (3) alternative assessments be developed for English-language learners and students with disabilities who cannot be included in the large-scale surveys, (4) contextual data regarding the educational experiences of these two groups of students be collected within the coordinated system of data collections that we have proposed in Chapter 1, (5) quantitative and qualitative reports of these students' achievements be prepared and disseminated, including contextual information that helps enhance the understanding of the educational needs of these students, and (6) NAEP's goals and plans for the participation, meaningful assessment, and reporting of results for these students be broadly disseminated.

The financial and operational ramifications of these goals are tremendous and the technical issues associated with implementing these goals are numerous. Reporting reliable summary achievement results for a single subgroup that includes all types of students with disabilities and for a single subgroup that includes all types of English-language learners requires extensive (and expensive) oversampling in order to produce samples of sufficient size to report reliable subgroup results at the national level. (The expense of producing reliable subgroup results at the state level may be prohibitive.) The development of alternative methods for students who cannot be assessed in the large-scale survey with accommodations will undoubtedly require a large financial investment, and, for many students, it is still not known what alternatives are best suited for assessing their achievements. The analysis and reporting of these students' achievements in relation to contextual data is an added expense not currently in NAEP's annual budget. However, the social obligation and the legislative mandate to include these groups of students in assessments and to understand their achievements and educational needs makes striving to overcome these obstacles a necessary goal for the federal government and for NAEP. Neither NAEP nor NCES can finance the steps necessary to accomplish these goals within current budgets. Additional appropriations must be forthcoming if NAEP is to make progress toward the same kinds of goals for participation and assessment of students with disabilities and English-language learners that Congress has mandated for state and district assessment programs.

Even with the availability of additional funding, significant technical issues are associated with the goals we have put forth. For example, although the provision of accommodations appears to increase the participation of students in NAEP, research to date has not resolved whether data obtained using modified versions of assessments or altered administrative conditions have the same meaning (i.e., reflect measurement of the same constructs) as data collected using standard assessment materials and conditions. NAEP's research agenda must address this lack of knowledge.

In addition, both groups for which we have recommended reporting subgroup results—students with disabilities and English-language learners—are very heterogeneous populations. The achievements and educational needs of students with learning disabilities could differ greatly from that of students with physical disabilities, and, even within subcategories, the skills of students with different types of learning or physical disabilities can be very different. There also can be differences in the achievements and educational needs of English-language learners based on native language, as well as within native language groups, depending on how much English is spoken within their home or their specific ethnic identification within their language group (e.g., Puerto Rican, Chicano, or Central American within the Spanish-speaking language group).

Reporting information on all English-language learners as a subgroup and all students with disabilities as a subgroup must be accompanied by clear caveats about the lack of certainty regarding the generalizability of this information to all types of language groups or types of students with disabilities within these large, heterogeneous, subgroups. Still, overall subgroup results can help alert the nation as to how these groups of students are performing—in the aggregate— compared with the nation as a whole.

Also, as mentioned above, for those English-language learners and students with disabilities who cannot be included in the large-scale survey with accommodations, it is not yet well established which types of alternative assessment methods are most appropriate for assessing different types of students within these major subgroups. States are now investigating and implementing such strategies in their own assessment programs, and NAEP should work in partnership with them to capitalize on progress to date in planning alternative assessment methods for NAEP.

These and additional technical issues are discussed further in the next section, which outlines a research agenda for enhancing the participation, meaningful assessment, and reporting of results for students with disabilities and English-language learners in NAEP and other large-scale assessments.

In previous chapters we described a new paradigm NAEP, one in which assessment methods were tightly matched to assessment purpose. We described a core NAEP in which large-scale surveys are an important method for reporting overall results in NAEP's core subjects. Based on the discussion in this chapter, we envision a core NAEP that includes as many students with disabilities and English-language learners as possible and reports reliable subgroup information for these two populations of students.

We also described a multiple-methods component of NAEP, and the discussion in this chapter outlines another purpose for such a component. NAEP should implement a variety of appropriate alternative assessment methods that capture the achievements of students with disabilities and English-language learners who cannot be included in the large-scale surveys (or whatever other methods are used to assess the general student population). Figure 3-1 shows the general structure of the new paradigm NAEP with multiple methods for assessing students with disabilities and English-language learners not included in the standard assessments.

A RESEARCH AGENDA

The implementation of the ambitious goals that we have outlined above cannot be accomplished without an increased federal commitment to and funding for research that extends beyond NAEP and NCES to the U.S. Department of Education. Much of this research has applications well beyond NAEP, extending to assessments at the state, district, and even classroom levels. NAEP clearly cannot bear the full responsibility for this research effort, but the program should serve as a leader in pushing the research agenda forward. Specifically, NAEP, NCES, and the U.S. Department of Education should define a research agenda that includes:

• the determination of the most appropriate methods for assessing and providing accommodations to students with disabilities and English-language learners and

• the effects of changes in inclusion criteria and accommodations over time on trends in achievement results.

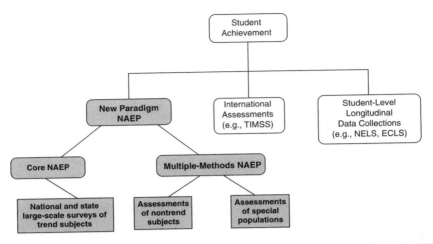

FIGURE 3-1 Measures of student achievement, including new paradigm NAEP. NOTE: TIMSS = Third International Mathematics and Science Study; NELS = National Education Longitudinal Study; ECLS = Early Childhood Longitudinal Study.

Methods for Assessing and Providing Accommodations

The research agenda to be defined must include attention to issues and questions such as the following:

- *The need for particular types of accommodations and the adequacy and appropriateness of the accommodations provided to various categories of students with disabilities and English-language learners.* Research in this area must include work on the demands (linguistic and nonlinguistic) made by different assessments on students with disabilities and English-language learners. For example, the NAEP reading assessment may place very different demands on the language abilities of students than does the mathematics assessment. Research on accommodations must also include attention to how different groups of students respond to different kinds of accommodations (e.g., students with language and speech disorders versus students with specific learning disabilities, or recently arrived English-language learners versus those who have received instruction in English over several years). Work also should focus on ways in which the appropriateness of particular accommodations for particular groups of students can be determined. Attention should also be given to the examination of whether different accommodations can provide students with disabilities and English-language learners a fair opportunity to answer questions across the range of item difficulties being tested.

- *The validity of different types of accommodations.* A reasonable accommodation should provide both students with disabilities and English-language learners access to tests through an adaptation of the assessment itself or a modification of the administration procedure that does not change the nature of the construct being measured. The accommodated scores should not be an irrelevant measure of the disability or the language limitation of examinees, but a reflection of what examinees know and are able to do.

• *The feasibility and cost-effectiveness of particularly expensive accommodations such as translation.* As discussed earlier in this chapter, the analysis of the recent use of translated versions of NAEP suggests that a number of nontrivial issues about the meaning of score data from translated assessments need to be resolved before the translation of instruments is adopted as a key accommodation method.

• *Scaling and reporting.* Research in this area should include attention to such questions as: What is the impact of accommodations on scores for students with disabilities and English-language learners? Does the NAEP scale accurately reflect results for respondents assessed under nonstandard conditions? Can the scores of students with disabilities and English-language learners be combined with scores of the general population for reporting NAEP results? If results for accommodated students cannot be reported on the NAEP scale, how might these results be best reported?

• *Questions about access to the curriculum and opportunity to learn.* Research in this area should include attention to such questions as: Do students with disabilities and English-language learners study the same curricula as other students? Is the content of the NAEP assessments appropriate for students with disabilities and English-language learners, given their educational experiences?

• *Alternative assessment methods for describing the achievements of students with disabilities and English-language learners who cannot participate in NAEP's assessments of the general student population.* To date, the focus of research efforts has been on strategies for including English-language learners and students with disabilities in large-scale survey assessments. However, the development of methods for assessing and reporting results for the diverse body of students not able to participate in the general assessments must also become a focus of research. Such research has the added benefit that it could provide the foundations for a generation of methodologies that are designed to assess student performance in ways that are appropriate for everybody.

Effects of Changes in Inclusion Criteria and Accommodations

As discussed previously, changes in inclusion criteria and in the availability of accommodations can potentially affect the measurement of trend results in two ways: (1) trends could be altered by the inclusion of students who previously would not have participated in NAEP but now are included in the national sample and (2) the availability of accommodations to students who previously would have participated in NAEP without them may have unknown impacts on their performance on the assessment.

Research currently being conducted as part of NAEP's explorations of enhanced participation and accommodations in the 1996 NAEP mathematics assessment will begin to address these issues. Comparisons of NAEP results—for the nation and for key subgroups—obtained from Sample 1 (old criteria, no accommodations) will be compared with those obtained from Sample 3 (new criteria, with accommodations). Equivalency of these two sets of results would indicate that the enhanced inclusion has no significant impact on overall NAEP scale score results and that trend lines could be continued with results from assessments administered with the new inclusion criteria and accommodations. If the two sets of results are not equivalent, then it may be necessary to continue to administer the assessment to both Sample 1 and Sample 3 in subsequent administrations or conduct other studies to gauge the effects of the use of new criteria and the provision of accommodations on trend lines. Results from this initial work will be forthcoming in fall 1998, but continued work of this nature will be required across NAEP's core subject-area assessments and over time to ensure that strategies for continuing trend lines are in place.

MAJOR CONCLUSIONS AND RECOMMENDATIONS

Conclusions

Conclusion 3A. **The participation and accommodation of students with disabilities and English-language learners are necessary if NAEP results are to be representative of the nation's students. There is currently a paucity of interpretable achievement data and accompanying contextual data on the performance and educational needs of these populations.**

Conclusion 3B. **Enhanced participation of students with disabilities and English-language learners in NAEP depends on (1) the consistent application of well-defined criteria to identify these students and (2) accurate collection and reporting of information about them.**

Recommendations

Recommendation 3A. **NAEP should include sufficient numbers of students with disabilities and English-language learners in the large-scale assessment so that the results are representative of the nation and reliable subgroup information can be reported.**

Recommendation 3B. Criteria for identifying students with disabilities and English-language learners for inclusion in the large-scale survey need to be more clearly defined and consistently applied.

Recommendation 3C. For those students who cannot participate in NAEP's standard large-scale surveys, appropriate, alternative methods should be devised for the ongoing collection of data on their achievement, educational opportunities, and instructional experiences.

Recommendation 3D. In order to accomplish the committee's recommendations, the NAEP program should investigate the following:

• Methods for appropriately assessing, providing accommodations, and reporting on the achievements of students with disabilities and English-language learners, and

• Effects of changes in inclusion criteria and accommodations on trends in achievement results.

4

Frameworks and the Assessment Development Process: Providing More Informative Portrayals of Student Performance

Summary Conclusion 4. The current assessment development process for main NAEP, from framework development through reporting, is designed to provide broad coverage of subject areas in a large-scale survey format. However, the frameworks and assessment materials do not capitalize on contemporary research, theory, and practice in ways that would support in-depth interpretations of student knowledge and understanding. Large-scale survey instruments alone cannot reflect the scope of current frameworks or of more comprehensive goals for schooling.

Summary Recommendation 4. The entire assessment development process should be guided by a coherent vision of student learning and by the kinds of inferences and conclusions about student performance that are desired in reports of NAEP results. In this assessment development process, multiple conditions need to be met: (a) NAEP frameworks and assessments should reflect subject-matter knowledge; research, theory, and practice regarding what students should understand and how they learn; and more comprehensive goals for schooling; (b) assessment instruments and scoring criteria should be designed to capture important differences in the levels and types of students' knowledge and understanding both through large-scale surveys and multiple alternative assessment methods; and (c) NAEP reports should provide descriptions of student performance that enhance the interpretation and usefulness of summary scores.

INTRODUCTION

Frameworks and the assessments that are based on them are central to the entire enterprise of NAEP. The framework documents describe the knowledge and skills to be assessed in each NAEP subject area, and the assessments represent the collection of measures (items, tasks, etc.) from which inferences about student performance in the subject area will be derived. Together they form the basis for describing student achievement in NAEP.

In this chapter we describe and evaluate NAEP's frameworks and the assessment development process for main NAEP. We use the term *assessment development process* here in a very broad sense, to describe the entire scope of activity from framework development through final assessment construction, scoring, and reporting. As background, we first provide an overview of the major steps in the development of an operational NAEP assessment, using the development of the 1996 NAEP science assessment for illustration. We then examine the conclusions and recommendations of previous evaluation panels most pertinent to our subsequent discussion. Our evaluation of NAEP's frameworks and assessment development process follows; in this discussion we make arguments for:

1. determining the kinds of inferences and conclusions about student performances that are desired in reports of NAEP results, and then using this vision of student achievement to guide the entire assessment development process,

2. improving assessment of the subject areas as described in current frameworks and including an expanded conceptualization of student achievement in future frameworks and assessments,

3. using multiple assessment methods, in addition to large-scale surveys, to improve the match of assessment purpose with assessment method,

4. enhancing use of assessment results, particularly student responses to constructed-response items, performance-based tasks, and other alternative assessment methods, to provide interpretive information that aids in understanding overall NAEP results, and

5. improving coherence across the many steps in the assessment development process as an essential prerequisite to successfully accomplishing goals 1 through 4.

In Chapter 1 we described the importance of enhancing NAEP's interpretive function by integrating its measures of student achievement with a larger system of indicators for assessing educational progress. This would provide an essential context for better understanding NAEP's achievement results in a given subject area. The focus in that discussion was on the collection and integration of data on relevant student-, school-, and system-level variables in ways that can elucidate student achievement and answer questions about "why the results are what they are."

In this chapter we discuss the analysis of students' responses to assessment items and tasks as another strategy for enhancing NAEP's interpretive function. By capitalizing on the currently unexploited sources of rich information contained in student responses (and patterns of responses), we describe how NAEP could answer questions about what students know and can do at a level of detail not currently reflected by summary scores. This type of interpretive information, gleaned from students' responses, provides insights about the nature of students' understanding in the subject areas. When combined with the broader-scale interpretive information that emerges from the coordinated system of indicators described in Chapter 1, qualitative and quantitative summaries of student achievement can help educators and policy makers begin to answer the key question that is asked when achievement results are released: "What should we do in response to these results?"

OVERVIEW OF NAEP'S CURRENT
ASSESSMENT DEVELOPMENT PROCESS

When this committee began its evaluation in spring 1996, the 1996 main NAEP science assessment was the focus, largely because the science achievement-level-setting process was undertaken concurrently with the term of this evaluation and because the science assessment included an unprecedented number and variety of constructed-response items and hands-on tasks. However, because each NAEP subject area has unique features, in terms of the content and structure of the domain and the methods used to assess the domain, it was necessary and useful to consider other NAEP subject-area assessments as well. Thus, although our evaluation maintains an emphasis on the 1996 science assessment, we have also considered NAEP's mathematics and reading assessments in some depth, since these subject areas are among the most important to educators and policy makers. Simultaneous consideration of science, mathematics, and reading also permits attention to issues that cut across subject areas, as well as those that are subject-specific.

The development of NAEP's frameworks and assessments is a complex multistep process. For any given subject area, the entire sequence of activities—from framework development, through assessment development and administration, to the reporting of initial results—spans approximately five years, barring funding interruptions or other changes in scheduling. An overview of the sequence of activities in the framework and assessment development process, based on the 1996 science assessment, is portrayed in Figure 4-1. The impressive effort that is mounted by the National Assessment Governing Board (NAGB), the National Center for Education Statistics (NCES), and their subcontractors each time a NAEP assessment is developed and administered is often looked to as a model for framework and assessment development by states, districts, and other developers of large-scale assessments.

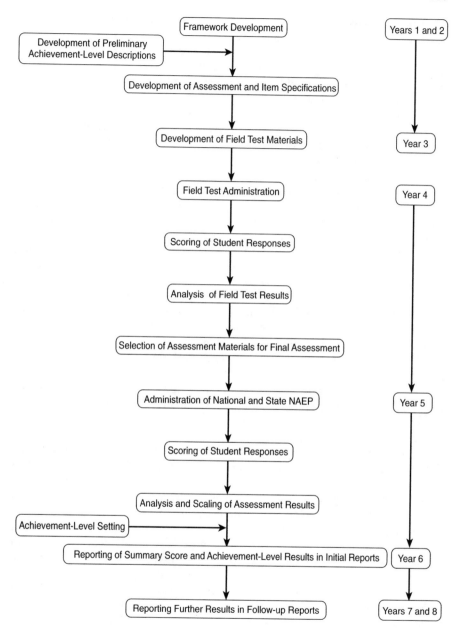

FIGURE 4-1 A generalized overview of NAEP's assessment development process.

Under NAGB's auspices, frameworks for the main NAEP assessments are developed by a planning committee (primarily subject-area experts—teachers, curriculum specialists, and disciplinary researchers) and a steering committee (a broad group of education administrators, policy makers, and subject-area experts) through a unique, broad-based consensus process. Through this consensus process, the planning and steering committee members reach a level of agreement about the subject-area knowledge and skills students should know and be able to do. Although there is never complete agreement among committee members about the scope and content of the frameworks, in general the outcome of the consensus process has been that the framework strikes a balance between reflecting current practice and responding to current reform recommendations.

Most NAEP frameworks specify that the subject-area assessments be constructed around two or more dimensions. In science, two major dimensions are "fields of science" and "ways of knowing and doing," which are supplemented by two underlying dimensions, "nature of science" and "themes." In reading, the major dimensions are "reading stance" and "reading purpose"; in mathematics, two primary dimensions, "content" and "mathematical abilities," are supplemented with a dimension designated "mathematical power." For each dimension, the frameworks also describe the proportions and types of items and tasks that should appear on the final version of the NAEP assessments. (See Figures 4-2, 4-3, and 4-4 for diagrammatic representations of the current main NAEP frameworks in science, reading, and mathematics.)

Following the development of the framework, test and item specifications are generated, also under the auspices of NAGB. These specifications, which provide a detailed blueprint for assessment development, are typically developed by a small subgroup of the individuals involved in the development of the framework, along with a subcontractor with experience in the development of specifications for large-scale assessments.

The framework and specifications documents thus serve as guides for the development of assessment materials in each subject area. Item development and field-test administration and scoring are currently carried out by staff at the Educational Testing Service (ETS—under contract to NCES) in consultation with an assessment development committee of subject-area experts, some of whom have been involved in the development of the framework. Items and draft scoring rubrics are developed by the committee, ETS staff, and external item writers identified by ETS and by the committee. Items are developed to include a mix of multiple-choice and a variety of constructed-response items and performance tasks as specified in the framework and specifications. ETS staff and assessment development committee members review and edit all assessment materials, which are also reviewed for potential sources of bias. When time has permitted, some of the more complex performance-based items have been piloted with two to three classes, and students have been interviewed about the items and

Fields of Science

Knowing and Doing	Earth	Physical	Life
Conceptual Understanding			
Scientific Investigation			
Practical Reasoning			
Nature of Science			
Themes: Models, Systems, Patterns of Change			

FIGURE 4-2 The 1996 main NAEP science framework matrix. NOTE: Nature of Science: the historical development of science and technology, and the habits of mind that characterize these fields, and the methods of inquiry and problem solving. Themes: the "big ideas" of science that transcend scientific disciplines and induce students to consider problems with global implications. SOURCE: National Assessment Governing Board (no date, d:13).

their responses to the items. It has not, however, been universal practice to pilot items before formal field testing.

Field tests are administered to samples of students by WESTAT and scored by National Computer Systems (NCS). ETS staff and development committee members participate in the selection of items for the final version of the assessment and the revision of scoring rubrics based on the initial wave of incoming student responses. Constructed-response items are then scored by trained readers. ETS documents state that items or sets of items (in the case of reading passages or hands-on science tasks) are selected for the final assessment based on their fit with the framework, their fit with preliminary achievement-level descriptions, and their general statistical properties (e.g., level of difficulty, item-test correlations).

Final assessment forms are again reviewed by the assessment development committee prior to administration by WESTAT to a nationally representative sample of students (generally a year after the field test was administered). Scoring is once again managed by NCS, with ETS staff and the assessment development committee overseeing any necessary revisions of the scoring guides prior to scoring by the trained readers.

The NAEP in Reading: Aspects of Reading Literacy

	READING STANCE: Constructing, Extending, and Examining Meaning			
	Initial Understanding	Developing Interpretation	Personal Reflection and Response	Demonstrating a Critical Stance
READING PURPOSE	Requires the reader to provide an initial impression or unreflected understanding of what was read.	Requires the reader to go beyond the initial impression to develop a more complete understanding of what was read.	Requires the reader to connect knowledge from the text with his/her own personal background knowledge.	Requires the reader to stand apart from the text and consider it.
Reading for Literary Experience				
Reading for Information				
Reading to Perform a Task				

FIGURE 4-3 The 1992-1998 main NAEP reading framework matrix. SOURCE: National Assessment Governing Board (no date, b:16-17).

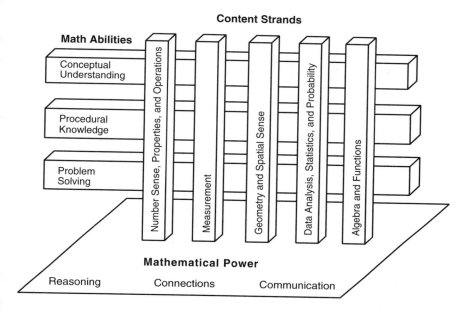

FIGURE 4-4 The 1996 main NAEP mathematics framework matrix. NOTE: Mathematical Power: consists of mathematical abilities within the broader context of reasoning and with connections across the broad scope of mathematical content and thinking. Communication is both a unifying threat and a way for students to provide meaningful responses to tasks. SOURCE: National Assessment Governing Board (no date, a:11).

Subsequent analysis of the results and production of the initial report (known as the *Report Card*) leads to the release of overall summary score results approximately 12 to 18 months after the administration of the assessment. Achievement-level setting and the release of achievement-level results also occur within the same time period, since it is NAGB's goal to include these results in the initial report. Following the release of initial summary score and achievement-level results, a series of follow-up reports that provide univariate analyses of student achievement in relation to contextual variables are released, and public-use NAEP datasets are made available to those who have site licenses.

NAGB's current plans call for NAEP final assessments to be readministered periodically (at 4-year intervals for reading, writing, mathematics, and science; see Table I-1). Because some assessment materials are released to the public after each administration of a final assessment, a new round of item development and field testing is conducted to replace those materials. The new materials and the revised final assessment are intended to reflect the goals of the original framework and specifications. Thus, the same framework serves as the basis for a series of assessments over time.

SELECTED FINDINGS FROM PREVIOUS NAEP EVALUATIONS

Our examination of NAEP's frameworks and the assessment development process has benefited greatly from the previous evaluations conducted by the National Academy of Education (NAE) and from a range of design initiatives and validity studies conducted by NAGB and NCES themselves. The NAE evaluations were mandated in NAEP's authorizing legislation and focused on the quality, validity, and utility of the NAEP assessments that were included as part of the trial state assessment program between 1990 and 1994 (the 1990 and 1992 mathematics assessments and the 1992 and 1994 reading assessments). Several major areas of observation and evaluation from the NAE studies are integral to discussions we present later in this chapter.

Framework Consistency with Disciplinary Goals

In general, the NAE panel found the NAEP frameworks for the 1990 and 1992 mathematics assessments and the 1992 and 1994 reading assessments to be reasonably well balanced with respect to current disciplinary reform efforts and common classroom practices in reading and mathematics. In reading, the panel concluded that the framework and the assessments were consistent with current reading research and practice, incorporating innovations in assessment technology such as interesting and authentic reading passages, longer testing time per passage, and a high proportion of constructed-response items (National Academy of Education, 1996:9). However, in their evaluation of the 1994 reading assessment, the panel contended that there were important aspects of reading not captured in the current reading framework, most notably differences in students' prior knowledge about the topic of their reading and contextual factors associated with differences in students' background, experiences, and interests (DeStefano et al., 1997).

In mathematics, the panel concluded that the 1990 frameworks and assessments reflected much of the intent of the *Curriculum and Evaluation Standards for School Mathematics* of the National Council of Teachers of Mathematics (1989) and that appropriate steps were taken to bring the 1992 assessment materials even more in line with those widely accepted standards. They did recommend, however, that the current content-by-process matrix, which requires items to be classified in a single content category and a single process category, be replaced with a model that better represents the integrated nature of mathematical thinking (National Academy of Education, 1992:20, 1993:69).

Fit of Items to Frameworks and Specifications

Analyses conducted for the NAE panel show that for the 1990 and 1992 mathematics assessments, the fit of the items to major dimensions of the framework was reasonable, particularly in the content categories. When a group of mathematics experts classified the items in the 1990 grade 8 mathematics assessment on the basis of the content and mathematical ability categories specified in the framework (see Figure 4-4), their classifications matched NAEP's classifications in content areas for 90 percent of the items, and they matched mathematical ability category classifications for 69 percent of the items (Silver et al., 1992). Nearly identical results were obtained when a similar study was conducted using the 1992 grade 4 items (Silver and Kenney, 1994). The lower congruence of classifications in the mathematical ability categories was judged to result from the fact that many items appeared to tap skills from more than one ability, making the classification of items into a single ability category a difficult task.

For the 1992 grade 4 reading assessment, a group of reading experts judged the item distribution across "reading purposes" to be a reasonable approximation of the goals specified in the framework, but they noted that the assessment was lacking in items that adequately measured the *personal response* and *critical stance* categories of the "reading stance" dimension (Pearson and DeStefano, 1994). The panel reiterated the lack of clarity in the stance dimension following the evaluation of the 1994 reading assessment (DeStefano et al., 1997), positing that the assessment of this dimension, as currently carried out, added little to the interpretive value of NAEP results.

Use of Constructed-Response and Other Performance-Based Items

Across the assessments that it evaluated, the NAE panel repeatedly applauded NAEP's continued move to include increasing numbers and variations of constructed-response and other performance-based item types, and it encouraged further development and inclusion of such items as mechanisms for assessing aspects of the framework not easily measurable through more constrained item formats. They also recommended that special studies should be used to assess aspects of the frameworks not easily captured in the range of item types administered in a large-scale survey assessment format (National Academy of Education, 1992:28-29, 1993:69-72, 1996:25-28).

Continuity Across Framework and Assessment Development Activities

Recognizing the complex, multistep nature of the NAEP assessment development process, the NAE panel recommended that mechanisms be implemented to ensure continuity throughout the process. The panel suggested that the mechanism could be a set of subject-specific oversight committees that monitor all steps of the process, from framework development to reporting, in order to ensure that the intentions of the framework developers were reflected in the assessment materials and in reports of NAEP results (National Academy of Education, 1992:30).

Time Allotted for Assessment Development

The NAE panel repeatedly noted the severe time constraints placed on the NAEP assessment development process, observing that "due to short authorization and funding cycles on one hand and time-consuming federal clearance procedures on the other, the actual development of the frameworks and assessment tasks has been squeezed into unconscionably short time frames" (National Academy of Education, 1996:27). The panel noted that such time constraints are antithetical to the iterative design and development processes required to develop innovative assessment tasks that measure aspects of student achievement not well measured through more constrained item formats.

A Broader Definition of Achievement

In their fifth and final evaluation report, *Assessment in Transition: Monitoring the Nation's Educational Progress* (National Academy of Education, 1997), the NAE panel provided arguments for the reconceptualization of the NAEP assessment domains to include aspects of achievement not well specified in the current frameworks or well measured in the current assessments. They recommended that particular attention be given to such aspects of student cognition as problem representation, the use of strategies and self-regulatory skills, and the formulation of explanations and interpretations. The NAE panel contended that consideration of these aspects of student achievement is necessary for NAEP to provide a complete and accurate assessment of achievement in a subject area.

THE COMMITTEE'S EVALUATION

Our evaluation of NAEP's frameworks and the assessment development process is organized around four topics: (1) an examination of the existing frameworks and assessment development process for main NAEP, (2) an argument for a broader conceptualization of student achievement in future NAEP frameworks and assessments, (3) a recommendation for the use of a multiple-methods strategy in the design of future NAEP assessments, and (4) a discussion of the types of portrayals of student achievement that can enable NAEP to better meet its interpretive function.

Two underlying themes regarding the assessment development process emerged during the course of our evaluation. These serve as a foundation for the discussion in this chapter and are central to the successful implementation of the process improvements we recommend.

First, we contend that the entire assessment development process must be guided by a clear understanding of the kinds of inferences and conclusions about student achievement that one wants to find in reports of NAEP results. For example, assume that the developers of a science framework determine that it is essential to describe and understand students' abilities to design and conduct scientific investigations. A primary goal of the framework should be to describe the kinds of inferences about students' knowledge and skills in scientific investigation that will eventually be made in reports of results. The method of assessment should then be appropriate for eliciting student performance in designing and conducting investigations. Scoring rubrics should capture critical differences in student responses that provide information needed to make the inferences about that performance.

However, for many large-scale assessment development efforts, including NAEP, too often the focus is *not* on the kinds of information that eventually are to be provided in the reports of results. Too often the focus of framework development is on the development of broad content outlines that include nearly everything that could be assessed in a subject area. Too often the focus of assessment development is on the production of large numbers of items that match categories of framework dimensions in very general ways. Too often scoring rubrics are designed for ease of training readers and scoring responses. Instead, the focus should be on defining what kinds of inferences about achievement are to be provided in reports and then designing a connected system of frameworks, assessments, and scoring rubrics so that they lead to the collection of the information from students' responses necessary to make such inferences.

The second theme is closely related to the first. In order for desired inferences about student achievement to guide the assessment development process, there must be a high degree of continuity from one step to another in the process, from the conceptualization of the framework, to the development of assessment materials and scoring rubrics, through the reporting of results. Too often the intentions of the developers of the framework can be diluted, and even unrealized, if there is not sufficient attention to carrying out the inferential goals described in the framework throughout the entire assessment development process. We discuss strategies for improving the coherence across the steps of the process later in this chapter.

NAEP's Frameworks and Assessment Development Process

In this section we evaluate NAEP's existing frameworks and the current assessment development process. We discuss (1) the content of main NAEP's frameworks in science, mathematics, and reading; (2) the fit of items to the framework dimensions in the 1996 NAEP science assessment; (3) assessment of the knowledge and skills described in the frameworks; (4) coherence across the assessment development process; and (5) the time frame available for completing assessment development activities.

Frameworks for Main NAEP Science, Mathematics, and Reading Assessments

Science   The consensus process through which NAEP's frameworks are developed has led to the production of comprehensive documents that cover a broad range of the content knowledge and skills within the potential subject-area domain. The committee observes that the framework for the 1996 science assessment continues this trend, specifying very broad and detailed coverage of subject-matter content across life, physical, and earth sciences, along with a range of process skills (*Science Assessment and Exercise Specifications for the 1996 NAEP*, National Assessment Governing Board, no date, c). These process skills are among those that are accorded high importance in national science standards documents, including those developed by the National Academy of Sciences, the American Association for the Advancement of Science's Project 2061 effort, and the National Science Teachers Association's Scope, Sequence, and Coordination framework. The process skills, defined in the NAEP framework as "ways of knowing and doing" are: *conceptual understanding, scientific investigation*, and *practical reasoning.* The science framework also includes two additional dimensions that are consonant with ideas promoted in the standards documents; these dimensions cut across the framework's content-by-process matrix:

- *"Themes"*—*systems, patterns of change, and models*—are described in the framework as the "big ideas" of science that transcend the scientific disciplines and enable students to consider problems with global implications (*Science Framework for the 1996 NAEP,* National Assessment Governing Board, no date, d:28).
- *"The nature of science"* includes the "historical development of science and technology, and the habits of mind that characterize those fields, and the methods of inquiry and problem-solving" (p. 15).

Thus, the framework for the 1996 NAEP science assessment includes both broad and detailed content coverage and the process skills that are accorded importance in national science curriculum standards. The structural matrix that summarizes the major components of the 1996 NAEP science assessment framework appears in Figure 4-2.

Mathematics   In mathematics, the framework also prescribes both broad content coverage and skills deemed to be important in national curriculum standards. NAEP has been attentive to ongoing input from the disciplinary and education communities and from previous evaluations in its revision of the mathematics framework in preparation for the 1996 mathematics assessment. The 1990-92 mathematics framework was modified for the 1996 assessment to include "mathematical power" as a component of the domain (see Figure 4-4). Mathematical power includes reform-endorsed measures of students' abilities "to reason in mathematical situations, to communicate perceptions and conclusions drawn from a mathematical context, and to connect the mathematical nature of a situation with related mathematical knowledge and information gained from other disciplines or through observation" (*Mathematics Framework for the 1996 NAEP;* National Assessment Governing Board, no date, a:37). In response to the NAE panel's evaluation of the 1990-92 mathematics framework, the 1996 framework dispensed with the rigidly structured content area-by-mathematical-ability matrix as a guide for specifying percentages of items to be included in the assessment (this matrix assumed that any given item assessed one, and only one, of three mathematical abilities—*conceptual understanding, procedural knowledge,* or *problem solving*). The revised framework is based on a single dimension comprised of five content strands that serve as the basis for specifying item percentages, but it recognizes that any given item, especially those that are complex in nature, can assess more than one aspect of mathematical ability or mathematical power (e.g., an item that assesses the content strand of *geometry and spatial senses* might also assess the mathematical abilities of *procedural knowledge* and *problem solving*). The goal during assessment development is to achieve a balance of coverage of mathematical abilities and mathematical power across the entire assessment, rather than focusing on developing a predetermined number of items that purport to measure each mathematical ability or aspect of mathematical power in a discrete fashion. Such a strategy supports current conceptions about the integrated nature of mathematical thinking.

Reading The framework used for the 1998 reading assessment remains unchanged from that used to guide the development of the 1992 and 1994 reading assessments. We concur with the NAE panel's evaluation that this framework reflects current theory and an understanding of research about reading processes. It successfully delineates characteristics of good readers and the complex interaction among the reader, the text, and the context of the reading situation. As described by NAGB (*Reading Framework for the National Assessment of Educational Progress:1992-1998*; National Assessment Governing Board, no date, b:9-10), the framework acknowledges a number of different aspects of effective reading and a number of variables that are likely to influence students' reading performance (see Figure 4-3).

NAEP has adequately addressed two aspects of effective reading: the extent to which "students read a wide variety of texts" and "form an understanding of what they read and extend, elaborate and critically judge its meaning" (National Assessment Governing Board, no date, b:9). This has been accomplished by including three types of texts in the assessment (literature, information, documents) and by asking questions at four levels of understanding or stances (initial understanding, developing interpretation, personal reflection and response, and demonstrating a critical stance). The NAEP reading framework also reflects current disciplinary goals for assessment by including a substantial number of extended response items whereby students are asked to write answers to comprehension questions rather than simply to recognize correct answers. However, as the NAE panel noted, there are important aspects of the reading model presented in the framework that are not captured in the organizing structure of stances and types of text.

Thus, we conclude, on the basis of studies conducted previously and on the committee's own observations, that NAEP's existing frameworks in science, mathematics, and reading generally reflect many goals of the disciplinary communities and have instituted some forward-looking, reform-oriented innovations. However, the frameworks still do not adequately reflect contemporary research and theory from cognitive science and the subject-area disciplines about how students understand and learn. Maintaining broad coverage of subject-area knowledge and skills is still a major focus of the frameworks, particularly in science and mathematics. Although breadth of coverage supports traditional assessment methodologies that result in summary scores as indicators of student achievement, it provides little insight about the level and depth of student understanding that is valued in many current views of student learning. It is also notable that none of the three frameworks reviewed specifically defines the kinds of inferences about student achievement that are most desired in reports of results. Instead, the user of the frameworks must make assumptions about the kinds of descriptions of student achievement that the framework developers intended to appear in results.

Fit of Items to the Framework Dimensions: 1996 NAEP Science

The construction of the main NAEP assessments, as is the case for most current large-scale survey assessments, has been predicated on the assumption that the goals of the framework can be measured through a broad array of discrete items (or sets of items that refer to a common reading passage or problem situation). Recognizing that some aspects of the framework are not best assessed in an objective (multiple-choice) format, NAEP has appropriately incorporated increasing numbers of short and extended constructed-response items into the assessments. The use of such items was more extensive in the 1996 NAEP science assessment than in any previous NAEP assessment (Table 4-1). Over 60 percent of the items required constructed responses, and approximately 80 percent of the students' assessment time was allocated to responding to these items. In addition, every student in the assessment was administered a hands-on task. In these tasks, students were provided with a set of materials and asked to carry out an activity according to provided instructions. They were then asked to respond to a series of discrete objective and constructed-response questions related to the activity.

The committee commissioned research to examine how well this diverse pool of multiple-choice and constructed-response items matched the major categories of the structural matrix of the NAEP science framework. The central findings of this work are summarized below. A detailed description of methods and results is presented in the volume of research papers that accompanies this report (Sireci et al., 1999).

In one study, 10 eighth-grade science teachers who were familiar with science education reform and the goals of the NAEP science framework were asked to study and discuss the framework and then classify items from the 1996 eighth-grade science assessment by content area and process area. They were also asked to indicate which, if any, of the three themes the items assessed, and to determine if each item assessed the nature of science. An item was considered to be "correctly" classified if at least 7 of 10 of the teachers classified the item in the category in which the item was classified by NAEP (the assessment development committee and the ETS staff).

In general, there was a high degree of congruence between content classifications of items assigned by the eighth-grade science teachers and those assigned by NAEP. Using the "7 of 10 raters" criterion, across the three content areas (life, physical, and earth sciences), 85 percent of the items were matched to the content area in which they were classified by NAEP. For more than half of the items, all 10 teachers matched the classifications assigned by NAEP. "Correct" classifications were relatively lower for the process dimension (60 percent). The percentages of correct classifications for conceptual understanding, practical reasoning, and scientific investigation were 70 percent, 53 percent, and 50 percent, respectively. For 12 percent of the items, all 10 teachers' classifications were congruent with those assigned by NAEP. This suggests that delineating process domains for these items is more difficult than delineating content domains. A likely reason is that many items may require students to draw on more than one cognitive skill simultaneously, an assessment feature that many in the science and education communities would support. Thus, we recommend that the science framework should be revised to parallel the changes to the framework for the 1996 mathematics assessment, in which the goal was to achieve a balance of coverage across process categories in the item pool as a whole rather than presuming that each item can assess only a single process category.

The results with regard to the themes and nature of science dimensions were problematic. Approximately 50 percent of the items in the science assessment were categorized in one of the three themes by NAEP, evenly distributed across the three themes (systems, models, and patterns of change). According to the judgment of the teachers in this study, virtually all of the items were thought to be measuring one of the three themes. Of the items that NAEP classified into one of the three themes, the match between the theme identified by the teacher and that designated by NAEP was only 50 percent. Likewise, the teachers also judged that virtually all of the items were assessing the nature of science dimension, while only 16 percent of the items were classified as "nature of science" by

TABLE 4-1 Items and Distribution of Assessment Time in NAEP Instruments

Items, Year	Number of Items			
	MC	SCR	ECR	Total
1992 Reading				
Grade 4	42	35	8	85
Grade 8	57	53	13	123
Grade 12	63	54	16	133
1994 Reading				
Grade 4	39	37	8	84
Grade 8	41	55	13	109
Grade 12	44	62	13	119
1992 Mathematics				
Grade 4	99	54	5	158
Grade 8	118	59	6	183
Grade 12	115	58	6	179
1996 Mathematics				
Grade 4	80	55	9	144
Grade 8	93	62	7	162
Grade 12	91	68	7	166
1994 Geography				
Grade 4	59	23	8	90
Grade 8	84	32	9	125
Grade 12	85	25	13	123
1994 History				
Grade 4	62	26	6	94
Grade 8	101	35	12	148
Grade 12	104	33	19	156
1996 Science				
Grade 4	51	73	16	140
Grade 8	74	100	20	194
Grade 12	70	88	30	188

NOTE: Main balanced incomplete block spiral only; excludes theme blocks and estimation blocks.
MC = multiple choice
SCR = short constructed response
ECR = extended constructed response

SOURCE: Johnson et al. (1997:4-5).

NAEP. The teachers' interpretation of the themes and the nature of science dimensions, as described in the framework and based on their own experiences with these concepts, appears to be so broad that they view nearly every item in the assessment as measuring both of these dimensions. Although it may truly be the case that these dimensions thread through all parts of the science assessment (and in ways that are perceived differently from one subject-matter expert to the next), it is clear that these dimensions must be more clearly and narrowly defined in the framework. Inferential goals for reporting achievement in these areas must be

Percent of Items			Percent of Time		
MC	SCR	ECR	MC	SCR	ECR
49%	41%	9%	28%	46%	26%
46%	43%	11%	25%	46%	29%
47%	41%	12%	25%	43%	32%
46%	44%	10%	25%	48%	26%
38%	50%	12%	19%	51%	30%
37%	52%	11%	19%	53%	28%
63%	34%	3%	43%	47%	11%
64%	32%	3%	44%	44%	11%
64%	32%	3%	44%	44%	11%
56%	38%	6%	34%	47%	19%
57%	38%	4%	37%	49%	11%
55%	41%	4%	35%	52%	13%
66%	26%	9%	41%	32%	28%
67%	26%	7%	44%	33%	23%
69%	20%	11%	43%	25%	33%
66%	28%	6%	43%	36%	21%
68%	24%	8%	44%	30%	26%
67%	21%	12%	39%	25%	36%
36%	52%	11%	18%	53%	29%
38%	52%	10%	20%	53%	27%
37%	47%	16%	18%	44%	38%

clearly stated, if these dimensions are to be successfully translated into assessment materials and have any interpretive utility.

Improved Assessment of Knowledge and Skills Described in the Frameworks

As stated earlier, the science, mathematics, and reading frameworks have incorporated many aspects of the standards-based goals of the disciplinary communities. In general, the assessment item pools are reasonably reflective of the goals for distributions of items set forth in the framework matrices, particularly in the content-area dimensions in mathematics and science.

However, the presence of standards-based goals in the frameworks and the general fit of the assessment item pools to categories in the major framework dimensions do not ensure that the goals of the framework have been successfully translated into assessment materials. Several lines of evidence indicate that NAEP's assessments, as currently constructed and scored, do not adequately assess some of the most valued aspects of the frameworks, particularly with respect to assessing the more complex cognitive skills and levels and types of students' understanding:

• Across the NAEP assessments, students' responses to some short constructed-response items and many extended constructed-response tasks are often sparse or simply omitted (up to 40 percent omit rates for some extended constructed-response items). Given that it is these very items that are often intended to assess complex thinking and understanding, the assessments are failing to gather adequate information on these aspects of the framework.

• Significant numbers of the scoring rubrics in the NAEP reading, mathematics, and science assessments award points for easily quantifiable aspects of the response (awarding higher scores for numbers of examples provided or reasons given, numbers of correct statements made, etc.) rather than for the quality of the response. Such quantitative rubrics do little to capture students' level of understanding. In addition, on some items, respondents can get partial credit while demonstrating no knowledge of the construct the item was designed to measure. On other items, the same level of partial credit is given to a variety of responses that suggest quite different understanding of the concepts the item was designed to measure. In many cases, rubrics are not well constructed to capture the potential complexity of student responses.

Silver et al. (1998) presented a paper at the 1998 annual meeting of the American Educational Research Association that corroborates these observations. They analyzed scoring rubrics and student responses for several extended constructed-response items from the 1996 main NAEP mathematics assessment and concluded that varying levels of sophistication in the reasoning used by students to respond to the items were not reflected in the rubrics they examined.

• When the NAEP science framework was developed in 1990-1991, the NAGB-appointed steering and planning committees believed that it was imperative that the assessment include measurement of student achievement via hands-on tasks. They specified that every student participating in the assessment should be administered one of these tasks. Initially this appeared to be a laudable method for promoting hands-on learning experiences in science instruction. However, the evidence is mounting that such tasks, when administered in standardized fashion as part of a large-scale survey assessment, are not an adequate way to measure student achievement in scientific investigation and related cognitive skills (Hamilton et al., 1997; Baxter and Glaser, in press). The standardized tasks in the NAEP science assessment (and other large-scale survey assessments) are necessarily highly structured, have a very heavy reading load, and appear to measure some general reasoning skills and the ability to read and follow directions at least as much as the scientific investigation skills highlighted in the framework. Also, the generalizability of similar types of science performance tasks appears to be rather low (Shavelson et al., 1993). Students' prior experience and their degree of engagement with a task set in a particular context may have a large (but probably unquantifiable) impact on their response to the task, and these impacts may vary when assessing similar aspects of achievement with a task set in a different context. The current technology for using performance-type measures in science (and in other NAEP subject areas) via the current large-scale survey assessment clearly has serious shortcomings.

These observations provide examples of ways in which current assessment items and tasks and the accompanying scoring rubrics fail to capture complex aspects of the NAEP frameworks in a satisfactory way. These challenges are certainly not unique to NAEP but are faced by virtually all large-scale survey assessments that attempt to measure even moderately complex student skills and understanding. NAEP is to be commended for developing frameworks that prescribe the assessment of some complex aspects of achievement and for taking a leadership role in exploring new methods for assessing such achievements. It is clear, however, that NAEP must continue to improve how various aspects of student achievement are assessed in the large-scale surveys. It is also clear that reliance on large-scale surveys alone is not adequate for the assessment of the more complex aspects of student achievement. More effort is needed, both by NAEP and by the assessment community, to find workable solutions to these problems. Some suggestions for how these challenges can be addressed, by improving the items and rubrics included in the large-scale surveys, as well as by broadening the range of methods used in NAEP's assessment system, are presented later in this chapter.

Specific recommendations and examples of how main NAEP's reading current assessment materials might be improved are presented in Appendix A. In this appendix, we provide a detailed analysis of a grade 8 reading passage and set of related items and scoring rubrics that were administered as part of the 1994 main NAEP reading assessment. In doing so, we illustrate how there is still much to be gained through improvements to the current large-scale assessment materials.

Improved Coherence Across the Assessment Development Process

As we stated earlier, the sequential, multistep NAEP assessment development process—framework development, item development, scoring of field test items, assembly of final forms, scoring, analysis, and reporting—can occur as somewhat discrete, fragmented events.

Efforts to reduce the fragmentation of the steps in the assessment development process in recent assessments have attempted to ensure that there is significant overlap among the experts who participate in framework development, the development of preliminary achievement-level descriptions, item development, scoring rubric development, and final form development. These experts have been given major decision-making roles, and this effort appears to have helped improve continuity. For example, during the development process for the 1996 NAEP science assessment, there was notable continuity of personnel involved in various stages of the process:

- the 2 leaders of the framework development effort also oversaw the development of the assessment and exercise specifications;
- 5 of 11 members of the NAGB-sponsored committee that developed the preliminary achievement-level descriptions had served on the committees that developed the framework, and 5 were also serving on the assessment development committee;
- 5 of 13 members of the assessment development committee had also served on the committees that developed the frameworks;
- many members of the assessment development committee played a large role in developing and refining scoring rubrics and rater training protocols;
- members of the assessment development committee were involved as leaders at various stages of the achievement-level-setting process;
- 3 members of the original committees that developed the framework in 1991 continued to participate as members of the assessment development committee through the 1996 assessment scoring sessions and were leaders in the 1996 and 1997 achievement-level-setting sessions.

In response to the recommendation by the NAE panel that subject-specific oversight committees monitor all steps of the process from framework development to the reporting of results, in 1996 NCES established four subject-area standing committees for NAEP (reading and writing; mathematics and science; arts; and civics) as well as a standing committee for students with disabilities and English-language learners. The stated purpose of the committees is "to ensure continuity throughout the development of assessments." Nevertheless, our observations of two meetings of one of these committees (mathematics and science) revealed that the committee was primarily used as an ad hoc advisory committee on NAEP issues of current interest to NCES. They did not seem to view their function as one of ensuring continuity across various phases of the development process. To some degree, this mismatch of stated purpose with actual committee activities is understandable, as this committee was formed long after the frameworks and assessment materials had been developed, when the recommended oversight role should have been taking place. However, when frameworks are revised or redeveloped and assessment materials begin to be developed for a largely new assessment, the intended role of these committees could be realized if their activities were focused on their stated purpose and the committee members were made aware of the goal of continuity across stages of the process that they are expected to oversee.

Although increased and continuing involvement of subject-area experts is likely to enhance coherence across the assessment development process, our observations indicate that there are still some critical stages in the process during which a lack of coherence seems apparent:

- *Translation of the goals of the frameworks into assessment instruments and scoring rubrics.* As stated earlier, current assessment items and tasks often are not well designed to measure complex aspects of student achievement described in the frameworks. Also, when items and tasks are well designed, the scoring rubrics are not consistently designed to attend to key differences in students' levels and types of understanding of the knowledge and skills specified in the framework. Rather, emphasis is often given to easily quantifiable aspects of a response with little consideration of the relevance of those distinctions to important differences in the levels of students' understanding.

- *Reflection of the goals of the frameworks in the reporting of results.* The current NAEP frameworks provide broad and detailed descriptions of the knowledge and skills to be covered in NAEP's subject-area assessments. However, NAEP reports, with their focus on summary score reporting, do little to portray any of the texture found in the frameworks. For example, "mathematical power" was added to the mathematics frameworks for the 1996 assessment, but no results, analysis, or even mention of student performance across this dimension is found in the *Report Card* of mathematics results (Reese et al., 1997). If goals specified in the frameworks are successfully translated into assessment materials, then NAEP should be able to provide descriptive, sometimes qualitative, information about student performance in all key aspects of the framework.

- *Reflection of the preliminary achievement-level descriptions in assessment materials.* The pools of items and tasks in current NAEP assessments have not been consistently constructed to measure knowledge and skills specified in the preliminary achievement-level descriptions presented in NAEP's framework documents. Although we discuss and evaluate NAEP's achievement-level setting in more detail in Chapter 5, it is important to note here that, if student performance is to be reported in relation to achievement levels, then the framework and assessment materials must be constructed with this goal in mind. The preliminary achievement-level descriptions must be integral parts of the frameworks, reflect the most valued aspects of the framework, and incorporate current, research-based understandings of levels of student performance in a discipline. The assessment must be designed to measure the knowledge and skills laid out in those descriptions, and the rubrics should be constructed to capture meaningful differences in the levels of students' understanding.

The NAE panel noted that assessment development for the NAEP reading and mathematics assessments had been squeezed into unconscionably short time frames (National Academy of Education, 1996:27). For the four new main NAEP large-scale survey assessments that have been developed since that time (the 1994 U.S. history and geography assessments; the 1996 science assessment; and the 1998 civics assessment), this has remained the case. The time from the awarding of the assessment development contract to the deadline for submission of all field test materials to the U.S. Department of Education and the Office of Management and Budget ranged from 5 to 8 months. The conception, development, piloting, review, and revision of all items and tasks to be field-tested occurs during this time, as does the initial development of scoring rubrics and necessary ancillary materials (such as kits used in the science hands-on performance tasks). In what may have been the worst-case scenario, between the time that the science assessment development contract was awarded (April 1993) and the deadline for submission (August 1993), the assessment development subcontractor (ETS) co-ordinated the development of over 220 multiple-choice items, 320 short con-structed-response items, 125 extended constructed-response items, and 17 hands-on tasks. Concern about compressing this critical development activity increases when one keeps in mind that not only do these items and tasks serve as the pool from which the final assessment will be built, but also they will be readministered in subsequent assessments to obtain trend information.

The impact of this compressed development was confirmed during discus-sions with individuals involved in recent NAEP assessment development efforts. They consistently reported that more time was needed to pilot and revise items, and that items and tasks should be piloted in settings in which it is possible to determine how students' responses are related to their understanding of the con-tent being assessed. This is particularly important for the extended constructed-response items and performance tasks. Individuals who have studied students' responses to these items have concluded that, in many cases, it was clear that students often did not appear to know what was expected of them in order to respond in ways that were consistent with the scoring guides. More specifically, these observations may indicate that (1) task goals may not have been clear to the students, or (2) tasks may not have been worded in ways that elicit knowledge-based differences in students' responses, or (3) scoring systems did not capture those differences.

Addressing these types of issues implies more than field-testing items under assessment conditions. Standard field-testing can work well for multiple-choice items for which there are well-established statistical procedures for determining item quality, but assessment materials designed to measure more complex perfor-mances require a different development strategy. It is important to understand how students solve problems and how they perceive the goals of the task. This involves using cognitive laboratories to talk with students or groups of students about their strategies, their perceptions of the task, and their understandings of the nature of the response that is required. Particular attention should be paid to refining scoring rubrics based on pilot-test and field-test results, focusing explicitly on distinguishing among the kinds of responses that indicate differential understanding.

NAEP's redesign plans initially extended assessment development by a year in order to provide 12 months for item and task development and field-testing (as occurs now) and an added year for a dry run of the final assessment. The purpose of this dry run was to obtain statistical information that would make it possible to perform data analyses and achievement-level setting more rapidly and efficiently following the administration of the operational assessment in the following year (and thus issue reports of initial results in a timely fashion). This plan was recently abandoned, however, apparently because of the high cost of conducting the dry run of the assessment.

We urge the NAEP program to reconsider adding a year to the assessment development cycle, but to devote it to the preliminary development and small-scale piloting that is needed to produce high-quality assessment materials that can better reflect the intent of NAEP's frameworks. This additional pilot test year is particularly important for constructed-response items, performance tasks, and the array of assessment methods that we envision as important components of NAEP in the future. Additional development time is essential if these assessment materials are to capture important differences in levels of students' understanding based on the current theory and research and if such differences are to be part of the interpretive information provided in reports of results. Development of assessment materials and scoring rubrics that accomplish this is not a simple task, and the extra year of development time is critical. Field-testing could then occur in the following year, followed by the administration of the operational assessment in the year after that.

Broader Conceptualization of Student Achievement

In addition to improving the assessment of important cognitive skills presented in the current frameworks, we contend that NAEP frameworks should incorporate a broader conceptualization of achievement, and that there is considerable research on cognition, learning, and development that could inform the design, conduct, and interpretation of NAEP (see also Greeno et al., 1997; National Academy of Education, 1997; National Research Council, 1999a). NAEP's frameworks currently do not adequately capitalize on current research and theory about what it means to understand concepts and procedures, and they are not structured to capture critical differences in students' levels of understanding. They also do not adequately describe more comprehensive goals for student achievement that go beyond subject-matter knowledge and focus on the skills and abilities that will be important to an educated person in the next century (see for example, SCANS Commission, 1991). Dimensions of achievement not adequately reflected in current frameworks and assessments include (National Academy of Education, 1997):

- *Problem representation:* building representations of problem-solving situations and drawing inferences to be used in problem solution, including planning steps for problem solution, planning for alternative outcomes, and planning steps to be taken as a result of those outcomes.
- *Use of strategies:* selection and execution of appropriate problem-solving steps needed to accomplish the goal (based on the understanding of the task).
- *Self-regulatory skills:* monitoring and evaluating strategies during problem solution and implementing corrective actions.
- *Explanation:* drawing on existing knowledge to explain concepts and principles; providing principled justification for steps taken in problem solving.
- *Interpretation:* synthesizing and evaluating information from various perspectives, understanding the relationships of claims, evidence, and other sources of information.
- *Individual contributions to group problem solving:* building and using knowledge resources while engaging in group problem solving; recognizing competence in others and using this information to judge and perfect the adequacy of one's own performance.

We contend, as did the NAE panel, that advances in the study of cognition provide valuable insights into problem solving, explanation, interpretation, and how complex understanding is achieved, and they can be used to inform the development of assessments that better measure these dimensions of achievement than can the current array of broadly used large-scale assessment technologies.

Theories of Cognition and Learning

The conceptualization of cognition that has emerged over the last decade views knowledge as not only residing in the "head of the individual," but as a derivative of how individuals operate collectively in a larger set of social settings and contexts. The latter perspective construes knowledge as being "situated" and views attempts to decontextualize it or fragment it as antithetical to the distributive, socially shared perspective on knowledge.

These perspectives on the nature of knowledge and skill raise serious questions about what should be assessed and the manner of assessment. With regard to the latter, it has been argued that the assessment technologies currently in use to develop, select, and score test items and tasks, and thus to determine NAEP's summary scores and achievement-level results, treat content domains and cognition as consisting of separate pieces of information, e.g., facts, procedures, and definitions. This fragmentation of knowledge into discrete exercises and activities is the hallmark of "the associative learning and behavioral objectives traditions," which dominated American psychology for most of this century (Greeno et al., 1997). This "knowledge in pieces" view has dominated learning theory and instructional practice in America, as well as assessment and testing technology. As noted by Mislevy (1993), "It is only a slight exaggeration to describe the test theory that dominates educational measurement today as the application of 20th century statistics to 19th century psychology" (p. 19). Much of current testing technology, notwithstanding changes made in scaling methods and measurement models, is based on an underlying theory that allows tasks to be treated as independent, discrete entities that can be accumulated and aggregated in various ways to produce overall scores. This model also allows for a simple substitution of one item for another or one exercise for another based on parameters of item difficulty.

In contrast to the approach currently employed in NAEP, contemporary cognitive theorists would argue that inferences about the nature of a student's level of knowledge and achievement in a given domain should not focus on individual, disaggregated bits and pieces of information as evidenced by questions students can answer correctly. More important is the overall pattern of responses that students generate across a set of items or tasks. The pattern of responses reflects the connectedness of the knowledge structure that underlies conceptual understanding and skill in a domain of academic competence. Thus, it is the pattern of performance, over a set of items or tasks explicitly constructed to discriminate between alternative models, that should be the focus of assessment. The latter can be used to determine the level of a given student's understanding and competence within a given domain of expertise. Such information is interpretive and diagnostic, highly informative, and potentially prescriptive.

Another important construct derivable from a contemporary cognitive perspective is that achievement is captured less by the specific factual, conceptual, or procedural knowledge questions that one can answer, and more by the extent to which such knowledge is transferable and applicable in a variety of tasks and circumstances. To know something is not simply to reproduce it but to be able to apply or transfer that knowledge in situations that range in similarity to the originally acquired competence. A third salient feature of contemporary views of cognition is that a person's knowledge, understanding, and skill are demonstrated by the capacity to carry out significant, sustained performances. Often, such performances may extend well beyond a few minutes and can extend to days, months, and even years (in the case of student research projects). A corollary is that such performances are often dependent on collaboration with others in a group. Especially significant are group situations that emphasize distributed expertise and the sharing of knowledge across individuals to enable successful performance of a major task.

These perspectives imply, first, that an assessment program such as NAEP can be truly informative about the nature of student achievement only if (1) it includes a wide array of tasks tapping the various facets of knowledge and understanding and (2) the information gathered from this array is not merely reduced to summary scores. This is true whether the subject area is mathematics, reading, science, or history. Second, it needs to involve extended individual and group performances. Even though NAEP has increasingly included more performance tasks and constructed-response items in lieu of heavy reliance on multiple-choice items, the kinds of extended items and tasks that can be administered under the constraints of large-scale survey conditions do not reflect the level of complexity that many feel is necessary for assessing achievement in subject areas.

A NAEP that is more reflective of contemporary perspectives on cognition would (1) assess a broader range of student achievements, (2) be more concerned with describing exactly what it is that students know rather than simply attempting to quantify their knowledge, and (3) would place increased emphasis on qualitative descriptions of students' knowledge as an essential supplement to quantitative scores. For example, in mathematics the goal would not be just to describe whether students could solve problems, but how they solved them or why they could not solve them. The implications of incorporating a cognitive perspective into NAEP on the types of results that can be reported is discussed in more depth in a later section of this chapter.

The arguments for including a broader conceptualization of achievement in NAEP are strengthened further when one examines the degree to which these aspects of student achievement are consistent with the more comprehensive goals for schooling that have been put forth as required skills and abilities for an educated person in the next century (Resnick, 1987; SCANS Commission, 1991; Murnane and Levy, 1996). These reports suggest, among other things, the critical importance of communication skills, reasoning skills, and the ability to work with others using technologies to accomplish meaningful tasks.

It is notable that there are a variety of skills emphasized in these reports, as well as in the dimensions of achievement that we have discussed here, that educational assessment techniques have no way to measure in a large-scale assessment setting, such as that in which NAEP is currently administered:

- solving complex, meaningful problems using technological tools,
- making persuasive presentations and arguments in conversation,
- finding and researching questions that are worth pursuing,
- figuring out what is going on in some complex situations and being able to diagnose problems with the process,
- designing artifacts and systems to accomplish meaningful goals,
- taking responsibility for completing a substantial piece of work,

- listening to what other people are saying and being able to make sense of different viewpoints,
- asking facilitative questions of other people and getting them to think about what they are doing,
- understanding deeply several domains of inquiry of particular interest to the student,
- reading on their own materials that relate to their interests and goals, and
- working well with others to plan and carry out tasks.

Re-creating these cognitively complex performances in assessment materials may not even be possible. However, extracting data from naturally occurring student performances by videotaping student activity and computer-based analysis of students' written work offers promise as alternative means of data gathering on these aspects of achievement. Given that the skills listed above are important goals for education, it is critical that a program that assesses educational progress in America find a way to assess such aspects of student performance—we propose a general model to address this issue in a later section.

Current Knowledge: Possibilities and Limits

We have argued that the assessment of student thinking should be a clearly articulated priority for NAEP, and, insofar as possible, the frameworks and assessments should take advantage of current research and theory (both from disciplinary research and from cognitive and developmental psychology) about what it means to know and understand concepts and procedures in a subject area. This strategy should be reflected in efforts to improve the assessment of subject areas delineated in the frameworks and to assess dimensions of achievement not currently emphasized in the frameworks.

In arguing for such an approach, we recognize that achieving this objective is an incremental process predicated on the existence of well-developed theories and sufficient research on student understanding to guide assessment development activities. Such knowledge does not exist for all portions of subject-area domains or for all dimensions of achievement. For example, there are major differences in the degree to which detailed theories and fine-grained descriptions exist for student understanding and performance in various aspects of reading, mathematics, and science. However, there is sufficient extant knowledge to significantly improve the design of current assessment materials and embark on the task of developing new ones.

In reading, the current NAEP assessment was developed around theories of reading that were evident in the framework, but more needs to be done to make assessment of important aspects of the framework possible. In some cases, important intentions of the framework are not evident in the assessment itself. For instance, the current assessment ignores the interaction between the type of text and the purpose of reading the text and does not fully assess the depth of understanding needed to explore literary texts or learn about challenging subject matter. The material in Appendix A provides illustrations of improvements that can be made in reading assessment materials that begin to address some of these issues. Additional examples could be generated for the various text types and for the different reading tasks specified within the current frameworks by drawing on the considerable body of research currently available on the text structure factors influencing comprehension, on the strategies used to effectively process texts given different reading purposes, and on the evaluation of students' representation of the various elements of a given text.

In mathematics, there is a growing body of research on students' understanding of mathematical concepts (see Grouws, 1996, for several examples). Thus, it is possible to pursue a type of task and item development strategy that focuses on differentiating specific levels and types of student understanding and to do so for a number of important topics in mathematics, including many that fall within the existing NAEP mathematics frameworks. Appendix C provides a concrete example of such a process of translating results from research about student learning into assessment tasks. A set of items is presented that systematically differentiates levels of student understanding for the conceptual domain of number patterns. The example provided, like the example shown in Appendix A for reading, starts from existing NAEP materials but significantly augments how items are structured individually and collectively, thereby enhancing what can be determined about levels of students' understanding in the domain. Later in this chapter, we discuss the relevance of this example in the context of recommendations for providing more informative portrayals of student achievement in NAEP reports.

In science, research is somewhat more limited than in the areas of reading and mathematics. Nonetheless, there are detailed investigations of how students build their understanding in various conceptual areas (e.g., electricity and circuits, force and motion) and how to assess the form and scope of such understanding, especially to assist instructional decisions (Minstrell, 1991; Minstrell and Hunt, 1992; White and Fredericksen, 1998). This type of systematic knowledge of the levels at which students understand and represent physical concepts, principles, and/or situations is a starting point for developing highly informative assessment tasks that could be used in large-scale survey assessments such as NAEP. An example of how these investigations can be used as a foundation for constructing assessment materials is shown in Appendix B and in a research paper by James Minstrell (1999) in a volume that accompanies this report.

The area of science performance assessment, which was discussed earlier as problematic in NAEP's 1996 assessment, provides an especially powerful example of how the design and evaluation of innovative assessments can be informed by cognitive theory and research on the nature of subject-matter expertise. As noted earlier, a major aspect of the recent NAEP science assessment

TABLE 4-2 Cognitive Activity and the Structure of Knowledge

Cognitive Activity	Structure of Knowledge	
	Fragmented (developmentally immature)	Meaningfully Organized (developmentally mature)
Problem representation	Surface features and shallow understanding	Underlying principles and relevant concepts
Strategy use	Undirected trial-and-error problem solving	Efficient, informative, and goal oriented
Self-monitoring	Minimal and sporadic	Ongoing and flexible
Explanation	Single statement of fact or description of superficial factors	Principled and coherent

SOURCE: Adapted from Baxter and Glaser (in press).

frameworks is the inclusion of scientific investigation and the use of hands-on performance tasks to assess these aspects of the domain. Such assessment innovations in large-scale surveys are highly laudable, but there are serious limitations to assessing these aspects of the domain in a large-scale format.

Baxter and Glaser (in press) have proposed an analytic framework for investigating the cognitive complexity of science assessments. Their framework juxtaposes the components of competence derived from studies of the development of expertise with the content and process demands of science subject matter. Table 4-2 from Baxter and Glaser (in press) illustrates critical aspects of cognition that are the desired targets of assessment in science (and other knowledge domains) and how these elements are typically displayed when the structure of a student's knowledge and understanding is fragmented and developmentally immature versus meaningfully organized and representative of higher levels of expertise and understanding. The cells in Table 4-2 provide capsule descriptions of the behaviors representative of a particular combination of cognitive activity and stage of knowledge structure development.

As argued by Baxter and Glaser, an analysis of the cognitive complexity of assessment tasks must take into account both the demands of the domain in which cognitive activities are manifested and their realization in the assessment situation. To capture the latter, they developed a simple content-process space (see Figure 4-5) that depicts the relative demands of the content knowledge and science process skills required for successful completion of a given science assessment task. In this space, task demands for content knowledge are conceptualized as falling on a continuum from rich to lean. At one extreme are knowledge-rich tasks that require in-depth understanding of subject-matter topics for task execu-

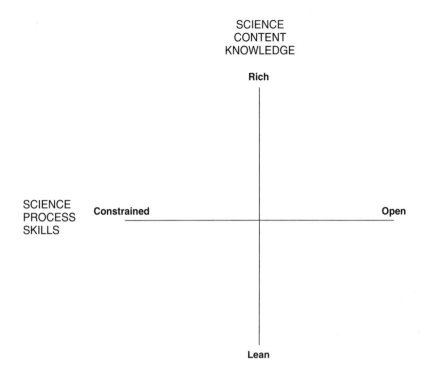

FIGURE 4-5 Content-process space. SOURCE: Baxter and Glaser (in press).

tion and completion. At the other extreme are tasks that are not dependent on prior knowledge or experience. Instead, performance is solely dependent on information given in the assessment situation. The task demands for process skills are also conceptualized as lying on a continuum from constrained to open. Process-constrained situations include those with step-by-step directions or highly scripted task-specific procedures for task completion. Hands-on science performance assessment tasks, as well as other innovative formats for science assessment (see Shavelson, 1997), can involve many possible combinations of content knowledge and process skills.

The content-process space, together with the components of competence mentioned in Table 4-2, provide a framework for examining the cognitive complexity of science assessments, including those currently in use in NAEP and any that might be developed under existing or modified frameworks. Analyses of a diverse range of science assessments illustrate matches and mismatches between the intentions of test developers and the nature and extent of cognitive activity elicited in an assessment situation. Such analyses also serve to illustrate the degree of correspondence between the quality of observed cognitive activity and performance scores (Baxter and Glaser, in press). As we noted earlier, many performance assessments constructed for large-scale survey instruments such as NAEP fall into the quadrant of Figure 4-5 described as knowledge-lean and process-constrained. In part, this is due to time limitations of the testing scenario and attempts to reduce sources of bias that could influence students' performance. However, the consequence is a limitation on the nature of what can be learned about some of the more cognitively complex aspects of science achievement incorporated into the NAEP frameworks. This is not a limitation of performance assessments per se but of their design and implementation within the constraints of typical large-scale survey administration. As we argue subsequently, creating performance assessments that sample from all aspects of the space represented in Figure 4-5 is probably a desired goal and may well require different methods and modes of data collection.

The examples we have provided of the application of cognitive theory and research to the design of enhanced assessment materials are only illustrative. Accepting the reality that there are limits to how extensively cognitive theory and research can be applied to task and item development, in areas for which such knowledge exists, it should play a central role in framework and assessment development. In portions of the subject-area domain for which little research exists, assessment development should take into account more than the content and structure of the discipline. For example, there are other sources of information about student thinking than those found in formal theory and research.

Teachers and other individuals who work intensively with students can offer informed perspectives regarding how students think about a subject. They can, for example, identify misconceptions, patterns of errors, and strategies. Furthermore, what we learn from the results of the assessment can and should be used to improve future assessments. Thus, an increased emphasis on student understanding and a broadening of the conceptualization of achievement assessed by NAEP is worthy of consideration, even if we accept the fact that assessment development cannot be grounded entirely in disciplinary and cognitive theory and research at present.

Multiple Methods for Measuring Achievement

The goals we have argued for in this chapter pose significant challenges for assessment development and assessment administration and operations. In this section we present a model for considering how the design of NAEP can evolve to accomplish these goals.

When considering the assessment of a domain, four general sets of questions should guide the framework and assessment developers:

- Have we been clear about the kinds of inferences we wish to make about achievement when we report results? Have the aspects of achievement about which we want to make inferences been clearly articulated in the framework? Have we specified exactly what aspects of student achievement we intend to measure?

- Assuming that the kinds of inferences to be made have been identified and articulated, what methods of assessment and types of assessment tasks provide students with appropriate opportunities to display their performance in the aspects of achievement of interest?

- Is the assessment task organized and presented in a way that elicits the levels and types of student responses that are needed to support the kinds of inferences that you wish to make?

- Does the scoring system capture critical aspects of student performance and permit distinguishing the relative quality of different performances?

If this set of questions is used as guidance, an assessment system designed to measure student achievement in the subject-area domains described in the frameworks—as well as the broader conceptualizations of achievement—would consist not only of the current large-scale survey assessments, but would also include a range of assessment methods—a new paradigm NAEP.

We propose that new paradigm NAEP adopt a design strategy whereby its assessments better match specific assessment technologies with the constructs to be assessed and the types of inferences to be drawn about student achievement. The types of technologies range along a continuum from large-scale survey assessments comprised primarily of multiple-choice and short constructed-response items to less-constrained, moderately open assessments (but still conducted at a single point in time) to relatively unconstrained observations of student performance obtained over longer time periods. The portion of the construct domain assessed also can range along a continuum, to some extent but not completely paralleling the continuum of assessment methods. Large-scale surveys can be used to assess individual cognitive constructs in the domain, not necessarily less complex or less important constructs, and each individual item assesses only a small slice of the domain. Families of items, such as the example in Appendix C, can assess a larger portion of the domain and levels of understanding within a cognitive construct. Moderately open assessments can assess related sets of cognitive constructs and also assess larger portions of the domain; highly open, less constrained tasks assess a range of simple and complex constructs in the domain and typically will cover large segments of the domain. The proposed continuum of assessment technologies and tasks also affords the opportunity to sample aspects of cognition and achievement that are otherwise difficult, if not impossible, to incorporate in restricted response tasks. These include some mentioned previously in this chapter such as problem representation, strategy use, self-regulation and monitoring, explanation, interpretation, argumentation, working with others, and technological tool use in problem solving.

As we stated in Chapters 1 and 2, a major component of this new paradigm NAEP is a core NAEP, consisting of large-scale survey instruments. Core NAEP would continue to track trends in achievement for both national NAEP and state NAEP in core subjects. Core subjects would include reading, mathematics, science, and writing, and any other subjects, such as U.S. history or geography, in which assessments are administered frequently enough to establish trend lines. However, core NAEP alone cannot assess all important aspects of student achievement. The second major component in our proposed design is multiple-methods NAEP, consisting of alternative surveys and assessments. These components should be used to assess (1) components of core subject area frameworks that are not well suited for assessment via large-scale surveys, (2) nontrend subject areas, (3) achievements of members of special populations who cannot participate in the large-scale surveys, and (4) achievements of students with specific instructional experiences (e.g., fine arts, advanced mathematics).

We contend that implementing a multiple-methods NAEP will be required in order to appropriately assess all aspects of the current frameworks as well as the broader conceptualizations of achievement discussed earlier in this chapter. Specifically, alternative methods will be required to assess aspects of student achievement not well assessed by large-scale surveys (e.g., performing investigations in science, solving problems in a group setting). In addition, multiple-methods NAEP is appropriate for assessing targeted samples of students with specific instructional experiences (e.g., advanced mathematics, fine arts, economics). An overview of the measures of student achievement in new paradigm NAEP is presented in Table 4-3.

Although we contend that a wider range of methodologies must have a place in new paradigm NAEP to appropriately assess all aspects of the current frameworks and to be able to assess broader dimensions of achievement, we simultaneously recognize that this would simply not be feasible, financially or logistically, if it were assumed that all assessment methods were administered to a sample of students as large as those to whom the current large-scale survey assessment instruments are administered. Smaller samples of students, and samples less fully representative of the nation should be used, as one moves along the assessment continuum. These issues, including costs associated with a multiple-methods NAEP, are considered in the next section.

Features of a Multiple-Methods Assessment System

If a multiple-methods approach were implemented, each core subject-area assessment would consist of a combination of the large-scale survey instruments and multiple alternative assessments. Insofar as possible, data from multiple-methods NAEP and core NAEP's large-scale surveys should be linked, and data from all methods administered across a subject area should be used to represent student achievement in NAEP's reports (i.e., summary scale score results from

TABLE 4-3 Overview of New Paradigm NAEP

	Assessment Method		
	---	---	---
	Core NAEP (Standard Large-Scale Survey)	Multiple-Methods NAEP	
Assessment Purpose		Alternative Surveys	Alternative Assessment Methods
Reporting trends using proficiency scores	X		
Reporting trends using achievement levels	X		
Assessment of students with special needs who cannot be included in standard assessments			X
Assessment of nontrend subjects		X	X
Assessment of samples of students with specific instructional experiences		X	X
Assessment of constructs not well assessed by large-scale surveys		X	X

large-scale assessment surveys should not be the only source of information used to represent student achievement).

Multiple-methods NAEP should explore such technologies as the use of clinical interviews and protocol analysis, assessment of group performance, and technology-based modes of assessment (e.g., computer-based analyses of collections of naturally occurring data on student classroom performances) as alternative methods for assessing how students think and learn. In the short term, NAEP should use alternative methods of assessment to administer components of the existing large-scale survey for which that method is not the most appropriate mode of data collection (e.g., science hands-on performance tasks).

Our recommendation for the use of multiple assessment methods is in some ways similar to one proposed by the current testing subcontractor, Educational Testing Service, in its 1997 report, *NAEP Redesigned,* one of several papers submitted to NCES to inform planning for the current redesign of NAEP (Johnson et al., 1997). In that document, ETS proposes a "modular" assessment design as one option for future NAEP. A key feature of the design is the proposal to administer more open, performance-based tasks to smaller samples of students, contending that the information needed to make appropriate inferences about student performances can be obtained from these more limited samples, if such samples can be linked to those taking the large-scale survey assessment. The proposal falls short, however, in one way; an assumption appears to be made that the constructed-response items and tasks that were originally developed for a large-scale assessment mode should be administered and scored as they previously had been—just to smaller samples of students. The multiple-methods approach that we are recommending should entail development of tasks and scoring rubrics that support collecting more in-depth descriptive information than what is currently gathered through even the most "open" items and tasks on the current main NAEP large-scale survey assessments.

Planning and Implementation Challenges

We make our recommendation for a multiple-methods NAEP with the recognition that full implementation of such a strategy is not immediately practical or feasible. Progress must be accomplished in three areas before multiple-methods NAEP could consist of the range of types of assessment methods that we have discussed in earlier sections of this chapter: (1) strategies for managing the costs of development, administration, scoring, and analysis of alternative surveys and assessments must be in place; (2) the research base for understanding the measurement attributes of such alternative methods must be expanded; and (3) current models used for the development of assessment materials must be changed.

Planning and implementation of a multiple-methods strategy must be undertaken with the recognition that trade-offs will be necessary to manage costs. We do not recommend that the broader array of assessment types be simply added on to the existing program. A portion of the funds currently devoted to the development, administration, and scoring of the extensive large-scale survey instruments will need to be diverted to multiple-methods NAEP. In our proposed design, some aspects of student achievement described in NAEP's frameworks would no longer be assessed via core NAEP and its large-scale survey instrumentation. The components of the current large-scale surveys that are intended to assess these aspects of achievement (extended-response questions, performance tasks) should therefore be reduced. Funds that are now devoted to developing these types of items and tasks, administering them to large samples of students, and scoring the large number of responses should be used to develop, administer, and score components of multiple-methods NAEP—to smaller samples of students.

The financial impact of a reduction in these types of items and tasks of the large-scale survey instruments is not insignificant. Detailed NAEP budgets were not available to us, but we did determine that approximately 35 percent of the budget for national NAEP is allocated for assessment development, field testing, and the scoring of student responses. On a per item basis, extended constructed-response and performance task item types require a disproportionate share of these funds. In fact, the increased representation of such items in NAEP's large-scale assessment has led to almost geometric increase in costs (Johnson et al., 1997). Thus, it is reasonable to conclude that significant savings would result from reducing the number of these item types in NAEP's large-scale survey.

NAEP's current assessment development and operations subcontractor, ETS, has presented analyses that show that such trade-offs—in which more complex (and expensive to administer and score) assessment materials are administered to smaller samples of students—could indeed be accomplished using NAEP's current financial resources; they could even result in cost savings (Johnson et al., 1997). Such savings could then be allocated to the development of the broader range of assessment materials needed to better assess the current frameworks and to adequately assess other aspects of achievement not currently measured by NAEP.

There are also considerable challenges associated with developing, administering, scoring, analyzing, and reporting results from alternative methods, and research and development efforts to date have not provided clear and complete solutions to these challenges. Developing assessment materials to assess complex constructs has been difficult, and there are no well-established strategies for developing such materials. In addition, the reliability and generalizability of such assessments has not been as high as is desirable. Data collection scenarios for multiple-methods NAEP must also circumvent the problem of the lack of student motivation that is the likely cause of the low response rates observed on extended-response items and tasks on the current large-scale survey. We anticipate that an increased reliance on the analysis of students' classroom work products may be necessary to ameliorate the lack of motivation exhibited by some students in a low-stakes assessment such as NAEP. Accelerated research regarding the use of naturally occurring student work as a basis for the assessment of student achievement is imperative.

Successful development of multiple-methods NAEP also requires that new models for the development of assessment materials be implemented. The development processes and "machinery" used by large testing subcontractors to rapidly develop large numbers of multiple-choice and short constructed-response items is inappropriate for the development of the types of assessments we envision for multiple-methods NAEP. Iterative review and revision based on a series of tryouts and follow-up discussions with individual students or small groups of students in cognitive laboratory settings will be needed, with an emphasis on the development of smaller quantities of assessment materials that more successfully assess complex performances and levels and types of student understanding. Such cognitive laboratory tryouts during the initial stages of assessment development are currently being used in efforts to improve NAEP's background questionnaires and in the development of reading and mathematics items for the proposed voluntary national test (National Research Council, 1999b).

It will also be important to include individuals with a broader range of expertise in assessment development activities than has previously been the case. Disciplinary specialists who conduct research about student learning and cognition as well as cognitive and developmental psychologists must be represented on committees that develop the frameworks and the assessment materials if implementation of the strategies we have recommended is to be accomplished.

In addition to an exemplary design team, a successful development process relies on iteratively updating frameworks and conceptions of student thinking based on research and practice. Indeed, if, as we envision, NAEP is but one component of a larger system of data collections for assessing educational progress, then the range of contextual, interpretive information gained from this system could inform the development of the next generation of frameworks and assessments in new paradigm NAEP.

Progress in the areas described above will not be easy to achieve and implementation of a multiple-methods NAEP will be incremental and evolutionary. For example, we anticipate that, largely for reasons of cost, multiple-methods NAEP would initially only be conducted as part of national NAEP, with the most feasible and informative components carried over to state NAEP administrations on a gradual, selected basis. However, despite the challenges posed by costs and funding reallocations, the need for an expanded research base, and the need to change assessment development models, the alternative is an unacceptable status quo—a NAEP that measures only those aspects of student achievement that can be assessed through a single, "drop-in-from-the-sky" large-scale survey and leaves other parts of the framework unaddressed. That alternative relegates NAEP to the role of an incomplete indicator of student achievement.

Portraying Student Achievement in NAEP Reports

Implementation of the committee's recommendations—to improve the translation of the goals of current frameworks into assessment materials and to evolve the frameworks to encompass broader conceptualizations of student achievement—would enable NAEP to produce broader and more meaningful descriptive information, both quantitative and qualitative. At a minimum, it would lead to an improved understanding of the current NAEP summary score results and, if capitalized on appropriately, would provide a much more useful picture of what it means to achieve in each subject area. This information would support the desires of NAEP's users for the enhanced interpretive function of NAEP discussed in Chapter 1. In this section, we further evaluate NAEP's current methods for portraying student achievement and describe how, even prior to the full implementation of the recommendations presented in this chapter, NAEP could improve the breadth and depth of how student achievement is portrayed.

NAEP's Current Portrayals of Student Achievement

A primary means by which NAEP currently describes student achievement is through summary scale scores, expressed on a proficiency scale from 0 to 300, 0 to 400, or 0 to 500. Summary scores (i.e., mean proficiencies) are reported for the overall national sample at each grade (4, 8, and 12) and for major demographic subgroups. In NAEP's 1996 mathematics and science *Report Cards*, the subgroups for which scale scores were reported were geographic regions, gender, race/ethnicity, level of parents' education, type of school, and socioeconomic level as indicated by a school's Title 1 participation and by free/reduced-price lunch eligibility (O'Sullivan et al., 1997; Reese et al., 1997). In previous *Report Cards* and in various follow-up reports, summary scores have been presented for additional subgroups (e.g., amount of television watching, time spent on homework). However, reporting by these types of variables in the *Report Cards* was recently abandoned by NAEP in an effort to streamline the reports, and because such stand-alone portrayals of student proficiency have been criticized for leading users to make inappropriate causal inferences about the effect of these single variables on student achievement.

This latter concern notwithstanding, in addition to the *Report Cards*, NAEP also produces a variety of briefer follow-up reports, which are generally released 12 to 30 months after the release of the *Report Cards*. These reports provide the results of univariate analyses in which mean proficiency scores are presented as a function of variables presumed to be related to achievement (i.e., summary scores in reading as a function of number and types of literacy materials in the home; summary scores in history as a function of amount of time spent discussing studies at home each day).

Another important means of reporting NAEP results is by the percentage of students performing at or above NAEP's basic, proficient, and advanced achievement levels. Achievement-level setting and the reporting of achievement-level results are discussed in Chapter 5.

Toward More Informative Descriptions of Student Achievement

In Chapter 1 we concluded that scores that summarize performance across items are, in general, reasonable and effective means for NAEP to fulfill the descriptive function of a social indicator. They provide a broad-brush view of the status of student achievement (albeit a more limited definition of achievement than we advocate) and do so in a way that can, when necessary, attract the attention of the public, educators, and policy makers to the results. However, summary scores should not be viewed as the only type of information needed to understand and interpret student achievement. In NAEP, we have argued that they represent performance on only a portion of the domain described in the frameworks, and thus they provide a somewhat simplistic view of educational achievement. On their own, do they not allow NAEP to adequately fulfill one of the interpretive functions of a social indicator—that is, they do not provide information that helps NAEP's users to think about what to do in response to NAEP results. More in-depth descriptive portrayals of student achievement are needed for this function to be fulfilled.

For example, much of the current debate regarding curriculum reform focuses on what should be taught, and decisions about what to teach are not entirely the province of curriculum developers and teachers. Policy decisions are made about content coverage and emphasis at state levels. NAEP could and should provide information that would assist those who make these decisions beyond simply portraying subject-area achievement as "better than it was four years ago" or "worse in one region of the country than in another." If one is faced with making a decision whether to shift emphasis in a state mathematics curriculum framework to focus on computational skills, as has recently been the case in California, it would be useful to have specific information about students' achievement in computational skills and how it relates to their understanding of underlying concepts and their ability to apply their skills to solve problems. A single score tells very little about where students' strengths and weaknesses are, nor does it help improve student achievement, whereas a more descriptive analysis of student achievement could provide guidelines for curriculum decisions.

How can NAEP provide the kinds of information about student achievement that is needed to help the public, decision makers, and education professionals understand strengths and weaknesses in student performance and make informed decisions about education? The new paradigm NAEP that we recommend, in which assessment method is optimally matched with the assessment purpose (and the kinds of inferences to be drawn), has great potential to provide an impressive array of information from which such portrayals could be constructed. This entails a shift to more qualitative measures of student achievement, with an emphasis on describing critical features of student knowledge and understanding. In order to make progress in this direction in the short term, the following initial guidelines should be implemented:

• Scoring rubrics for constructed-response items and tasks (whether included as part of the large-scale survey assessments of core NAEP or in multiple-methods NAEP) should be constructed to describe critical differences in levels and types of student understanding; for example, rubrics should not be constructed simply to capture easily quantifiable differences in numbers of correct examples given or reasons cited. Thus scale scores generated from the accumulation of student responses would be more valid reflections of the intent of both current and envisioned frameworks.

• Scoring rubrics for constructed-response items and tasks should allow for the accumulation of information about more than one aspect of a student's performance. Although current scaling and analysis methodologies may not enable all such information to be reflected in summary scores, information gleaned from student responses can be used to provide informative and useful descriptions of achievement.

• Assessment instruments should include families of related items, designed to support inferences about the levels of student understanding in particular portions of the frameworks. Analysis of patterns of student responses across these items can reflect the knowledge structure that underlies students' conceptual understanding, providing a richer interpretive context for understanding overall achievement results. In such a scenario, families of items serve as the unit of analysis; that is, each item is not simply a discrete source of information unconnected to other items. If we presume that these responses also contribute to summary scores, then this has implications for scaling—and appropriate modifications to existing scaling methodology would need to be explored and implemented.

• Finally, in an ideal situation, the reporting of information that provides an interpretive context for understanding patterns of achievement results would be released along with the *Report Card* that presents summary score results for the nation and major subgroups. However, given the current pressures to release summary results on an accelerated schedule, providing interpretive analyses in the *Report Cards* may not be feasible, at least in the short term. NAEP's current type of univariate interpretive follow-up reports represents a first-order type of interpretive reporting. We envision much more in-depth analyses, such as those described in the example in the following section. This level of analysis undoubtedly will present challenges to NAEP's time frames for reporting, which have been focused on presenting summary score results as shortly as possible after the administration of the assessment. Nevertheless, reports that provide interpretive context should be released by NCES as quickly as possible after the release of *Report Cards*, accompanied by the same kinds of high profile press conferences and press release packets that are used for the release of reports of national and state summary results. Although timely reporting of summary score results is a necessary and laudable goal, when these results are released in the absence of information that provides an interpretive context for helping users understand results, then the value of NAEP as an indicator is much diminished.

A Successful First Step: NCTM's Interpretive Reports

A multiple-methods NAEP has the potential to provide an array of in-depth information about achievement in NAEP disciplines; still, it is a relatively easy task to glean more detailed information from the current assessments than presently occurs. Examination of data (particularly students' responses to constructed-response items) from the current assessments provides a basis for profiling student knowledge. For example, it is possible to analyze students' specific errors, examine the quality of their explanations, and interpret overall performance on relevant clusters of items in ways that characterize what students can and cannot do.

Since the first mathematics assessment, the National Council of Teachers of Mathematics has written interpretive reports based on the analysis of students' responses to individual NAEP items. These reports, supported by funding external to NAEP, characterize student performance at different levels of detail appropriate for different audiences. For example, the most recent monograph, reporting on the sixth NAEP mathematics assessment, administered in 1992, includes an analysis of students' understanding of basic number concepts and properties, their computational skills, and their ability to apply number concepts and skills to solving problems, based on examinations of items that assess these skills and concepts (Kenney and Silver, 1997). The report includes data across approximately 100 individual NAEP items. For some items, responses are analyzed in some detail; for others, p-values are reported. The reports, however, go well beyond cataloging the results for individual items. Patterns of responses and errors are analyzed to draw conclusions about student performance on specific topics. For example, the authors of the 1996 report concluded (Kenney and Silver, 1997:137-138):

> [S]tudents at all three grade levels appear to have an understanding of place value, rounding and number theory concepts for whole and rational numbers in familiar, straightforward contexts. Students' understanding improves across grade levels but falls when the contexts are unfamiliar or complex. Students at all three grade levels perform well on addition and subtraction word problems with whole and rational numbers that are set in familiar contexts and only involve one step calculation. . . .[S]ome students at all three grade levels attempt to solve multistep problems as though they involved single-step procedures. . . .
>
> The most troubling results were the low performance levels associated with students' ability to justify or explain their answers to regular and extended, constructed-response items.

The NCTM interpretive teams have consistently documented that the most critical deficiency in students' learning of mathematics at all ages is their inability to apply the skills that they have learned to solve problems. This conclusion is consistently supported by the fine-grained analysis of student performance in virtually every content area of the mathematics framework. The analyses also provide a perspective on relations between skill acquisition and the development of understanding of fundamental concepts. These conclusions, based on interpretive analyses of students' responses, address issues that are at the core of public debate regarding curriculum choices. NAEP should help inform this debate and provide a basis for more informed policy decisions by integrating these types of analyses and reports into plans for assessments in all NAEP subject areas.

A good step in this direction was NAEP's establishment of collaborative relationship with arts organizations to develop reports and dissemination strategies for the 1997 NAEP arts assessment. The collaboration with NCTM to conduct and report the results of interpretive analyses should be continued, and similar collaborations with organizations in NAEP's other subject areas should be established (e.g., the National Council of Teachers of English, the International Reading Association, the National Science Teachers Association, the National Council for Social Studies).

Although the NCTM interpretive teams have learned a great deal by analyzing student performance, the NAEP mathematics assessment is not specifically designed to support these kinds of within- and across-item analyses. Much could be improved in the structure of NAEP items and rubrics to better capture students' understanding in mathematics. Because the response data are not accumulated in ways that facilitate these analyses (Kenney and Silver, 1997), the interpretations are less explicit than they might be if the assessment were specifically designed to support them. The conclusions identify both specific and general areas of student weakness, but it is not possible to aggregate data to provide specific percentages of students who demonstrated understanding of core concepts or proficiency in essential skills or who meet benchmark criteria for applying concepts and skills to solve problems, because the assessments were not designed to include sets of items that ensured that this sort of analysis and reporting would be possible.

The NCTM reports provide an example of the educationally useful and policy-relevant information that can be gleaned from students' responses in the current assessments, and they point toward the even more useful information that could be provided if assessments were developed with these analyses in mind. A first step in this assessment development strategy—the development of families of items for use in large-scale assessments—is discussed next.

Recommended Next Step: Developing Item Families

The notion of item families in NAEP was first articulated in the framework for the 1996 main NAEP mathematics assessment. However, an analysis conducted by Patricia Kenney for this committee showed that the sets of items included in the 1996 mathematics assessment exhibited few of the characteristics of either of the two kinds of families of items described in the framework (Kenney, 1999). The framework describes two types of item families: a vertical family and a horizontal family. A vertical family includes items or tasks that measure students' understanding of a single important mathematics concept *within* a content strand (e.g., numerical patterns in algebra) but at different levels, such as providing a definition, applying the concept in both familiar and novel settings, and generalizing knowledge about the concept to represent a new level of understanding. A horizontal family of items involves the assessment of students' understanding of a concept or principle *across* the various content strands in the NAEP program within a grade level or across grade levels. For example, the concept of proportionality can be assessed in a variety of contexts, such as number properties and operations, measurement, geometry, probability, and algebra. The framework also suggested that a family of items could be related through a common context that serves as a rich problem setting for the items.

In the volume of research papers that accompanies this report, Minstrell (1999) and Kenney (1999) describe strategies for developing families of items for use in future NAEP large-scale assessments of science and mathematics. One such item family in mathematics and the rationale underlying its construction is presented in Appendix C. This family of items assesses the progression of grade 4 students' understanding of numerical patterns; it was constructed using a combination of items from the 1996 main NAEP assessment, supplemented with new items that together form a coherent family. This example illustrates one way in which improved interpretations of students' achievements can be generated by making relatively modest changes to NAEP's current assessment development strategy.

We close this section by reiterating one of the chapter's underlying themes: frameworks and assessments must be designed with goals for reporting as a guide. We urge the implementation of a strategy for reporting NAEP results in which reports of summary scores are accompanied by, or at the very least quickly followed by, interpretive reports produced by disciplinary specialists and based on analyses of patterns of student responses across families of items as well as across multiple assessment methodologies.

A VISION FOR ASSESSMENT DEVELOPMENT IN NAEP

The goals that we have set forth in this chapter are ambitious. They are very challenging from the standpoints of assessment development and assessment administration and operations. These goals—improving the assessment of more complex aspects of the current frameworks, expanding the conceptualization of NAEP's dimensions of achievement; implementing a multiple-methods design, and extracting and reporting more in-depth interpretive information from students' responses—may even seem overwhelming. However, each is critical if an already respected program is to better fulfill its mission of assessing academic achievement and be well positioned to meet the information demands of its users in the next century.

If these goals are implemented, what would be accomplished? What would the new paradigm NAEP look like? How would it differ from what exists now? If the recommendations presented in this chapter were implemented, NAEP would be characterized by:

- an assessment development process that is guided by a vision of the kinds of inferences and conclusions about student achievement to be described in reports of NAEP results,

- an assessment design in which assessment purpose is aligned with assessment method,
- core NAEP subjects that are assessed using the current large-scale survey (for measurement of trends) and whatever multiple methods are best suited to assess aspects of the framework not well assessed through large-scale surveys,
- nontrend subjects assessed using whatever combination of surveys and alternative assessment methods is best suited to meet the goals described in the subject area's framework,
- an array of alternative assessment methods to assess the broader conceptualizations of achievement that are included in future NAEP frameworks, and
- subject-specific reports of achievement results that include in-depth portrayals of student achievement gleaned from the entire array of methods used to assess a subject area; in core subjects, such reports ideally would also include summary proficiency scores from large-scale assessments and results from achievement level setting.

In Figure 4-6 we present a further-developed view of new paradigm NAEP and other measures of student achievement within the coordinated system of educational indicators that we proposed in Chapter 1.

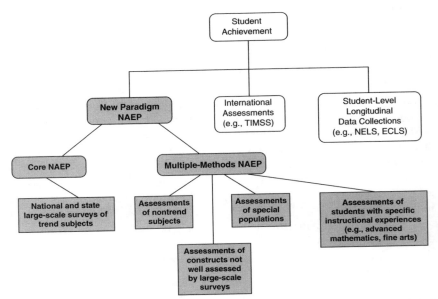

FIGURE 4-6 Measures of student achievement, including new paradigm NAEP. NOTE: TIMSS = Third International Mathematics and Science Study; NELS = National Education Longitudinal Study; ECLS = Early Childhood Longitudinal Study.

MAJOR CONCLUSIONS AND RECOMMENDATIONS

Conclusions

Conclusion 4A. **The current development of NAEP frameworks and assessments is not guided by a clear vision of the kinds of inferences to be drawn from the results.** These frameworks and assessments support neither the reporting of achievement levels nor in-depth interpretations of student performance.

Conclusion 4B. **There are many complex steps between framework development and reporting, and the intentions of the framework developers are often lost in this sequence of activities.** Although NAEP has made progress in improving continuity from one step to another, attending to the lack of coherence across steps is still a challenge.

Conclusion 4C. **Currently, NAEP focuses on the assessment of subject-area knowledge and skills but does not adequately capitalize on contemporary research, theory, and practice in ways that would support in-depth interpretations of student knowledge and understanding.**

Conclusion 4D. **Measuring student achievement only through NAEP's current large-scale survey precludes adequate assessment of (1) the more cognitively complex portions of the domains described in the current frameworks and (2) expanded domains represented by conceptions of achievement that are responsive to the changing demands of society.**

Conclusion 4E. **NAEP's current reporting metrics fail to capitalize on interpretive information that can be derived from responses to individual items or sets of items.**

Conclusion 4F. **Insufficient time is allotted to assessment development, which restricts activities needed for developing the kinds of materials that support more interpretive analyses and more informative reporting.**

Recommendations

Recommendation 4A. The inferences to be made about student performance in NAEP reports should guide the development of NAEP frameworks. These inferential goals should also guide a coherent set of assessment development activities.

Recommendation 4B. NAEP's frameworks and assessments should capitalize on research, theory, and practice about student learning in the content domains to guide (1) the development of items, tasks, scoring rubrics, and assessment designs that better assess the more complex aspects of the content domains and (2) the development of integrated families of items that support in-depth interpretations of student knowledge and understanding.

Recommendation 4C. NAEP needs to include carefully designed targeted assessments to assess the kinds of student achievement that cannot be measured well by large-scale assessments or are not reflected in subject-area frameworks.

Recommendation 4D. NAEP reports should provide interpretive information, derived from analyses of patterns of students' responses to families of related items, in conjunction with the overall achievement results.

Recommendation 4E. More time, attention, and resources are needed for the initial stages of assessment development (task development, scoring, tryouts, and field tests) to produce a rich array of assessment materials.

Recommendation 4F. In order to accomplish the committee's recommendations, NAEP's research and development agenda should emphasize the following:

- development of materials (items, tasks, families of items, and scoring rubrics) that support improved assessment of current frameworks in NAEP's large-scale survey assessment,
- development of targeted assessments that tap components of the current frameworks and expanded achievement domains not well assessed via large-scale survey methods,
- methods for producing and presenting more in-depth interpretive information in NAEP reports to make overall results more un-

derstandable, minimize improper or incorrect inferences, and support the needs of users who seek information that assists them in determining what to do in response to NAEP results, and

• development and implementation of sampling, scaling, and analysis models that accommodate the use of families of interdependent items in the large-scale survey assessment.

5

Setting Reasonable and Useful
Performance Standards

Summary Conclusion 5. **Standards-based reporting is intended to
be useful in communicating student results, but the current process
for setting NAEP achievement levels is fundamentally flawed.**

Summary Recommendation 5. **The current process for setting
achievement levels should be replaced. New models for setting
achievement levels should be developed in which the judgmental
process and data are made clearer to NAEP's users.**

INTRODUCTION

The current NAEP authorizing legislation, the Improving America's Schools
Act (P.L. 103-328), states that "The National Assessment Governing Board . . .
shall develop appropriate student performance levels for each age and grade in
each subject area to be tested under the National Assessment. . . . " The National
Assessment Governing Board (NAGB) first began its groundbreaking work on
the development of the performance standards for student achievement in 1990.
Since that time, results from most of the main NAEP assessments have been
reported not only in descriptive terms—summary scores that reflect *what students know and can do* in NAEP's subject areas—but in evaluative terms—
percentages of students that reach specific levels of performance defined by *what
students should know and be able to do.* In keeping with its historic commitment
to reporting results on metrics understandable to policy makers and the public,
NAGB has used these performance standards, more commonly known as NAEP

achievement levels, to chart the progress of the nation's students toward high academic achievement. Reporting results in relation to performance standards is a mechanism by which NAEP currently fulfills the evaluative needs of its users— their need to understand whether student achievement, as presented in descriptive results, is "good enough."

In this chapter, we begin by providing an overview of NAEP's performance standards and the achievement-level-setting process as it was conducted through the 1996 main NAEP assessments. We then summarize the major findings of previous evaluations and research efforts that have examined this process and present a detailed accounting and evaluation of the achievement-level-setting process as it was applied to the 1996 NAEP science assessment. We follow with a discussion of the committee's major conclusions regarding performance standards and the achievement-level-setting process, and then present recommendations that lay out constructive steps by which NAEP can improve how it fulfills this critical evaluative function.

NAEP PERFORMANCE STANDARDS AND THE ACHIEVEMENT-LEVEL-SETTING PROCESS

Goals of Standards-Based Reporting

As described earlier, in the 1970s and early 1980s, NAEP reports were built around the assessment materials themselves; by displaying individual assessment items and associated student performance data, initial reports allowed NAEP users to review the types of tasks students could and could not do. Since the implementation of the first redesign of NAEP in 1984, data on item responses have been summarized across items to provide a picture of overall performance for the nation and for key demographic subgroups. Group (or subgroup) performance has been reported on a 300-, 400-, or 500-point scale and, until recently, has been accompanied by descriptions of the knowledge and skills typical of performance at given scaled score levels. Current NAEP *Report Cards* for both main NAEP and trend NAEP continue the convention of reporting overall performance as a summary scale score (Pellegrino et al., 1998).

NAGB's recent, congressionally mandated work on performance standards for NAEP has added fundamentally new data to the reporting of main NAEP results. NAGB has established policy definitions for three levels of student achievement—basic, proficient, and advanced (Reese et al., 1997:8):

• *Basic:* partial mastery of prerequisite knowledge and skills that are fundamental for proficient work at each grade.
• *Proficient:* solid academic performance for each grade assessed. Students reaching this level have demonstrated competence over challenging subject

matter, including subject-matter knowledge, application of such knowledge to real-world situations, and analytical skills appropriate to the subject matter.

- *Advanced:* superior performance.

This innovative system for standards-based reporting allows information on what students know and can do to be compared with consensus judgments about what students at each grade level should know and be able to do. Thus, in addition to providing scale scores that portray the overall performance of groups of students, standards-based reporting provides percentages of the groups of students that are at or above the basic, proficient, and advanced performance levels. The NAEP approach to standards-based reporting offers many potential benefits:

- *Aiding communication.* Many, including NAGB and Congress, contend that standards-based reporting metrics hold more meaning for policy makers and other NAEP users than do reports on the current, arbitrary 300-, 400-, or 500-point reporting scales. Proponents believe that standards-based reporting facilitates communication and understanding of achievement results, stimulates public discourse, and serves to generate support for education. The current achievement levels are rigorous and allow policy makers to talk about goals for increasing the numbers of students performing at high levels.

Performance standards serve an important evaluative function for NAEP's users. During the last decade, many state and commercial testing programs have adopted standards-based reporting metrics, and many educators, policy makers, and parents have come to expect reports that state whether observed performance levels are "good enough." It would be very difficult for NAEP to recuse itself from the current movement toward standards-based reporting.

- *Providing detailed descriptions of prerequisite skills and knowledge.* Proponents also contend that educators, curriculum developers, and other subject-area specialists will benefit from having descriptions of what it means to be basic or proficient or advanced in a discipline to help focus curriculum and instruction in key areas. However, even more detailed descriptions may be required if educators and curriculum experts are to get the most from NAEP results.

- *Promoting improved performance.* Another reason for developing and reporting challenging standards for achievement is to encourage teachers to teach and students to learn to high levels. NAGB contends that achievement levels will prompt America's progress toward high academic attainment. To date, however, there is a paucity of evidence to indicate whether this is the case.

Although standards-based reporting offers much of potential value, there are also possible negative consequences as well. The public may be misled if they infer a different meaning from the achievement-level descriptions than is intended. (For example, for performance at the advanced level, the public and policy makers could infer a meaning based on other uses of the label "advanced," such as advanced placement, that implies a different standard. That is, reporting that 10 percent of grade 12 students are performing at an "advanced" level on NAEP does not bear any relation to the percentage of students performing successfully in advanced placement courses, although we have noted instances in which this inference has been drawn.) In addition, the public may misread the degree of consensus that actually exists about the performance standards and thus have undue confidence in the meaning of the results. Similarly, audiences for NAEP reports may not understand the judgmental basis underlying the standards. All of these false impressions could lead the public and policy makers to erroneous conclusions about the status and progress of education in this country.

The Achievement-Level-Setting Process

During the development of frameworks for each of the main NAEP subject areas, NAGB's policy definitions of achievement levels are applied, resulting in more detailed subject-specific descriptions of performance expectations for each of the three achievement levels; these are known as the "preliminary achievement-level descriptions." As an integral part of the framework, these descriptions are intended to provide guidance for the development of items and tasks for the assessment. After the administration of the assessment, these performance standards are applied to the assessment results in a process known as achievement-level setting, the outcome of which is the reporting of NAEP results in terms of percentages of students performing at basic, proficient, and advanced achievement levels. Once achievement levels are set for a NAEP subject, they stay fixed for multiple administrations of the assessment, providing a mechanism to observe changes in these percentages over time and presumably a more policy-relevant reporting metric. When a new NAEP assessment based on a new or highly revised framework is developed and administered, new achievement levels would be set.

In the NAEP achievement-level-setting process, through 1996 NAGB employed the most prevalent approach to standard setting currently in use. Using the Angoff approach and its variants, panels of raters are convened, are trained on the knowledge and skills of examinees at different levels, and, in the case of NAEP, are asked to refine the preliminary achievement-level descriptions and then estimate the probability that a hypothetical student at the boundary of a given achievement level will get an item correct. Thus, for each multiple-choice item on the assessment, panelists estimate three probabilities: (1) the probability that a student whose performance is on the border between basic and below basic will correctly answer the item, (2) the probability that a student whose performance is on the border between proficient and basic will correctly answer the item, and (3) the probability that a student whose performance is on the border between advanced and proficient will correctly answer the item. For constructed-response items with multiple possible score levels, panelists are asked to estimate mean item scores for students at each of these same three boundaries. Item judgments are averaged across items and panelists to arrive at cutscores that distinguish the levels of performance. (For a detailed accounting of this methodology, see National Academy of Education, 1993a; Cohen et al., 1997; and Reckase, 1998.)

Through 1997, NAGB has set and reported achievement levels in mathematics, reading, history, geography, and, most recently, science. (See Linn, 1998, for a brief review of NAEP's achievement-level-setting efforts from 1990 through 1996.) Although the impact of reporting by achievement levels is not yet clear, many evaluators and researchers have been critical of the process and the results. Key findings from past evaluations of the NAEP's achievement levels and the achievement-level-setting process are described next.

SELECTED FINDINGS FROM PAST NAEP EVALUATIONS AND RESEARCH

NAGB's achievement-level-setting procedures and results have been the focus of considerable review: Linn et al. (1991), for the NAEP Technical Review Panel; Stufflebeam et al. (1991), under contract to NAGB; the U.S. General Accounting Office (1993); and the National Academy of Education (1992, 1993a, 1993b, 1996). Collectively, these reviewers agreed that:

- *The judgment task posed to raters is too difficult and confusing.* In the application of the Angoff procedure to the NAEP achievement-level-setting context, raters are asked to estimate the probability that a hypothetical student at the boundary of a given achievement level will get an item correct. This requires raters to delineate the ways the student could answer the item, relate these to cognitive processes that students may or may not possess, and operationally link these processes with the categorization of performance at three different levels (Pellegrino et al., 1998). This judgment process represents a nearly impossible cognitive task (National Academy of Education, 1993a, 1996).
- *There are internal inconsistencies in raters' judgments for different item types.* On past NAEP assessments, notable differences were observed in the cutscores set for each achievement level depending on item difficulty, number of score levels specified in the item scoring rubrics, and response format—e.g., multiple choice versus constructed response. Method variance of this kind is problematic because it renders cutscore locations dependent on the mix of item types in the assessment, in addition to rendering questionable the verbal description of the meaning of achievement at each level (National Academy of Education, 1993a, 1996; Linn, 1998).
- *The NAEP item pools are not adequate to reliably estimate performance*

at the advanced levels. Evaluators have contended that, particularly at the advanced level, the item pools do not represent well the types of knowledge and skills that the NAEP achievement-level descriptions (and national subject-area content standards) portray as being required of students demonstrating advanced performance (Stufflebeam et al., 1991; National Academy of Education, 1996).

• *Appropriate validity evidence for the cutscores is lacking.* There has been a lack of correspondence between NAEP achievement-level results and external evidence of student achievement, such as course-taking patterns and data from other assessments (for example, the advanced placement examinations) on which larger proportions of students perform at high levels. Numerous external comparison studies conducted by the National Academy of Education supported the conclusion that NAEP cutscores between the proficient and advanced levels and between the basic and proficient levels are consistently set too high, with the outcome of achievement-level results that do not appear to be reasonable relative to numerous other external comparisons (National Academy of Education, 1993a, 1996; Linn, 1998).

• *Neither the descriptions of expected student competencies nor the exemplar items are appropriate for describing actual student performance at the achievement levels defined by the cutscores.* Discrepancies between the achievement-level descriptions and the locations of the cutscores create a mismatch between what students in the score range defined by the cutscores are said to be able to do and what it is they actually did on the assessment (Linn, 1998). Also, evaluators have repeatedly concluded that the knowledge and skills assessed by exemplar items do not match up well with the knowledge and skill expectations put forth in the achievement-level descriptions, nor do the exemplars provide a reasonable view of the range of types of performance expected at a given achievement level (National Academy of Education, 1993a, 1993b, 1996).

Counterarguments are presented by Hambleton and Bourque (1991), Kane (1995), Mehrens (1995), and Brennan (1998).

Collectively, past evaluators (Linn et al., 1991; Stufflebeam et al., 1991; U.S. General Accounting Office, 1993; National Academy of Education, 1992, 1993a, 1993b, 1996) have concluded that the achievement levels are flawed; they have recommended that the current achievement-level-setting results not be used for NAEP reporting, unless accompanied by clear and strong warnings that the results should be interpreted as suggestive rather than definitive because they are based on a methodology that has been repeatedly questioned in terms of its accuracy and validity (National Academy of Education, 1996:106). In its final report, the National Academy of Education panel reiterated its position on achievement-level setting. The panel stated (1997:115):

> Given the growing importance and popularity of performance standards in reporting assessment results, it is important that the NAEP standards be set in defensible ways. Because we have concerns that the current NAEP perfor-

mance standards are flawed, we recommend that the Governing Board and NCES undertake a thorough examination of these standards, taking into consideration the relationship between the purposes for which standards are being set, and the conceptualization and implementation of the assessment itself. In addition, any new standards need to be shown to be reliable and valid for the purposes for which they are set.

1996 SCIENCE ACHIEVEMENT-LEVEL SETTING

The NAEP achievement-level-setting process has evolved over time, in part in response to the evaluations summarized above, although variants of the modified Angoff procedure have remained in place. In accordance with the committee's charge from Congress, we reviewed the processes used to develop achievement-level descriptions and set achievement levels for the 1996 main NAEP science assessment, the most recent achievement level setting to be completed. Our review of the science achievement-level setting informed our evaluation of the current achievement-level-setting model and, in conjunction with the previous evaluations and research cited above, led us to conclusions about the current standards and process, as well as recommendations for future achievement-level-setting efforts.

Although it would be hard to argue that earlier achievement-level-setting efforts were satisfactory, achievement-level setting for the 1996 science assessment was particularly troubling. The process suffered from many of the same difficulties identified by the National Academy of Education in previous efforts, and the solutions for dealing with these challenges ultimately led to the issuing of a report on science achievement levels that blurred the distinction between "what students can do" and "what students should be able to do" that standards-based reporting is intended to make clear.

To set achievement levels for the 1996 NAEP science assessment, NAGB and its subcontractor for achievement-level setting, American College Testing, Inc. (ACT), used the same general modified Angoff method that was used in other disciplines. The result of this process (as in previous efforts) was that, at all three grade levels, very low percentages of students scored at or above the proficient level and almost no students reached the advanced level; at grade 4, an unusually high percentage (in comparison to other subjects) performed at or above the basic cutscore. For the first time in NAEP achievement-level setting, a rater group said they were dissatisfied with the process and their results; the grade 8 raters said they were not confident that their group held a common conception of student performance at the different levels.

To examine and rectify the grade 8 problem, ACT reconvened the grade 8 raters to discuss their discontent and to reconsider the ratings, cutscores, and achievement-level definitions that they had generated at the initial rating session. In that session, the reconvened raters lowered the cutscores (increasing slightly the percentages of students scoring at or above proficient). It is important to note that, originally and at the reconvention, the ratings by representatives of the public were more stringent than those of the educator and nonteacher educator raters. For past subjects, there were only minimal differences between the judgments of teachers, nonteacher educators, and general public representatives. In addition, there were also minimal differences when raters' judgments were aggregated and analyzed based on gender, racial/ethnic status, region, and school district size. At the same time, ACT explored a number of methods for recalculating the cutscores; however, none of these adjustments corrected the fundamental problem—that some cutscores appeared to be unreasonably high and others too low.

In February 1997, NAGB's achievement-level committee met to consider the original results and the reconvention results and used their own expert judgments—in this case, representing a policy perspective rather than a disciplinary one—to set "reasonable" science cutscores. The committee examined the 1996 results in combination with external comparative information, including grade 8 results from the Third International Mathematics and Science Study (TIMSS), advanced placement examination results from the same cohort of students as the NAEP grade 12 sample, and NAEP achievement-level results in other disciplines. The achievement-level committee recommended resetting seven of the nine cutscores. In an undocumented process, the committee moved four cutscores up, five cutscores down, and left two cutscores as set by the science raters. Based on the resetting of the cutscores, as many as 40 items (from grade-level pools of approximately 190) moved from one achievement level to another (i.e., items that previously had been mapped as "proficient" now mapped as "advanced"). These post hoc adjustments to the cutscores recommended by the raters indicated that NAGB now questioned the method it had relied on previously to justify the setting of high standards in other disciplines (e.g., history and geography) and reiterated the findings of previous evaluation panels that cutscores derived through the current process lead to unreasonable results. Thus, in the case of science, NAGB's own examination of the external comparative data led it to the same conclusion that multiple evaluation panels had reached: that the results of the achievement-level-setting process were not believable. NAGB then continued to pursue consideration of their own reset cutscores.

In March 1997, the full National Assessment Governing Board adopted the adjusted cutscores as interim results and asked ACT and NAGB staff to develop new achievement-level definitions that would correspond to these new cutscores and to continue examining the results, using then-forthcoming TIMSS results for other grades and other external data.

In April 1997, NAGB staff charged a group of science educators who had been involved with the development of the 1996 NAEP science framework and assessment with developing new achievement-level descriptions to correspond to the adjusted levels. This group examined the new cutscores and the items positioned at those cuts and determined that new achievement-level descriptions based on those items would be at variance with NAGB's policy definitions; that is, they judged that the knowledge and skills tested by items bounded by the new cutscores were inconsistent with generic descriptions of basic, proficient, and advanced performance and with NAGB's press for high standards. They elected not to author definitions. Given this science panel's conclusions, NAGB's executive committee decided later in April to defer issuing the interim science achievement levels, which had been scheduled to be issued with the *NAEP 1996 Science Report Card* in early May (O'Sullivan et al., 1997).

In June 1997, NAGB impaneled another group of science educators to examine the full range of items that mapped to each new achievement level, determine the knowledge and skills assessed by these items, and author descriptions based on their observations of the items and student response data. The panel used behavioral anchoring techniques to describe the levels and select exemplar items. The three grade groups successfully completed the tasks and generated new descriptions. They offered little note of any discord between the behavioral anchoring-based descriptions and the policy definitions; although such discord would have been predicted based on the April science panel's conclusion that the items bounded by the new cutscores were no longer consistent with the policy definitions. It is important to note that the behavioral anchoring-based descriptions differ from both the preliminary achievement-level descriptions and the achievement-level descriptions developed by the original group of raters, in that they do not describe *what students should know and be able to do* in science at basic, proficient, and advanced levels; instead, they portray *what students currently know and can do* in science at levels prescribed by the adjusted cutscores approved by NAGB. Thus, instead of laying out performance standards and then determining what percentages of students met those standards, NAGB determined cutscores that, based on their policy judgment, provided reasonable percentages of students at each of the three levels, and then asked the science educators to use behavioral anchoring techniques to analyze items and describe what students at those set levels could do.

NAGB met in August 1997 to consider these results and make recommendations about science achievement-level reporting. At that meeting, NAGB's achievement-level committee reviewed the data, new definitions, and exemplar items; it considered whether the new levels describe what U.S. students currently know and can do or depict what they should know and be able to do. The committee argued that Congress charged them to develop "useful" performance levels, and that the adjusted cutscores and resulting definitions better met that end than the descriptions and levels that had been produced through the original achievement-level-setting process.

The achievement-level committee recommended that NAGB release the new achievement-level descriptions and the adjusted achievement-level results. NAGB expressed satisfaction with the application of behavioral anchoring methods to replace the original achievement-level descriptions; they approved the adjusted cutscores, definitions, and exemplar items and recommended that results be reported.

The science achievement-level report was issued in October 1997. Recognizing that the achievement-level descriptions developed through the behavioral anchoring no longer represented conceptions of what students *should* know and be able to do, in the summary report, titled *What Do Students Know?*, NAGB presented the definitions of basic, proficient, and advanced as "what students know and are able to do" (National Assessment Governing Board, 1997). It is not clear that the significance of this distinction was recognized by the press, public, or other users of NAEP results.

In summary, in the 1996 NAEP science achievement-level-setting effort, instead of reporting achievement results relative to an established standard of performance as in NAEP's previous achievement-level reports, the science report presented results that were based on NAGB's judgment as to what constituted reasonable percentages of students at the three achievement levels. NAGB had rejected the achievement-level-setting process that it had previously used to set achievement levels in other subjects, replacing it with an ad hoc process in which NAGB reset many of the cutscores. However, neither the process nor the judgments used were described in any detail in the report on science achievement levels.

THE COMMITTEE'S EVALUATION

The Value of Standards-Based Reporting in NAEP

Despite the very serious continuing difficulties with the achievement-level-setting process and the blurring of the "can do"/"should be able to do" distinction that occurred in reporting NAEP's achievement-level results for science, the concept of standards-based reporting still appears to have the potential to be a significant improvement in communicating about student achievement to the public and to policy makers. However, there is not an extensive body of research on the ways in which standards-based information is interpreted and used by the various audiences for NAEP reports. In a study of press reports from the 1994 main NAEP reading assessment and the 1996 main NAEP mathematics assessment, Barron and Koretz (in press) found that achievement levels were the most popular reporting metric, with the most commonly reported statistic being the percentage of students reaching the proficient level. In a similar, earlier analysis of press reports from the 1990 main NAEP mathematics assessment, Koretz and Deibert (1995/1996) found that the achievement-level metrics were used extensively in reporting national and state results, but less often in reporting differences between major subgroups. Much of the additional research that does exist has focused on alternative forms of standards-based reporting (Hambleton, 1997; Koretz and Deibert, 1995/1996; Burstein et al., 1996). One likely reason for the dearth of detailed research about how NAEP's users interpret and use achievement-level results is that the idea of reporting performance against standards is such an obvious improvement over an abstract and artificial proficiency scale that the perceived need for or value of such research is low.

The NAEP performance standards developed by NAGB represent an extension of the national educational goals first proposed by President George Bush and the state governors in 1989 (Alexander, 1991). In its report on the science achievement levels, NAGB (1997:5) makes it clear that the goal is that "all students should be proficient." Having such a goal provides a clearer basis for assessing progress, since the significance of a 10-point gain on a 0 to 500 proficiency scale is difficult to assess. Viewing improvement as the percentage of students at or above the proficient level of achievement—with a target of 100 percent—provides added meaning in a clear and easy to understand metric.

Evidence of the perceived value of NAEP's standards-based reporting is given by the fact that *Education Week's* report *Quality Counts* (1998) reported NAEP state-level mathematics and science results entirely in terms of the percentage of students at or above the proficient level of achievement, even though the initial NAEP science *Report Card* had presented results only on the numeric proficiency scale (O'Sullivan et al., 1997) and even though the report of science achievement results provided achievement-level descriptions of student performance based on what students "can do" rather than what students "should be able to do." State assessment programs also increasingly are taking NAEP's lead in reporting by performance standards.

Another cited benefit of standards-based reporting is the potential impact on curriculum development and instruction; however, there also has been a lack of good research on the impact of the achievement-level descriptions on these areas. Rich, multifaceted descriptions of student knowledge and skills at each achievement level could help teachers, teacher educators, and curriculum developers focus their instruction on areas judged to be most critical to proficient performance. However, because NAEP does not provide student-level or school-level data, it is difficult to conceive of it as a source of information whereby teachers would know where their own classes stand relative to the achievement levels. Furthermore, the lack of systematic diagnostic information related to particular elements in the achievement-level descriptions limits the capacity to identify specific deficiencies at either the state or the national level. Improvements in this area are possible, however; in Chapter 4, we urged NAEP to produce more in-depth interpretations of student performance that can be derived from analyses of student responses across and within items; such interpretations are likely to enhance understanding of the meaning of performance at each of NAEP's achievement levels and may have the potential to provide some basic guidance to educators about areas of strength and weakness at state and national levels.

We also recommend an addition to the current reporting of NAEP achievement-level results—the provision of descriptions of what students who are "below the basic level" can do. The 1996 mathematics achievement level results showed that 50 percent, 48 percent, and 42 percent of students at grades 4, 8, and 12, respectively, performed below the basic achievement level. A total of 33 percent (grade 4), 39 percent (grade 8), and 43 percent (grade 12) performed below the basic level on the 1996 science assessment. Despite the large proportions of students performing below the basic level, no descriptions of the performance of these students were provided in reports of achievement-level results. Results of a recent study of state testing directors' perceptions of the usefulness of NAEP results indicated that this important group of NAEP users also recommended the reporting of descriptions of student performance below the basic level (Bullock and DeStefano, 1998). Such descriptions could be developed using behavioral anchoring methods after the achievement-level cutscores are set. Subject-area specialists could develop descriptions of those items anchoring on the NAEP scale below the basic-level cutscore.

In summary, despite the continuing serious failings of the current standard-setting process, NAEP should continue its commitment to finding valid and useful ways of reporting standards-based achievement results. The ability to evaluate whether achievement results meet well-defined expectations as embodied in achievement standards is likely to enhance the usefulness of NAEP results for policy makers, and, in addition, the detailed descriptions of student performance that accompany the achievement levels are potentially useful to educators.

The Judgmental Nature of Achievement-Level Setting

The concept of setting standards implies judgments that vary across individuals. Most people would agree that one person's idea of what constitutes high standards will often differ from another person's idea of them. However, as NAEP achievement-level setting has evolved over the course of this decade, the detailed way in which the composition of the achievement-level panels is specified and the complex process of collecting, aggregating, reviewing, and revising item-level judgments from these panels has left many with the impression that this is primarily a scientific process. The notion is that something like the mean of everyone's judgment about what constitutes proficient (or basic or advanced) performance on the NAEP assessment reflects an absolute truth to be approximated as accurately as possible through sampling and aggregation procedures.

In fact, "true" achievement levels do not exist. Standard setting rests on informed judgment; thus, there are no right or wrong standards (although the meaning of the standards that are set can be poorly or inappropriately communicated). However, despite the judgmental nature of the process, the process itself and the mechanism whereby decisions are reached in achievement-level setting should be well documented and clearly communicated.

In the report on achievement-level results for science, NAGB noted that they did not accept some of the panel's recommendations because they "did not meet its criterion of reasonableness" (National Assessment Governing Board, 1997:5). This reasonableness criterion is not further discussed, nor is any reference to a further discussion provided. We are concerned that the process by which the science achievement levels were set is not readily replicable, primarily because the criterion used to judge reasonableness and the rules or process used to make adjustments when initial results failed the reasonableness criterion are not well documented. The report mentions TIMSS, advanced placement information, and NAEP results from other disciplines as points of comparison in judging the reasonableness of the proposed science achievement levels. In order to ensure some level of consistency in future efforts, it would be helpful to understand how this other information was used, the criterion for determining how large a discrepancy between proposed achievement-level results and external data would lead to a change in achievement-level cutscores, and how the magnitude and direction of a change in the location of cutscores was decided.

The report of science achievement levels states clearly that the levels are based on the judgment of the National Assessment Governing Board. The judgmental nature of the achievement levels was less clear in earlier reports. The committee recommends that NAGB should more explicitly communicate that the achievement levels result from an inherently judgmental process to avoid any false impressions that the achievement levels reflect some deeper scientific truth. The reports also should describe more fully the means by which judgments are made and criteria applied in determining the reasonableness of the achievement levels that result from these judgments.

The Achievement-Level-Setting Process

Prior reviews, beginning with the Stufflebeam et al. review (1991), which was commissioned and then rejected by NAGB, and continuing through reviews by Linn et al. (1991), the U.S. General Accounting Office (1993), the National Academy of Education's Trial State NAEP evaluation panel (1992, 1993a, 1993b, 1996), have all expressed concern with the process and the results of NAEP achievement-level-setting procedures. After reviewing the process and the results of the achievement-level setting for science, we concur with these past evaluators that NAEP's procedures and results are fundamentally flawed.

Our conclusion that the current procedures are fundamentally flawed is based on three factors. First, the results are not believable. A primary concern is that too few students are judged to be advanced relative to many other common conceptions of advanced performance in a discipline (e.g., advanced placement course work). NAGB itself did not accept that the numbers of students judged to be advanced in science at all three grades were reasonable on the basis of results of the current process.

A second reason is that achievement-level-setting results vary significantly depending on the type and difficulty of the items used in the judgment process. Constructed-response items typically result in higher cutscores than those set using multiple-choice items. A similar result holds for easier versus difficult items.

A third reason for our conclusion is research that suggests that panelists have difficulty in estimating accurately the probability that test items will be answered correctly by students with specified characteristics (Shepard, 1995). Panelists have particular difficulty in estimating the probability that an item will be answered correctly by a hypothetical student whose performance is at the borderline of two achievement levels (Impara and Plake, 1998). Even if panelists could judge the relative difficulty of different items, any constant error in estimating p-values will accumulate to a potentially significant bias in the overall sum (Linn and Shepard, 1997). The same concerns apply to the mean estimation procedures used with constructed-response items with multiple possible score levels. These concerns are particularly critical with respect to the advanced level. Students at this level will get most of the items right most of the time. Systematic biases toward overestimating high probabilities and underestimating low probabilities (e.g., a tendency to "round up," for example from 0.95 to 1.00) will create the bias toward higher achievement levels that has been of great concern in the NAEP achievement-level-setting results.

NAGB's own rejection of the results of the science achievement-level-setting and the imposition of their own judgment to set final levels demonstrates the critical need for an alternative paradigm and methods. We recommend that the current model for setting achievement levels be abandoned. A new approach is needed for establishing achievement levels in conjunction with the development of new NAEP frameworks for assessments to be administered in 2003 and later. Alternatives should be explored—including those that avoid complex item-level judgments and rest instead on judgments about larger aggregations of student performance data.

Although we (and many critics) have pointed to deficiencies with current procedures, no clearly proven alternatives exist. We are not optimistic that substantial improvement will be realized by the modest alternatives currently being considered by NAGB's technical advisers and contractors, most of which represent minor variations on the way item-by-item judgments are collected and processed, although the contrasting groups method (National Academy of Education, 1993a; McLaughlin et al., 1993) and some newer alternatives, such as the "bookmark" procedure (Lewis et al., 1996), which does not involve averaging item-by-item estimates, may be worthy of investigation for NAEP's future achievement-level-setting efforts. In Appendix D, we present the initial conceptual framing for a model that (1) relies on the solicitation of judgments about aggregates of student performances, (2) uses comparative data to help ensure the reasonableness of the results, and (3) brings policy makers and educators together to set standards in a setting in which each group can benefit from hearing and understanding the perspectives of the other. We hope that it can stimulate discussion about future achievement-level-setting alternatives.

In the authorizing legislation for NAEP (P.L. 103-382) Congress stated that

NAEP's student performance levels shall be used on a developmental basis until the commissioner of NCES determines, as a result of a congressionally authorized evaluation, that such levels are reasonable, valid, and informative to the public. Given the flawed current achievement-level-setting process, attendant concerns about the validity of the current achievement levels, and the lack of proven alternatives, NAEP's current achievement levels should continue to be used on a developmental basis only. If achievement-level results continue to be reported for re-administrations of assessments in which achievement levels have already been set (e.g., the 1998 reading report, the 2000 mathematics report), then the reports should adhere to the following guidelines:

- Strongly and clearly identify the developmental basis of the achievement levels, emphasizing that they should be interpreted and used with caution, given the continuing serious questions about their validity and
- Focus on the content of the reports on the change, from one administration of the assessment to the next, in the percentages of students in each of the categories determined by the existing achievement-level cutscores (below basic, basic, proficient, and advanced), rather than focusing on the percentages in each category in a single year. Even when the process used to determine cutscores and ascribe meaning to the achievement-level categories is flawed, tracking changes in the percentages of students performing at or above those cutscores (or in fact, any selected cutscore) can be of use in describing changes in student performance over time (see also Linn, 1998).

Regardless of the specific alternative that is used for future achievement-level settings, three general aspects of the process should be addressed: (1) the role of preliminary achievement-level descriptions in assessment development, (2) the role of various participants in the achievement-level-setting process, and (3) the use of normative and external comparative data to evaluate the reasonableness of the achievement levels during and after the level-setting process. We next discuss each of these and present related recommendations for future achievement-level-setting efforts.

Role of the Preliminary Achievement-Level Descriptions

The function of preliminary achievement-level descriptions in assessment development for the main NAEP assessments has not been not well specified or well documented. The current science assessment was the first NAEP subject-area assessment for which preliminary achievement-level descriptions were developed along with the frameworks and, even so, they were somewhat of an afterthought. (A subset of the science framework steering and planning committees was reconvened after the framework had been completed and given limited time to develop the preliminary achievement-level descriptions that were included in the framework document.) Furthermore, as discussed in Chapter 4, it is not clear to what degree NAEP's final item pools have reflected the knowledge and skills put forth in the preliminary achievement-level descriptions.

Preliminary achievement-level descriptions should guide the development of assessment items and exercises (see also National Academy of Education, 1993a). Because reporting results in terms of achievement levels is a primary goal, the frameworks and assessments must be developed with this in mind. Preliminary achievement-level descriptions should be an integral part of NAEP's frameworks and should play a key role in guiding the development of assessment materials, including scoring rubrics. Furthermore, items and tasks should be written and rubrics defined to address the intended achievement levels. Items and tasks should be developed to maximize information about student achievement at the three critical cutscores and, to the extent that individual items are used as exemplars, they should be closely aligned with the knowledge and skills identified in the achievement-level descriptions.

Thus, greater attention should be devoted to the development of preliminary achievement-level descriptions during the framework development process. This effort must involve educators in the subject area who are familiar with levels of student work in the target subjects and grades. After the framework and the preliminary achievement-level descriptions are developed, it is critical to have continued communication between the committee that developed the framework and the descriptions and those groups that have responsibility for developing the assessment (the assessment development committee and NAEP's assessment development subcontractors). At the very least, members of the framework committee should review assessment materials and provide feedback at an early stage of the development process regarding the degree to which the assessment materials reflect the framework and the preliminary achievement-level descriptions. (The existing NAEP subject-area standing committees should play an important role in ensuring that this review and feedback occurs.) This strategy reiterates one of our major recommendations from Chapter 4—the need for greater coherence across all phases of the framework and assessment development process.

A tighter alignment between the assessment materials and the preliminary achievement-level descriptions is important, and accomplishing this is likely to require that the preliminary achievement-level descriptions be more informative than they are currently. Table 5-1 shows an analysis (rearrangement) of the preliminary and final achievement-level descriptions for eighth-grade science at the proficient level.[1] The preliminary description on the left is quite general and

---

[1]As noted previously in this chapter, the final science achievement-level descriptions were unusual in that they were developed inductively from item-level data using behavioral anchoring methods after NAGB had reset the achievement levels. NAGB warns against comparing these descriptions to the preliminary descriptions or descriptions for achievement levels in other subject areas because of this difference in how they were developed. We use them here simply to provide an example of a level of detail that one should include in preliminary achievement-level descriptions if they are to be helpful in guiding assessment development.

TABLE 5-1 Analysis of Preliminary and Final Achievement-Level
Descriptions for the Grade 8 Proficient Level

Preliminary	Final
Experiments and Data	**Experiments and Data**
1. Collect basic information and apply it to the physical, living, and social environments	6. Design plans to solve problems
	2. Design an experiment and have an emerging understanding of variables and controls
4. Design experiments to answer simple questions involving two variables	1. Create, interpret, and make predictions from charts, diagrams, and graphs based on information provided to them or from their own investigations
5. Isolate variables	
6. Collect and display data and draw conclusions from them	3. Read and interpret geographic and topographic maps
	17. Are able to develop their own classification system based on physical characteristics
Relationships	**Relationships**
2. Link simple ideas in order to understand payoffs and trade-offs	4. Use and understand models
3. Understand cause-and-effect relationships such as predator/prey and growth/rainfall	5. Partially formulate explanations of their understanding of scientific phenomena
7. Draw relationships between two simple concepts;	
8. Begin to understand relationships (such as force and motion and matter and energy)	
Other Subject-Area Knowledge	**Other Subject-Area Knowledge (Physical)**
9. Begin to understand the laws that apply to living and nonliving matter	11. Have an emerging understanding of the particulate nature of matter, especially the effect of temperature on states of matter
	12. Know that light and sound travel at different speeds
	13. Can apply their knowledge of force, speed, and motion
	7. Begin to identify forms of energy and describe the role of energy transformations in living and nonliving systems
	8. Have knowledge of organization, gravity, and motions within the solar system
	10. Have some understanding of properties of materials
	Other Subject-Area Knowledge (Biological)
	15. Understand that organisms reproduce and that characteristics are inherited from previous generations

TABLE 5-1 Continued

Preliminary	Final
	16. Understand that organisms are made up of cells and that cells have subcomponents with different functions
	14. Demonstrate a developmental understanding of the flow of energy from the sun through living systems, especially plants
	Other Subject-Area Knowledge (Earth Science)
	9. Can identify some factors that shape the surface of the Earth
	18. Can list some effects of air and water pollution
	19. Demonstrate knowledge of the advantages and disadvantages of different energy sources in terms of how they affect the environment and the economy

NOTE: Numbers indicate the sequence in which the listed phrases occurred in the actual text of the grade 8 proficient achievement-level descriptions.

does not appear to be very useful in developing item content or adjusting factors that may affect item difficulty. The final description on the right provides a good deal of information to inform the content of items that may differentiate proficient from basic performance, as well as some information to inform skills (e.g., experimental design, interpretation of graphical information) that may be assessed. It is important to note, however, that although these more prescriptive descriptions would be helpful in future assessment development, there is also a danger that they could be overly limiting. They provide examples of many but not all of the areas in the framework, and it would be a mistake to limit assessment development to just the areas touched on in these descriptions.

Role of Various Participants in the Achievement-Level-Setting Process

NAEP's current achievement-level-setting process is designed to include individuals with a range of perspectives and areas of expertise. Panelists include teachers and curriculum specialists in the subject area for which achievement levels are being set, as well as members of the public, many of whom apply knowledge of the subject area in their work. The composition of the achievement-level-setting panels has been specified in detail and the process for identifying participants has been carefully planned, carried out, and documented. In the end, however, NAGB rejected the 1996 science panel's recommendations on the basis of reasonableness, largely on the basis of normative and comparative data that were not available to the panelists.

NAGB has both the authority and the responsibility to make final decisions with respect to NAEP achievement levels. The carefully balanced, bipartisan composition of NAGB should make it well suited to balance policy, practical, and technical considerations in setting goals for student achievement. It is not clear, however, that NAGB is making the best possible use of the different forms of expertise available to inform its judgments. The many types of individuals selected for the panels bring important knowledge and perspectives to bear on the achievement-level-setting process. Curriculum specialists understand how different areas of achievement relate to curricular objectives; teachers have a deep understanding of students in a given grade and what can reasonably be expected of them; members of the business community and the public provide important input on the importance of different skills for success later in life.

We recommend that the roles of educators, policy makers, the public, NAGB, and other groups in developing achievement-level descriptions and setting achievement levels should be specified more precisely. In particular, the roles of disciplinary specialists and policy makers should be better integrated throughout the achievement-level-setting process. Curriculum specialists and teachers should play a larger role in providing information about how and why achievement-level cutscores are set when final, policy-informed decisions about setting achievement-level cutscores are made. In addition, members of NAGB should be involved in the achievement-level-setting discussions among curriculum specialists, teachers, and the public so that they better understand the rationale underlying the panelists' recommended cutscores. All of these groups, through NAGB, should have a role in establishing and reviewing the process and the resulting achievement levels.

Use of Normative and External Comparative Data

Many experts argue that the data-based and policy consequences of the results of standard setting should be known to the achievement-level-setting raters early in their deliberations; thus normative student performance data and external comparative data should be considered by raters in setting NAEP achievement levels, primarily for use in evaluating the reasonableness of level-setting decisions.

NAEP raters have learned about the consequences of their cutscore decisions—that is, the numbers of students scoring at or above the levels that they had just set—at the close of achievement-level setting, not during the determination of the levels. In adjusting the problematic standards for the 1996 NAEP science assessment, however, benchmark data from other assessments (advanced placement examinations, the SAT, TIMSS) played an important role in NAGB's designation of cutscores. Existing internal and external consequences or comparative data should also be available to inform achievement-level-setting panelists' judgments.

In the future, we hope that a broader range of data on consequences would be available to inform achievement-level-setting efforts. During a December 1996 workshop on standard setting that the committee sponsored as part of our evaluation of NAEP, different types of data on consequences were discussed. (Papers presented at the workshop were published in the January 1998 issue of *Applied Measurement of Education*.) In other arenas in which standards are set, explicit consideration is given to what would happen if standards are or are not met. Military enlistment standards, for example, are set based on the likelihood that individuals at different score levels will be able to successfully complete training (Hanser, 1998). Training standards are set based on the likelihood that an individual will perform adequately on the job. Environmental and nutritional standards are set on estimates of the probability of illness or fatalities at different levels (Goldberg, 1998; Jasanoff, 1998). However, we are far from having a clear consensus on the kinds of educational consequences (e.g., college entrance and success, career success, good citizenship) to which student achievement should be linked. Nonetheless, longitudinal data do exist, and more could be collected over time, allowing achievement scores at different age and grade levels to be related to a variety of consequences. For example, if twelfth-grade performance standards were based, in part, on the likelihood of success in college, then eighth-grade standards may be set on the basis of the likelihood of meeting the twelfth-grade standards and fourth-grade standards set on the basis of the likelihood of meeting eighth-grade standards. At the very least, such information could be corroborative, providing additional checks on the reasonableness of proposed or existing achievement-level standards.

ACHIEVEMENT-LEVEL SETTING IN
FUTURE NAEP ASSESSMENTS

Achievement-level setting in NAEP is still very much in a developmental stage. As new models are explored and efforts undertaken in conjunction with assessments based on new or revised subject-area frameworks, the focus should be on standard setting for the large-scale survey assessments in the core subjects of reading, writing, mathematics, and science.

In previous chapters of this report, we have recommended the use of multiple assessment methods in NAEP, both for assessing those aspects of the core subject-area frameworks that are not well assessed in a large-scale survey format and for assessing subject areas that are not assessed frequently enough to establish ongoing trend lines. Data obtained through these multiple methods would undoubtedly provide a rich source of information to aid in setting achievement levels but would also add to the complexity of the process; however, in the short term, it is judicious to focus on achievement-level setting using data from the large-scale survey portions of the NAEP reading, mathematics, writing, and science assessments. Thus, in our proposed structure of new paradigm NAEP, achievement-level setting and reporting of results would initially be focused on the core NAEP component only. It seems more important to "get it right" in these subject areas, using data from one assessment methodology, than to devote resources to setting achievement levels based on multiple methods or in all of NAEP's subject areas. Eventually, however, we envision an achievement-level-setting process in which all available information that describes student achievement in a subject area, gleaned from across multiple assessment methods, would be used to inform the setting of NAEP's achievement levels.

MAJOR CONCLUSIONS AND RECOMMENDATIONS

Conclusions

Conclusion 5A. **Standards-based reporting is intended to be useful in communicating student results to the public and policy makers. However, sufficient research is not yet available to determine how various audiences interpret and use NAEP's achievement-level results.**

Conclusion 5B. **Standard setting rests on informed judgment, but the complexity of NAEP's current achievement-level-setting procedures can create the misleading impression that level setting is a highly objective process, rather than a judgmental one.**

Conclusion 5C. **The role of the preliminary achievement-level descriptions in item development is not well specified.**

Conclusion 5D. **The roles of various participants in the achievement-level-setting process are not well integrated across the stages of the process.**

Conclusion 5E. **NAEP's current achievement-level-setting procedures remain fundamentally flawed. The judgment tasks are difficult and confusing; raters' judgments of different item types are internally inconsistent; appropriate validity evidence for the cutscores is lacking; and the process has produced unreasonable results. Furthermore, NAGB rejected as unreasonable the outcomes of the 1996 achievement-level setting for science.**

Recommendations

Recommendation 5A. The current process for setting achievement levels should be replaced. New models are needed for establishing achievement levels in conjunction with the development of assessments based on new NAEP frameworks.

Recommendation 5B. NAEP's current achievement levels should continue to be used on a developmental basis only. If achievement-level results continue to be reported for future administrations of assessments in which achievement levels have already been set, the reports should strongly and clearly emphasize that the achievement levels are still under development, and should be interpreted and used with caution. Reports should focus on the change, from one administration of the assessment to the next, in the percentages of students in each of the categories determined by the existing achievement-level cutscores (below basic, basic, proficient, and advanced), rather than focusing on the percentages in each category in a single year.

Recommendation 5C. NAGB should explicitly communicate that achievement levels result from an inherently judgmental process. They should describe more fully the means by which judgments are made. NAGB should also clearly explain the criteria for determining the reasonableness of the achievement levels that result from these judgments.

Recommendation 5D. Preliminary achievement-level descriptions should be an integral part of NAEP's frameworks and should play a key role in guiding the development of assessment materials, including scoring rubrics. Items and tasks should be written and rubrics defined to address the intended achievement levels. Preliminary achievement levels for advanced performance in the content domains need to be clarified.

Recommendation 5E. The roles of educators, policy makers, the public, NAGB, and other groups in developing achievement-level descriptions and setting achievement levels should be specified more precisely. In particular, the roles of disciplinary specialists and policy makers should be better integrated throughout the achievement-level-setting process. All stakeholder groups, perhaps through NAGB, should have a role in establishing and reviewing the process and the resulting achievement levels.

Recommendation 5F.   Normative student performance data and external comparative data should be considered by raters in setting NAEP achievement levels, primarily for use in evaluating the reasonableness of level-setting decisions.

Recommendation 5G. Achievement-level reports should provide information about what students below the basic level can and cannot do.

Recommendation 5H. In order to accomplish the committee's recommendations, NAEP's research and development agenda should emphasize the following:

• documentation and analysis of the impacts of standards-based reporting in NAEP on understanding and use of the results,
• development and implementation of alternate achievement-level-setting models,
• investigation and implementation of the use of normative and comparative data in determining achievement levels and evaluating their reasonableness, and
• analysis of similarities and differences between results of NAEP achievement-level-setting efforts and those associated with state and other testing programs.

6

Strategies for Implementing the Committee's Recommendations for Transforming NAEP

In this report we have argued that many of the demands placed on NAEP are a function of the unfilled need for better information about many aspects of the American student population and education system. We have asserted that the nation needs a new definition of educational progress, one that provides a more comprehensive picture of education in America and one that supports the policy interests that drive NAEP's authorization. Our argument rests on the premise that student achievement on a set of large-scale assessments should not be the nation's only marker of educational progress. We argue that policy makers and the public must be informed about other important educational outcomes and about the associations between student achievement and education. We also argue that the NAEP program cannot assume the burden of providing all of the information needed on educational performance and progress and that it should focus instead on improving methods for providing high-quality information about student academic achievement.

In this final chapter, we make suggestions for reconfiguring NAEP to play a key role in a coordinated system of education indicators. We begin with an overview of committee recommendations that have procedural implications for upcoming programmatic activity. We then offer and develop suggestions for effecting the changes we recommend for NAEP. In discussing them, we review work recently undertaken by the U.S. Department of Education that lays a foundation for the assessment changes we describe. When we can, we relate our suggestions for implementation to the timelines and priorities of ongoing activity at the National Center for Education Statistics (NCES) and the National Assessment Governing Board (NAGB).

RECAPITULATION OF THE PRIMARY RECOMMENDATIONS

In Chapters 1 through 5, we discussed the creation of a coordinated system of education indicators. We made recommendations for streamlining NAEP's design, enhancing the participation and meaningful assessment of all students in NAEP, providing more informative portrayals of student performance in NAEP reports, and improving achievement-level setting. We argued that:

• Educational progress is not synonymous with student achievement results on NAEP. The assessment of educational progress should be reconceptualized as a broader, coordinated system of education indicators that includes, but goes beyond, measures of student achievement. Data on curriculum and instruction, academic standards, technology use, financial allocations, and other indicators of education inputs, practices, and outcomes should be collected using a range of methods and included in the coordinated system for assessing educational performance and progress.

• NAEP's frameworks, achievement measures, performance levels, and results are only one component of the more inclusive system we describe.

• Within this larger system, the sampling and administration designs for NAEP's survey-based student achievement measures should be streamlined.

• At the same time, the measurement of achievement by NAEP needs to be reconceptualized so that it capitalizes on contemporary research, theory, and practice in NAEP subjects in ways that support in-depth interpretations of student knowledge and understanding.

• The student achievement measures should be broadened beyond large-scale assessment methods. Although current instruments can be improved to better assess portions of the current NAEP frameworks, alternative methods are better suited to assessing broader conceptualizations of achievement that include complex skills. Academic achievement should be more broadly defined and measured using methods that are appropriately matched to the subjects, skills, and populations of interest. A multiple-methods design should be included in new paradigm NAEP to better assess:

—aspects of student achievement not well addressed by large-scale survey methods (e.g., scientific investigation, self-regulatory skills),

—noncore subject areas for which testing frequency generally prohibits the establishment of trend lines,

—subject areas (or portions of subject areas) in which not all students receive instruction (e.g., fine arts, advanced mathematics),

—the accomplishments of special populations (e.g., English-language learners, students with disabilities), and perhaps

—the educational experiences and postsecondary plans of high school seniors.

- Furthermore, NAGB should explore and implement a new model for achievement-level setting.

We made this set of arguments more concrete by providing a model for a coordinated system of education indicators. The model suggests the types and range of indicators that might be included in an integrated system. We provided it to illustrate, but not prescribe, an indicator model and repeat it here as groundwork for the discussion in this chapter. Figure 6-1 shows possible components of a coordinated system and depicts the measures of student achievement within the broader system. In the model we show new paradigm NAEP with its core NAEP and multiple-methods NAEP components.

Our recommendations regarding the NAEP program have significant ramifications for the programs and plans of the National Center for Education Statistics and the National Assessment Governing Board. We organize our discussion of implementation strategies around four additional committee recommendations:

- First and foremost, the U.S. Department of Education and the National Center for Education Statistics should quickly initiate the activities necessary for reconfiguring NAEP and developing a coordinated system of education indicators.
- Responsibility for the design and implementation of the coordinated system should lie with NCES. NCES should develop the conceptual and structural framework for the system and should house, manage, and refine the data system. Within this structure and for new paradigm NAEP, the National Assessment Governing Board should have responsibility for determining what areas of student achievement are to be assessed and for setting expectations for student performance. NCES should determine how to measure the areas of achievement identified by NAGB and should develop and implement the assessments, collect and analyze the data, and report the results.
- The transitional contract for NAEP should be amended to address many of the recommendations put forward in Chapters 2 through 5. The more expansive changes we outline should build on these and be introduced with the generation of assessments for which new frameworks are developed.
- The U.S. Department of Education should quickly fund efforts to design, test, and evaluate new methods for assessing student achievement.

In Chapter 1 we discussed strategies and activities to be pursued by the U.S. Department of Education and NCES in developing the coordinated system of education indicators. In the remainder of this chapter, we provide suggestions for activities that should be pursued to transform the NAEP program and create new paradigm NAEP to play a critical role in the coordinated system.

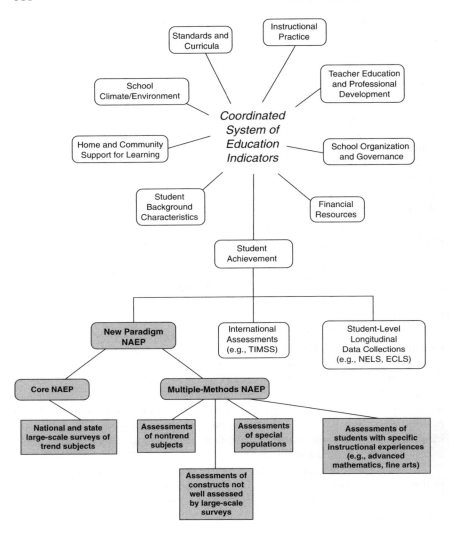

FIGURE 6-1   Proposed coordinated system of education indicators, including new paradigm NAEP.   NOTE: TIMSS = Third International Mathematics and Science Study; NELS = National Education Longitudinal Study; ECLS = Early Childhood Longitudinal Study.

RECENT WORK THAT PROVIDES A FOUNDATION FOR NEW PARADIGM NAEP

In August 1996 the National Assessment Governing Board adopted policies for redesigning national assessment that would "carry NAEP into the next millennium" (National Assessment Governing Board, 1996). Soon thereafter, the NAEP program began laying plans for implementing the adopted policies. Implementation planning was supported by suggestions from a series of planning grants, commissioned papers, stakeholder surveys, and public hearings. At its November 1997 meeting, NAGB passed a resolution that guides implementation of NAEP's redesign (National Assessment Governing Board, 1997).

NAGB and NCES are planning a staged implementation of the redesign initiatives; they have funded a transitional procurement covering the NAEP administrations from 2000 through 2002 and a redesign procurement covering the NAEP administrations from 2003 through 2006, years during which new assessment frameworks will be introduced. The transitional contract implements as many of the redesign goals as is practicable and conducts research and development to prepare for full implementation. Additional work on redesign initiatives will be undertaken through NCES's NAEP secondary analysis program, validity studies program, and as described in this and other evaluation reports.

Some of NAGB's redesign policies, if successfully implemented, will lay the groundwork for the assessment changes we describe; they are discussed in NAGB's implementation plan entitled, "Bridging Policy to Implementation: A Resolution" (National Assessment Governing Board, 1997). NAGB's priorities for future NAEP include:

- *Combining the long- and short-term trend designs.* In their policy statement, NAGB says that a plan should be developed in concert with the transitional contract to "ensure that the current cross-sectional assessment shall become the future long-term trend (replacing the current long-term trend) when new assessment frameworks are brought on-line." They ask for research and development to support a combined design. This priority parallels our recommendations for streamlining NAEP's design.
- *Streamlining the national and state samples.* Here, too, our recommendations are paralleled by NAGB's intentions; they ask for sampling plans for future assessments that are more efficient and less burdensome. State samples, they say, should be "developed to the largest extent possible by augmenting the national samples in states."
- *Exploring market-basket reporting.* NAGB has stated that secondary analysis grants or validity studies projects should be funded to examine market-basket reporting and cost options. We support these explorations to seek more easily understood metrics for describing NAEP's large-scale assessment results.

• *Issuing policy and practitioner reports.* NAGB's resolution calls for issuance of simple, accurate, and jargon-free reports for practitioners and the public. We also contend that national and state policy makers should receive targeted, policy-relevant reports.

• *Implementing multiple-methods assessments.* NAGB's resolution makes some initial inroads toward the implementation of a multiple-methods program. For the year 2000, for example, they specify that hands-on science blocks should be administered to the minimum number of students needed for accurate estimation and comparability of trend data to the past. They also ask for research and development on possible simplified designs for NAEP data collections. They note that the NAEP assessment development contractor will conduct small-scale pilot studies to examine potential designs. While these initial explorations are positive steps in the direction of more closely matching assessment method with assessment purpose, our recommendations regarding multiple-methods NAEP extend well beyond these steps.

• *Facilitating interpretive uses of NAEP data.* The redesign implementation resolution states that NAEP users should have access to data in forms that support efforts to improve education. This priority is not inconsistent with the more expansive initiatives for serving the interpretive needs of educators and policy makers that we have recommended throughout this report. Again, Chapter 4 made suggestions for obtaining interpretive information from NAEP, and Chapter 1 discussed the coordinated system.

The earlier mentioned planning grants, recently authored by the Educational Testing Service (Johnson et al., 1997), American College Testing (Bay et al., 1997), and the American Institutes for Research (1997), as well as work by NCES and NAGB, provide additional input on a number of issues addressed in this report. As described in Chapter 4, the ETS proposal, for example, discusses first steps for multiple-methods designs in some detail. ETS suggests modular assessment for NAEP, as had NAGB's Design/Feasibility Team in 1996 (Forsyth et al., 1996). ETS recommended partitioning the subject-area frameworks into aspects of achievement that can be efficiently assessed using large-scale surveys—consisting primarily of multiple-choice and short constructed-response items—and those more appropriately assessed with extended constructed-response tasks that rely on higher levels of engagement and development. The first set of achievements should be assessed, it stated, under the current NAEP model and the second with smaller groups of examinees, perhaps with more extensive collection of ancillary data on student background variables and on the learning practices of students (Johnson et al., 1997). The small-scale data collections would support deeper analysis and richer reporting. In their design document, ETS acknowledged that tasks in the second category may not contribute to the derivation of scaled scores, but their information value may lie "closest to the exercises themselves" (p. 4-29). ETS suggested that portions of the large-scale survey assessment be given to students performing extended tasks, however, so that the relationships among assessment components could be evaluated. These proposals are reasonable first steps toward a multiple-methods NAEP.

NCES efforts to expand inclusion criteria and offer a range of testing accommodations in 1996 lay the groundwork for continued effort in this area. As they currently do, NCES should continue to support and conduct research on the meaningful assessment of English-language learners and students with disabilities in NAEP, and it should implement promising procedures for enhancing inclusion, accommodation, meaningful assessment, and meaningful reports for special populations.

In issuing their most recent request for proposal and in work with their advisers (the Technical Advisory Committee on Standard Setting), NAGB has stated its clear desire to consider and explore alternate models for achievement-level setting. The changes planned and being implemented for the upcoming civics and writing assessments adjust the current standard-setting model and procedures in relatively minor ways. NAGB is open, however, to a more fundamental recasting of the current process. To date, however, attractive and realistic alternatives have not been forthcoming. (Several shortcomings of the current model and suggestions for future standard-setting research were described in Chapter 5.)

OPERATIONALIZING CHANGES TO THE NAEP PROGRAM

The changes we recommend to the NAEP program are multifaceted and would need to be phased in over time. There is an opportunity for those responsible for NAEP to pursue strategies that enhance the likelihood of an effective transformation over the next two decades. As mentioned earlier in this chapter, the NAEP redesign plan involves a transitional contract covering assessment administration through the year 2002. During this period, tests based on existing frameworks will be administered. We see this as an excellent opportunity for effecting change and conducting some of the foundational research that should precede implementation of several of our recommendations. We recommend that NCES and NAGB make the changes described in this section in the context of activity funded under the transitional contract and in subsequent administrations of subjects under the current main NAEP and trend NAEP frameworks. Table 6-1 provides a summary of the NAEP administrations scheduled during the transitional period and as new frameworks are introduced.

Some of the following changes may be possible with minor modification to awarded tasks and with later administrations under the current frameworks:

- Extended-response and other performance tasks should be administered to samples of students using a modular approach.
- NCES should further their efforts to represent all students in NAEP and

TABLE 6-1 Scheduled NAEP Contracts and Administrations by Framework, Subject, and Grade/Age

NAEP Contract/ Administration Dates	National NAEP		
	Framework	Subject	Grade/Age
Transitional contract Assessments administered in 2000-2002	Current main	Mathematics Science U.S. History Geography Reading Writing	Grades 4, 8, 12
Redesign contract Assessments administered in 2003-2006	Current main	Civics Science Writing	Grades 4, 8, 12
	New main	Mathematics Reading	Grades 4, 8, 12
	New main	Foreign Language World History Economics	Grade 12
Future work Assessments administered in 2007-2010	New main	Arts Mathematics Science U.S. History Geography Reading Writing	Grades 4, 8, 12

[a]Trend assessments are not based on formal framework but are collections of items administered in past assessments.

SOURCE: NAEP program documents.

meaningfully portray the performance of English-language learning students and students with disabilities.

• Improved development of items, tasks, and scoring rubrics should be undertaken within the current frameworks. These changes could be directed at better assessment of currently tested knowledge and skills and extend beyond these to more complex aspects of achievement described by the frameworks, but that are currently not adequately assessed. New materials could be included in replacement blocks for the current generation of assessments.

State NAEP			Trend NAEP		
Framework	Subject	Grade/Age	Framework[a]	Subject	Grade/Age
Current main	Mathematics Science Reading Writing	Grades 4, 8			
Current main	Science Writing	Grades 4, 8	Current trend instruments	Reading Mathematics Science	Ages 9, 13, 17
				Writing	Grades 4, 8, 11
New main	Mathematics Reading	Grades 4, 8			
New main	Mathematics Science Reading Writing	Grades 4, 8	Current trend instruments	Reading Mathematics Science	Ages 9, 13, 17
				Writing	Grades 4, 8, 11

• Improved coherence across the steps of development, administration, analysis, and reporting should be an immediate priority. The recently established subject-area standing committees provide a basis from which to begin the work of more coherent assessment and reporting.

• As they do with the National Council of Teachers of Mathematics, the NAEP program should work with disciplinary organizations to generate reports that provide in-depth analyses of student response data for individual items and groups of items. The NAEP program recently developed similar relationships with various arts organizations for the fine arts assessment, and it should continue this practice to enhance the utility and visibility of NAEP products.

  • In the resolution for redesign implementation, NAGB stated that field tests should be embedded as feasible in regular testings. We extend this idea to suggest that alternatives for streamlined sampling and administration designs for upcoming frameworks should be explored in conjunction with the 2000 and 2002 administrations. The feasibility, likely accuracy, and efficiency of alternate designs could at least partially be examined on a field-test basis in upcoming administrations.

  • Similarly, alternate assessment formats should be field-tested in conjunction with operational testing in 2000 and 2002 for possible use with new frameworks. Furthermore, small targeted studies should be conducted to assemble some of the building blocks of multiple-methods NAEP. New constructs, item types, item families, measurement methods, sampling plans, scoring approaches, and reporting schemes could be tried in concert with the core program.

  • Finally, alternate standard-setting models should be explored in 2000 and 2002 along with the current approach. This would allow NAGB and its contractors to explore the efficacy and outputs of possible future models.

These changes are summarized in Table 6-2, which lists the modifications we propose under the transitional contract and in concert with NAEP administrations under existing frameworks. These changes would provide strong grounding for more expansive revision with subjects administered under new frameworks.

More ambitious changes to the assessment program undoubtedly are better tied to the introduction of new frameworks in the year 2003 and beyond. Improvements that could be made under the redesign contract and in future work also are summarized in Table 6-2. These improvements include:

  • Introduction of combined trend NAEP and main NAEP designs as discussed in Chapter 2 and slated for research development under the transitional procurement,

  • Implementation of more efficient national and state sampling designs—again, as earlier described and under consideration in the next procurement,

  • Design of a NAEP assessment system that includes large-scale survey methods and an array of smaller-scale, alternative measures, using, for example, video assessment, interviews, computer-based analyses of natural student work, and other measurement techniques, in ways that better align assessment method with assessment purpose,

  • As earlier described, implementation of an expanded array of alternative assessments using multiple methods for noncore subject areas, special populations, and other aspects of achievement and populations not well addressed by large-scale survey methods,

TABLE 6-2 Proposed Introduction of Changes Associated with New Paradigm NAEP

NAEP Contract/ Administration Dates	Framework	Goals associated w/ assessments	Proposed Introduction of Changes
Transitional contract Assessments administered in 2000-2002	Current main	Goals associated w/ assessments based on current frameworks (and beyond)	• Administration of extended-response and performance tasks to targeted samples • Continued efforts to meaningfully assess English-language learners and students with disabilities • Improved development of items, tasks, and rubrics for replacement blocks • Improved coherence across development, administration, analysis, reporting
Redesign contract Assessments administered in 2003-2006	Current main		• Work with disciplinary organizations to report in-depth analyses of student response information • Exploration of alternatives for streamlined designs • Research and field-testing of new item types/families, measurement methods, scoring approaches, and reporting schemes
	New main	Goals associated w/ assessments based on new frameworks	• Exploration of new achievement-level-setting models • Introduction of combined main and trend designs • Implementation of more efficient national and state sampling designs • Development of assessments with multiple methods in which methods are better aligned to purposes
Future work Assessments administered in 2007-2010	New main		• Administration of alternative assessments for noncore subjects, special populations, and constructs not well measured by large-scale survey methods • Research and instrument development to support assessment of broader conceptions of achievement • Implementation of a new achievement-level-setting model

• Research to support the assessment of broader conceptualizations of student achievement as described in Chapter 4, and
• Operational use of a new model for achievement-level setting.

Distribution of Responsibility for New Paradigm NAEP

The new paradigm NAEP we argue for in this report has several components that differ in significant ways from the existing NAEP program. In our judgment, it is important to make clear how responsibility for the components of an operational new paradigm NAEP should be distributed. The following is our recommended partitioning of responsibility across the varied facets of the program:

• *Development of frameworks for the assessment of student achievement.* As it has historically and in keeping with their authority to set policy for NAEP (P.L. 103-382, Section 412), NAGB should specify the disciplines to be assessed and develop NAEP's frameworks. NAGB should stop short of specifying methodology and technical designs for the assessments.
• *Specification of measurement methods and development of measures for the achievement variables.* This should be accomplished by NCES and its advisers and contractors.
• *Data collection and database development.* Again, NCES should accomplish this work with its contractors.
• *Determination of performance standards for the survey-based achievement measures.* NAGB and its advisers should continue in their evaluative role.
• *Initial analysis and reporting.* NCES should analyze and report data with help from advisers and contractors.

The according of responsibilities for new paradigm NAEP described above entails some changes in the current legislatively authorized responsibilities of NAGB and NCES. In the current legislative authorization for NAEP, NCES, and NAGB (Improving America's Schools Act of 1994, P.L. 103-382), one of the duties of NAGB is to "design the methodology of the [NAEP] assessment. . . ." Because the implementation of new paradigm NAEP is an extraordinary design challenge—both technically and operationally—we recommend that responsibility for the design of assessment methodologies in new paradigm NAEP should rest with the body with demonstrated technical and operational expertise—NCES.

CONCLUSION

The U.S. Department of Education, NCES, and NAGB have an important opportunity to take the steps that are appropriate to NAEP's continued evolution and its rich history as the preeminent program for assessing academic achievement in America. It is our hope that the activities we advocate, within the time frame proposed, will be seriously and vigorously pursued. NAEP cannot remain stagnant if it is to fulfill its mission of informing its constituents about important aspects of academic achievement.

It is also clear that NAEP cannot fill the role of providing all information necessary and appropriate to portraying and pursuing improvements in education in America. Awareness of the complex relationships between student characteristics, teaching, learning, and achievement should mark public debate about the progress of American education. The system described in this report, of which NAEP is an integral component, would (1) support better understanding of student achievement data, (2) expand the measurement of academic achievement and other educational outcomes to include nontest-based indicators, and (3) serve policy planning by raising awareness of the complexity of the system and providing a basis for hypothesis generation about educational success and its school, demographic, and family correlates.

The operational implications of the recommendations we make in this report are substantial. The development and implementation challenges of an improved NAEP within a coordinated system of education indicators will be great. It is our contention, however, that substantial efforts to these ends will result in the provision of important and useful descriptive, evaluative, and interpretive information about American academic achievement and educational progress.

References

INTRODUCTION

Alexander, Lamar
  1991   *America 2000.* Washington, DC: U.S. Department of Education.
Alexander, Lamar, and H. Thomas James
  1987   *The Nation's Report Card: Improving the Assessment of Student Achievement.* Stanford, CA: National Academy of Education.
Applied Measurement in Education
  1998   Special issue: Setting consensus goals for academic achievement. *Applied Measurement in Education* 11(1).
Jones, Lyle V.
  1996   A history of the National Assessment of Educational Progress and some questions about its future. *Educational Researcher* (October):1-8.
Messick, Samuel, Albert Beaton, and Frederic Lord
  1983   *National Assessment of Educational Progress Reconsidered: A New Design for a New Era.* Princeton, NJ: Educational Testing Service.
National Academy of Education
  1996   *Quality and Utility: The 1994 Trial State Assessment in Reading,* Robert Glaser, Robert Linn, and George Bohrnstedt, eds. Panel on the Evaluation of the NAEP Trial State Assessment. Stanford, CA: National Academy of Education.
  1993   *The Trial State Assessment: Prospects and Realities,* Robert Glaser, Robert Linn, and George Bohrnstedt, eds. Panel on the Evaluation of the NAEP Trial State Assessment. Stanford, CA: National Academy of Education.
  1992   *Assessing Student Achievement in the States,* Robert Glaser, Robert Linn, and George Bohrnstedt, eds. Panel on the Evaluation of the NAEP Trial State Assessment. Stanford, CA: National Academy of Education.
National Assessment Governing Board
  no   Draft Statement of Purposes for the National Assessment of Educational Progress. Na-
  date   tional Assessment Governing Board, Washington, DC.

1996   *Redesigning the National Assessment of Educational Progress.* Washington, DC: National Assessment Governing Board.

National Center for Education Statistics
1974   *NAEP General Information Yearbook.* Washington, DC: U.S. Department of Education.

National Commission on Excellence in Education
1983   *A Nation at Risk: The Imperative for Educational Reform.* Washington, DC: U.S. Government Printing Office.

National Council of Teachers of Mathematics
1989   *Curriculum and Evaluation Standards for School Mathematics.* Reston, VA: National Council of Teachers of Mathematics.

National Research Council
1999   *Grading the Nation's Report Card: Research from the Evaluation of NAEP,* James W. Pellegrino, Lee R. Jones, and Karen J. Mitchell, eds. Committee on the Evaluation of National and State Assessments of Educational Progress, Board on Testing and Assessment. Washington, DC: National Academy Press.
1996a   *National Science Education Standards.* Washington, DC: National Academy Press.
1996b   *Evaluation of "Redesigning the National Assessment of Educational Progress."* Committee on the Evaluation of National and State Assessments of Educational Progress, Board on Testing and Assessment. Washington, DC: National Academy Press.

Office of Technology Assessment
1992   *Testing in American Schools: Asking the Right Questions.* Office of Technology Assessment, OTA-SET-519; February. Washington, DC: U.S. Government Printing Office.

Tyler, Ralph
1966   The development of instruments for assessing educational progress. Pp. 95-101 in *Proceedings of the 1965 Invitational Conference on Testing Problems.* Princeton, NJ: Educational Testing Service.

CHAPTER 1

Barron, Sheila, and Daniel Koretz
in   *Interpretation and Use of the NAEP TSA Results by the Media.* Washington, DC: U.S.
press   Department of Education.

Beatty, Alexandra S., Clyde M. Reese, Hilary R. Persky, and Peggy Carr
1996   *NAEP 1994 U.S. History Report Card: Findings from the National Assessment of Educational Progress.* Washington, DC: U.S. Department of Education.

Bohrnstedt, George W.
1997   Connecting NAEP Outcomes to a Broader Context of Educational Information. Unpublished paper presented at the annual meeting of the American Educational Research Association, March 24-28, 1997.

Boruch, Robert, and George Terhanian
1999   Putting data sets together: Linking NCES surveys to one another and to data sets from other sources. In *Grading the Nation's Report Card: Research from the Evaluation of NAEP,* James W. Pellegrino, Lee R. Jones, and Karen J. Mitchell, eds. Committee on the Evaluation of National and State Assessments of Educational Progress, Board on Testing and Assessment. Washington, DC: National Academy Press.

Boruch, Robert, and Erling Boe
1994   On "Good, Certain, and Easy Government": The policy uses of statistical data and reports. Pp. 23-36 in *Effective Dissemination of Clinical and Health Information,* L.D. Sechrest, T.E. Becker, E.M. Rogers, T.S. Campbell, and M.L. Grady, eds. Rockville, MD: U.S. Department of Health and Human Services.

Bryk, Anthony S., and Kim L. Hermanson
  1993   Educational indicator systems: Observations on their structure, interpretation, and use.
          Linda Darling-Hamilton, ed. *Review of Research in Education* 19:451-484.
Burstein, Leigh
  1980   The analysis of multilevel in educational research and evaluation. David C. Berliner, ed.
          Review of Research in Education 8:158-233.
Burstein, Leigh, Daniel Koretz, Robert Linn, Brenda Sugrue, John Novak, Eva L. Baker, and Elizabeth Lewis Harris
  1996   Describing performance standards: Validity of the 1992 National Assessment of Educa-
          tional Progress achievement level descriptors as characterizations of mathematics perfor-
          mance. *Educational Assessment* 3(1):9-51.
Burstein, Leigh, Lorraine M. McDonnell, Jeannette Van Winkle, Tor H. Ormseth, Jim Mirocha, and
          Gretchen Guiton
  1995   *Validating National Curriculum Indicators.* Prepared for the National Science Founda-
          tion, Document No. MR-658-NSF. Santa Monica, CA: RAND.
Council of Chief State School Officers
  1989   *State Education Indicators.* Washington, DC: Council of Chief State School Officers.
de Neufville, Judith I.
  1975   *Social Indicators and Public Policy: Interactive Processes of Design and Application.*
          New York: Elsevier Scientific Publishing Company.
Finn, Chester
  1989   News release, November 29. National Assessment Governing Board, Washington, DC.
Forsyth, Robert, Ronald Hambleton, Robert Linn, Robert Mislevy, and Wendy Yen
  1996   *Design/Feasibility Team: Report to the National Assessment Governing Board.* Wash-
          ington, DC: National Assessment Governing Board.
Grissmer, David W., and Ann Flanagan
  1997   Improving the NAEP Data for Policy Analysis. Draft prepared for the National Center
          for Education Statistics.
Hartka, Liz, and Fran Stancavage
  1997   Perspectives on the impact of the Trial State Assessments: State assessment directors,
          state mathematics specialists, and state reading specialists. Pp. 429-489 in *Quality and
          Utility: The 1994 Trial State Assessment in Reading: Background Studies,* Robert Glaser,
          Robert Linn, and George Bohrnstedt, eds. Panel on the Evaluation of the NAEP Trial
          State Assessment, Stanford, CA: National Academy of Education.
Hilton, T., ed.
  1992   *Using National Databases in Education Research.* Hillsdale, NJ: Lawrence Erlbaum
          Associates, Inc.
Hoachlander, Gary, Jeanne E. Griffith, and John H. Ralph
  1996   *From Data to Information: New Directions for the National Center for Education Statis-
          tics.* NCES 96-901, August. Washington, DC: U.S. Department of Education.
Koretz, Daniel M., and Edward Deibert
  1995/   Setting standards and interpreting achievement: A cautionary tale from the National
  1996   Assessment of Educational Progress. *Educational Assessment* 3(1):53-81.
KPMG Peat Marwick LLP, and Mathtech, Inc.
  1996   A Review of the National Assessment of Educational Progress: Management and Meth-
          odological Procedures. Prepared for National Center for Education Statistics, June 4.
Linn, Robert L.
  1998   Validating inferences from National Assessment of Educational Progress achievement-
          level setting. *Applied Measurement in Education* 11(1):23-47.
Linn, Robert L., and Eva L. Baker
  1998   Back to basics: Indicators as a system. *The CRESST Line* Winter:1-3.

McDonnell, Lorraine M.
1994   *Policymakers' View of Student Assessment.* RAND Institute on Education and Training, prepared for Office of Educational Research and Improvement, U.S. Department of Education. Santa Monica, CA: RAND.

Mullis, Ina V., Jay R. Campbell, and Alan E. Farstrup
1993   *NAEP 1992 Reading Report Card for the Nation and the States: Data from the National and Trial State Assessments.* NCES Report No. 23-ST06; September. Washington, DC: U.S. Department of Education.

National Academy of Education
1997   *Assessment in Transition: Monitoring the Nation's Educational Progress,* Robert Glaser, Robert Linn, and George Bohrnstedt, eds. Panel on the Evaluation of the NAEP Trial State Assessment. Stanford, CA: National Academy of Education.
1996   *Quality and Utility: The 1994 Trial State Assessment in Reading,* Robert Glaser, Robert Linn, and George Bohrnstedt, eds. Panel on the Evaluation of the NAEP Trial State Assessment. Stanford, CA: National Academy of Education.

National Assessment Governing Board
1996   *Policy Statement on Redesigning the National Assessment of Educational Progress.* Washington, DC: National Assessment Governing Board.

National Center for Education Statistics
1997   *A School Reform Framework for the Redesign of SASS.* National Center for Education Statistics School and Staffing Survey staff. Washington, DC: U.S. Department of Education.

National Research Council
1996   *Evaluation of "Redesigning the National Assessment of Educational Progress."* Committee on the Evaluation and State Assessments of Educational Progress, Board on Testing and Assessment. September. Washington, DC: National Academy Press.
1993   *A Collaborative Agenda for Improving International Comparative Studies in Education,* Dorothy M. Gilford, ed. Board on International Comparative Studies in Education, Commission on Behavioral and Social Sciences and Education. Washington, DC: National Academy Press.
1985   *Youth Employment and Training Programs: The YEDPA Years,* Charlie L. Betsey, Robinson G. Hollister, Jr., and Mary R. Papageorgiou, eds. Washington, DC: National Academy Press.

National Research Council and Institute of Medicine
1995   *Integrating Federal Statistics on Children: Report of a Workshop.* Committee on National Statistics and Board on Children, Youth, and Families. Washington, DC: National Academy Press.

Odden, Allan
1990   Educational educators in the United States: The need for analysis. *Educational Researcher* 19(7):24-29.

Peak, Lois
1996   *Pursuing Excellence: A Study of U.S. Eighth-Grade Mathematics and Science Teaching, Learning, Curriculum, and Achievement in International Context.* NCES 97-198. Washington, DC: U.S. Department of Education.

Porter, Andrew C.
1996   SCASS Science Opportunity-to-Learn Survey. Prepared for Council of Chief State School Officers Large-Scale Assessment Conference, June 23-26.
1991   Creating a system of school process indicators. *Educational Evaluation and Policy Analysis* 13(1):13-29.

Porter, Andrew, Michael Kirst, E. Osthoff, J. Smithson, and S. Schneider
  1993   *Reform Up Close: An Analysis of High School Mathematics and Science Classrooms.*
          Madison, WI: Wisconsin Center for Education Research.
Richards, C.E.
  1988   Indicators and three types of education monitoring systems: Implications for design. *Phi
          Delta Kappan* 69(7):490-498.
Rivlin, Alice M.
  1973   Measuring performance in education. Pp. 411-437 in *Studies in Income and Wealth,* M.
          Moss, ed. New York: Columbia University Press.
Shavelson, Richard J.
  1987   Historical and Political Considerations in Developing a National Indicator System. Un-
          published paper presented at the annual meeting of the American Educational Research
          Association, April.
Sheldon, E.B., and R. Parke
  1975   Social indicators. *Science* 188:693-699.
Smith, Thomas M., Beth Aronstamm Young, Yupin Bae, Susan P. Choy, and Nabeel Alsalam
  1997   *The Condition of Education, 1997.* NCES 97-388. Washington, DC: U.S. Department of
          Education.
Special Study Panel on Education Indicators
  1991   *Education Counts: An Indicator System to Monitor the Nation's Educational Health.*
          Report to the Acting Commissioner of Education Statistics; September. Washington,
          DC: U.S. Department of Education.
Stigler, James, and Michelle Perry
  1999   Developing classroom process data for the improvement of teaching. In *Grading the
          Nation's Report Card: Research from the Evaluation of NAEP,* James W. Pellegrino, Lee
          R. Jones, and Karen J. Mitchell, eds. Committee on the Evaluation of the National and
          State Assessments of Educational Progress, Board on Testing and Assessment. Washing-
          ton, DC: National Academy Press.
Stigler, James, and James Hiebert
  1997   Third International Mathematics and Science Study: Videotape Classroom Study Ex-
          amples Tape and Guide. Available: http://nces.ed.gov/timss/video.
Stufflebeam, Daniel L., Richard M. Jaeger, and Michael Scriven
  1991   Summative Evaluation of the National Assessment Governing Board's Inaugural 1990-91
          Effort to Set Achievement Levels on the National Assessment of Educational Progress.
          Prepared for the National Assessment Governing Board, August 23.
U.S. General Accounting Office
  1993   *Educational Achievement Standards: NAGB's Approach Yields Misleading Interpreta-
          tions.* GAO/PEMD-93-12. Washington, DC: U.S. General Accounting Office.

CHAPTER 2

Allen, Nancy L., James E. Carlson, and Christine A. Zelenak
  1998a   *The 1996 NAEP Technical Report.* Washington, DC: U.S. Department of Education.
Allen, Nancy L., Spencer S. Swinton, Steven P. Isham, and Christine A. Zelenak
  1998b   *Technical Report of the NAEP 1996 State Assessment Program in Science.* Prepared by
          Educational Testing Service, No. NCES 98-480; January. Washington, DC: U.S. De-
          partment of Education.
Allen, Nancy L., Debra L. Kline, and Christine A. Zelenak
  1996   *The NAEP 1994 Technical Report.* Washington, DC: U.S. Department of Education.

Barron, Sheila I.

1999 Difficulties associated with secondary analysis of NAEP data. In *Grading the Nation's Report Card: Research from the Evaluation of NAEP,* James W. Pellegrino, Lee R. Jones, and Karen J. Mitchell, eds. Committee on the Evaluation of National and State Assessments of Educational Progress, Board on Testing and Assessment, Washington, DC: National Academy Press.

Campbell, Jay R., Kristin E. Voelkl, and Patricia L. Donahue

1997 *NAEP 1996 Trends in Academic Progress: Achievement of U.S. Students in Science, 1969 to 1996; Mathematics, 1973 to 1996; Reading, 1971 to 1996; and Writing, 1984 to 1996.* NCES 97-985. Washington, DC: U.S. Department of Education.

Carlson, James E.

1996 Information Provided by Polytomous and Dichotomous Items on Certain NAEP Instruments. Unpublished paper presented at the annual meeting of the American Educational Research Association, April.

DeVito, Pasquale J.

1996 Issues Relating to the Future of National Assessment of Education Progress: The State Perspective. Unpublished paper presented at the annual meeting of the American Educational Research Association, April, 1996.

Forsyth, Robert, Ronald Hambleton, Robert Linn, Robert Mislevy, and Wendy Yen

1996 *Design/Feasibility Team: Report to the National Assessment Governing Board.* Washington, DC: National Assessment Governing Board.

Hambleton, Ronald K.

1997 Enhancing the Validity of NAEP Achievement Level Score Reporting. Presentation at the National Assessment Governing Board Achievement Levels Committee meeting, Boulder, CO, August 20-22.

Hambleton, Ronald K., and Sharon C. Slater

1996 Are NAEP Executive Summary Reports Understandable to Policy Makers and Educators? Presented at the annual meeting of the National Council on Measurement in Education, April.

Hartka, Elizabeth, and Donald H. McLauglin

1994 A study of the administration of the 1992 National Assessment of Educational Progress Trial State Assessment. Pp. 479-552 in *The Trial State Assessment: Prospects and Realities: Background Studies,* Robert Glaser, Robert Linn, and George Bohrnstedt, eds. Panel on the Evaluation of the NAEP Trial State Assessment. Stanford, CA: National Academy of Education.

Hartka, Elizabeth, Jin-Ying Yu, and Don McLaughlin

1997a A study of the administration of the 1994 Trial State Assessment. Pp. 109-190 in *Quality and Utility: The 1994 Trial State Assessment in Reading: Background Studies,* Robert Glaser, Robert Linn, and George Bohrnstedt, eds. Panel on the Evaluation of the NAEP Trial State Assessments. Stanford, CA: National Academy of Education.

Hartka, Elizabeth, Marianne Perie, and Don McLaughlin

1997b Public school nonparticipation study. Pp. 191-222 in *Quality and Utility: The 1994 Trial State Assessment in Reading: Background Studies,* Robert Glaser, Robert Linn, and George Bohrnstedt, eds. Panel on the Evaluation of the NAEP Trial State Assessments. Stanford, CA: National Academy of Education.

Hedges, Larry V., and Richard L. Venesky

1997 The 1994 reading anomaly: Report to the National Academy of Education on the drop in the National Assessment of Educational Progress main assessment (short-term trend) scores. Pp. 295-350 in *Quality and Utility: The 1994 Trial State Assessment in Reading: Background Studies,* Robert Glaser, Robert Linn, and George Bohrnstedt, eds. Panel on the Evaluation of the NAEP Trial State Assessments. Stanford, CA: National Academy of Education.

Heitjan, D.F., and Roderick J.A. Little
  1991   Multiple imputation for the fatal accident reporting system. *Applied Statistics* 40:13-29.
Jaeger, Richard M.
  1997   Reporting the Results of the National Assessment of Educational Progress. Unpublished
          paper prepared for the NAEP Validity Studies Panel, December 18.
  1996   Reporting Large-Scale Assessment Results for Public Consumption: Some Propositions
          and Palliatives. Unpublished paper presented at the annual meeting of the National Coun-
          cil on Measurement in Education, April.
  1992   General issues in reporting the results of the NAEP Trial State Assessment results. Pp.
          285-344 in *Assessing Student Achievement: Background Studies,* Robert Glaser, Robert
          Linn, and George Bohrnstedt, eds. Panel on the Evaluation of the NAEP Trial Assess-
          ment. Stanford, CA: National Academy of Education.
Kish, L., and M.R. Frankel
  1974   Inference from complex samples. *Journal of the Royal Statistical Society, Series B* 36:1-
          22.
Kolen, Michael J.
  1999a   Issues in phasing out trend NAEP. In *Grading the Nation's Report Card: Research from
          the Evaluation of NAEP,* James W. Pellegrino, Lee R. Jones, and Karen J. Mitchell, eds.
          Committee on the Evaluation of National and State Assessments of Educational Progress,
          Board on Testing and Assessment. Washington, DC: National Academy Press.
  1999b   Issues in combining state NAEP and main NAEP. In *Grading the Nation's Report Card:
          Research from the Evaluation of NAEP.* James W. Pellegrino, Lee R. Jones, and Karen J.
          Mitchell, eds. Committee on the Evaluation of National and State Assessments of Educa-
          tional Progress, Board on Testing and Assessment. Washington, DC: National Academy
          Press.
KPMG Peat Marwick LLP, and Mathtech, Inc.
  1996   A Review of the National Assessment of Educational Progress: Management and Meth-
          odological Procedures. Prepared for National Center for Education Statistics, June 4.
Mislevy, Robert J.
  1985   Estimation of latent group effects. *Journal of the American Statistical Association* 80:993-
          997.
Mislevy, Robert J., Eugene G. Johnson, and Eiji Muraki
  1992   Scaling procedures in NAEP. *Journal of Education Statistics* 17:131-154.
Muraki, Eiji
  1992   Application of Multigroup Partial Credit Model to Differential Item Functioning. Unpub-
          lished paper presented at the annual meeting of the American Educational Research Asso-
          ciation, April.
National Academy of Education
  1997   *Assessment in Transition: Monitoring the Nation's Educational Progress,* Robert Glaser,
          Robert Linn, and George Bohrnstedt, eds. Panel on the Evaluation of the NAEP Trial
          State Assessment. Stanford, CA: National Academy of Education.
  1996   *Quality and Utility: The 1994 Trial State Assessment in Reading,* Robert Glaser, Robert
          Linn, and George Bohrnstedt, eds. Panel on the Evaluation of the NAEP Trial State
          Assessment. Stanford, CA: National Academy of Education.
  1993   *The Trial State Assessment: Prospects and Realities,* Robert Glaser, Robert Linn, and
          George Bohrnstedt, eds. Panel on the Evaluation of the NAEP Trial State Assessment.
          Stanford, CA: National Academy of Education.

1992   *Assessing Student Achievement in the States,* Robert Glaser, Robert Linn, and George Bohrnstedt, eds. Panel on the Evaluation of the NAEP Trial State Assessment. Stanford, CA: National Academy of Education.

National Assessment Governing Board

1997   *Bridging Policy to Implementation: A Resolution.* Washington, DC: National Assessment Governing Board.

1996   *Redesigning the National Assessment of Educational Progress.* Washington, DC: National Assessment Governing Board.

National Research Council

1999   *Grading the Nation's Report Card: Research from the Evaluation of NAEP,* James W. Pellegrino, Lee R. Jones, and Karen J. Mitchell, eds. Committee on the Evaluation of National and State Assessments of Educational Progress, Board on Testing and Assessment. Washington, DC: National Academy Press.

O'Sullivan, Christine Y., Clyde M. Reese, and John Mazzeo, eds.

1997   *NAEP 1996 Science Report Card for the Nation and the States.* Washington, DC: U.S. Department of Education.

Reese, Clyde M., Karen E. Miller, John Mazzeo, and John Dossey

1997   *NAEP 1996 Mathematics Report Card for the Nation and the States: Findings from the National Assessment of Educational Progress.* Washington, DC: U.S. Department of Education.

Rubin, D.B.

1987   *Multiple Imputation for Nonresponse in Surveys.* New York: John Wiley and Sons.

Rust, Keith

1996   Sampling issues for the redesign. Appendix 1 in *Design/Feasibility Team: Report to the National Assessment Governing Board.* Washington, DC: National Assessment Governing Board.

Rust, Keith, and J. P. Shaffer

1997   Sampling. In E.G. Johnson's E. Lager, and C.Y. O'Sullivan, NAEP Reconfigured: An Integrated Redesign of the National Assessment of Educational Progress. Working Paper No. 97-31. Washington, DC: U.S. Department of Education.

Silver, Edward A., and Patricia Ann Kenney

1997   An examination of relationships between the 1990 mathematics scores for grade 8 and selected themes from the NCTM. *Journal for Research in Mathematics Education* 24: 159-167.

Sireci, Stephen G., H. Jane Rogers, Hariharan Swaminathan, Kevin Meara, and Frederic Robin

1999   Evaluating the scale structure of the 1996 grade 8 NAEP science assessment. In *Grading the Nation's Report Card: Research from the Evaluation of NAEP,* James W. Pellegrino, Lee R. Jones, and Karen J. Mitchell, eds. Committee on the Evaluation of National and State Assessments of Educational Progress, Board on Testing and Assessment. Washington, DC: National Academy Press.

Spencer, Bruce D.

1997a   Combining state and national NAEP. Pp. 47-60 in *Assessment in Transition: Monitoring the Nation's Educational Progress: Background Studies,* Robert Glaser, Robert Linn, and George Bohrnstedt, eds. Panel on the Evaluation of the NAEP Trial State Assessment. Stanford, CA: National Academy of Education.

1997b   School and student sampling in the 1994 Trial State Assessment: An evaluation. Pp. 51-108 in *Quality and Utility: The 1994 Trial State Assessment in Reading: Background Studies,* Robert Glaser, Robert Linn, and George Bohrnstedt, eds. Panel on the Evaluation of the NAEP Trial State Assessment. Stanford, CA: National Academy of Education.

U.S. General Accounting Office
  1993   *Educational Achievement Standards: NAGB's Approach Yields Misleading Interpreta-
         tions.* GAO/PEMD-93-12. Washington, DC: U.S. General Accounting Office.
Wainer, Howard
  1997   Improving tabular displays, with NAEP tables as examples and inspirations. *Journal of
         Education and Behavioral Statistics* 22(1):1-30.
Widmeyer Group, Inc.
  1993   *Dissemination Strategies for the National Assessment of Educational Progress.* Prepared
         for the National Assessment Governing Board. Washington, DC: The Widmeyer Group,
         Inc.
Yu, Feng, and Ratna Nandakumar
  1996   Dimensionality of NAEP Data. Unpublished paper presented at the annual meeting of the
         American Educational Research Association, April, 1996.
Zhang, Jinming
  1997   A New Approach for Assessing the Dimensionality of NAEP Data. Unpublished paper
         presented at the annual meeting of the American Educational Research Association, March
         24-28, 1997.
Zieleskiewicz, Jennifer
  1999   Subject-matter experts' perceptions of the relevance of NAEP long-term trend items in
         science and mathematics. In *Grading the Nation's Report Card: Research from the
         Evaluation of NAEP,* James W. Pellegrino, Lee R. Jones, and Karen J. Mitchell, eds.
         Committee on the Evaluation of National and State Assessments of Education, Board on
         Testing and Assessment. Washington, DC: National Academy Press.
Zwick, Rebecca
  1991   Effects of item order and context on estimation of NAEP reading proficiency. *Educa-
         tional Measurement: Issues and Practice* (Fall):10-16.

CHAPTER 3

Abedi, Jamal, Carol Lord, and Joseph R. Plummer
  1997   *Final Report of Language Background as a Variable in NAEP Mathematics Performance.*
         National Center for Research on Evaluation, Standards, and Student Testing/University
         of California, Los Angeles. Los Angeles, CA: University of California.
Anderson, N.E., and J. Olson
  1996   *Puerto Rico Assessment of Educational Progress: 1994 PRAEP Technical Report.* Au-
         gust. Princeton, NJ: Educational Testing Service.
Anderson, N.E., F.F. Jenkins, and K.E. Miller
  1996   *NAEP Inclusion Criteria and Testing Accommodations: Findings from the NAEP 1995
         Field Test in Mathematics.* Princeton, NJ: Educational Testing Service.
August, Diane, and Edith McArthur
  1996   *Proceedings of the Conference on Inclusion Guidelines and Accommodations for Limited
         English Proficient Students in the National Assessment of Educational Progress, Decem-
         ber 5-6, 1994.* NCES 96-861; May. Washington, DC: U.S. Department of Education.
August, Diane, and Julia Lara
  1996   *Systemic Reform and Limited English Proficient Students.* Washington, DC: Council of
         Chief State School Officers.
August, Diane, Kenji Hakuta, and D. Pompa
  1994   For all students: Limited English proficient students and Goals 2000. *Occasional Papers
         in Bilingual Education* 10:4.

Bond, Lloyd. A.

1996   *Statewide Assessment of Students with Disabilities.* Council of Chief State School Offic-
        ers and North Central Regional Educational Laboratory; January. Oak Brook, IL: North
        Central Regional Educational Laboratory.

Bond, Lloyd A., D. Braskamp, and Edward Roeber

1996   *The Status Report of Assessment Programs in the United States: State Student Assess-
        ment Programs Database, School Year 1994-95.* Council of Chief State School Officers
        and North Central Regional Educational Laboratory. Oak Brook, IL: North Central
        Regional Educational Laboratory.

Bradby, D.

1992   *Language Characteristics and Academic Achievement: A Look at Asian and Hispanic
        Eighth Graders in NELS:88.* Washington, DC: U.S. Department of Education.

Butler, Frances A., and Robin Stevens

1997   Accommodation Strategies for English Language Learners on Large-Scale Assessments:
        Student Characteristics and Other Considerations. National Center for Research on Evalu-
        ation, Standards, and Student Testing/University of California, Los Angeles.

Center for Equity and Excellence

1997   *Statewide Assessment Programs: Policies and Practices for the Inclusion of LEP Stu-
        dents.*

Cheung, Oona M., Barbara S. Clements, and Y. Carol Mieu

1994   *The Feasibility of Collecting Comparable National Statistics about Students with Limited
        English Proficiency.* Washington, DC: Council of Chief State School Officers.

Council of Chief State School Officers

1991   *Summary of State Practices Concerning the Assessment of and the Data Collection about
        LEP Students.* Washington, DC: Council of Chief State School Officers.

Educational Testing Service

no   *Testing Persons with Disabilities: A Report for ETS Programs and Their Constituents.*
date   Educational Testing Service Committee on People with Disabilities. Princeton, NJ: Edu-
        cational Testing Service.

Fleischman, Howard L., and Paul J. Hopstock

1993   *Descriptive Study of Services to Limited English Proficient Students: Volume I, Summary
        of Findings and Conclusions.* Prepared for Office of the Under Secretary, U.S. Depart-
        ment of Education. Washington, DC: U.S. Department of Education.

Hafner, A.

1995   Assessment Practices: Developing and Modifying Statewide Assessment for LEP Stu-
        dents. Paper presented at the Council of Chief State School Officers Conference on
        Large-Scale Assessment; June. School of Education, California State University, Los
        Angeles.

Hakuta, Kenji, and Guadalupe Valdés

1997   A study design to evaluate strategies for the inclusion of limited English proficient stu-
        dents in the National Assessment of Educational Progress state trial assessment. Pp. 69-
        80 in *Assessment in Transition: Monitoring the Nation's Educational Progress: Back-
        ground Studies,* Robert Glaser, Robert Linn, and George Bohrnstedt, eds. Panel on the
        Evaluation of the NAEP Trial State Assessment. Stanford, CA: National Academy of
        Education.

Houser, J.

1995   *Assessing Students with Disabilities and Limited English Proficiency.* National Center
        for Education Statistics, Policy and Review Branch, Data Development Division, Work-
        ing Paper No. 95-13; March. Washington, DC: U.S. Department of Education.

Lewit, Eugene M., and Linda Schuumann Baker
    1996   Children in special education. Issue on Special Education for Students With Disabilities,
            Spring. *The Future of Children* 6(1):139-151.

Mazzeo, John
    1997   Toward a More Inclusive NAEP. Unpublished paper presented at the annual meeting of
            the American Educational Research Association, March 24-28, 1997.

Mazzeo, J., J. Carlson, K. Voekl, and A. Lutkus
    1998   *Increasing the Participation of Students with Disabilities and Limited English Proficient
            Students in the National Assessment of Educational Progress: A Special Report on 1996
            Research Activities.* Washington, DC: U.S. Department of Education.

National Academy of Education
    1997   *Assessment in Transition: Monitoring the Nation's Educational Progress,* Robert Glaser,
            Robert Linn, and George Bohrnstedt, eds. Panel on the Evaluation of the NAEP Trial
            State Assessment. Stanford, CA: National Academy of Education.

    1996   *Quality and Utility: The 1994 Trial State Assessment in Reading,* Robert Glaser, Robert
            Linn, and George Bohrnstedt, eds. Panel on the Evaluation of the NAEP Trial State
            Assessment. Stanford, CA: National Academy of Education.

    1993   *The Trial State Assessment: Prospects and Realities,* Robert Glaser, Robert Linn, and
            George Bohrnstedt, eds. Panel on the Evaluation of the NAEP Trial State Assessment.
            Stanford, CA: National Academy of Education.

National Center on Educational Outcomes
    1995a   *A Compilation of States' Guidelines for Accommodations in Assessments for Students
            with Disabilities.* Martha L. Thurlow, D.L. Scott, and J.E. Ysseldyke, eds. Synthesis
            Report 18. Minneapolis, MN: National Center on Educational Outcomes, University of
            Minnesota.

    1995b   *A Compilation of States' Guidelines for Including Students with Disabilities in Assess-
            ments.* Synthesis Report 17. Minneapolis, MN: National Center on Educational Out-
            comes, University of Minnesota.

    1994a   *Recommendations for Making Decisions About the Participation of Students with Dis-
            abilities in Statewide Assessment Programs.* Synthesis Report 15. Minneapolis, MN:
            National Center on Educational Outcomes, University of Minnesota.

    1994b   *Making Decisions About the Inclusion of Students with Disabilities in Large-Scale As-
            sessments: A Report on a Working Conference to Develop Guidelines on Inclusion and
            Accommodations.* Synthesis Report 13. Minneapolis, MN: National Center on Educa-
            tional Outcomes, University of Minnesota.

    1993   *Testing Accommodations for Students with Disabilities: A Review of the Literature.*
            Synthesis Report 4; March. Minneapolis, MN: National Center on Educational Out-
            comes, University of Minnesota.

National Research Council
    1997   *Educating One and All: Students with Disabilities and Standards-Based Reform,* Lorraine
            M. McDonnell, Margaret J. McLaughlin, and Patricia Morison, eds. Committee on Goals
            2000 and the Inclusion of Students with Disabilities, Board on Testing and Assessment.
            Washington, DC: National Academy Press.

National Research Council and Institute of Medicine
    1997   *Improving Schooling for Language-Minority Children: A Research Agenda,* Diane Au-
            gust and Kenji Hakuta, eds. Committee on Developing a Research Agenda on the Educa-
            tion of Limited-English-Proficient and Bilingual Students, Board on Children, Youth, and
            Families. Washington, DC: National Academy Press.

Olson, John F. and Arnold A. Goldstein
    1997   *The Inclusion of Students With Disabilities and Limited English Proficient Students in
            Large-Scale Assessments: A Summary of Recent Progress.* Washington, DC: U.S. De-
            partment of Education.

O'Sullivan, Christine Y., Clyde M. Reese, and John Mazzeo
  1997   *NAEP 1996 Science Report Card for the Nation and the States.* Washington, DC: U.S. Department of Education.
Reese, Clyde M., Karen E. Miller, John Mazzeo, and John Dossey
  1997   *NAEP 1996 Mathematics Report Card for the Nation and the States.* Washington DC: U.S. Department of Education.
Reschly, Daniel P.
  1996   Identification and assessment of students with disabilities. Issue on Special Education for Students With Disabilities, Spring. *The Future of Children* 6(1):40-53.
Rivera, Charlene
  1995   How Can We Ensure Equity in Statewide Assessment Programs? Findings from a national survey of assessment directors on statewide assessment policies for LEP students, presented at the Council of Chief State School Officers' National Conference on Large-Scale Assessment, June 18. Washington, DC: Institute for Equity and Excellence in Education, George Washington University, Washington, DC.
Secada, Walter G.
  1994   Issues in the development of Spanish-language versions of the National Assessment of Educational Progress. Pp. 377-400 in *The Trial State Assessment: Prospects and Realities: Background Studies,* Robert Glaser, Robert Linn, and George Bohrnstedt, eds. Panel on the Education of the NAEP Trial State Assessments. Stanford, CA: National Academy of Education.
Spencer, Bruce D.
  1994   A study of eligibility exclusions and sampling: 1992 Trial State Assessment. Pp. 1-68 in *The Trial State Assessment: Prospects and Realities: Background Studies,* Robert Glaser, Robert Linn, and George Bohrnstedt, eds. Panel on the Evaluation of the NAEP Trial State Assessment. Stanford, CA: National Academy of Education.
Stancavage, Fran, Don McLaughlin, Robert Vergun, Cathy Godlewski, and Jill Allen
  1997a   Study of exclusion and assessability of limited English proficiency students in the 1994 Trial State Assessment of the National Assessment of Educational Progress. Pp. 223-244 in *Quality and Utility: The 1994 Trial State Assessment in Reading: Background Studies,* Robert Glaser, Robert Linn, and George Bohrnstedt, eds. Panel on the Evaluation of the NAEP Trial State Assessment. Stanford, CA: National Academy of Education.
  1997b   Study of exclusion and assessability of students with disabilities in the 1994 Trial State Assessment of the National Assessment of Educational Progress. Pp. 245-294 *Quality and Utility: The 1994 Trial State Assessment in Reading: Background Studies,* Robert Glaser, Robert Linn, and George Bohrnstedt, eds. Panel on the Evaluation of the NAEP Trial State Assessment. Stanford, CA: National Academy of Education.
U.S. Department of Education
  1996   *To Assure the Free and Appropriate Public Education of All Children with Disabilities.* Eighteenth Annual Report to Congress on the Implementation of the Individuals with Disabilities Education Act. Washington, DC: U.S. Department of Education.
Valdés, Guadalupe, and Richard A. Figueroa
  1994   *Bilingualism and Testing: A Special Case of Bias.* Norwood, NJ: Ablex.
Valdes, K.A., C.L. Williamson, and M. Wagner
  1990   *The National Longitudinal Transition Study of Special Education Students. Statistical Almanac, Volume 1.* Menlo Park, CA: SRI International.
Weston, Tim
  1997   Investigating the Validity of the Accommodation of Oral Presentation: Proposal for Research. Prepared for September 12, 1997, NVS Panel meeting.
Willingham, Warren, M. Ragosta, Randy E. Bennett, Henry Braun, Donald A. Rock, and Donald Powers
  1988   *Testing Handicapped People.* Boston: Allyn and Bacon, Inc.

CHAPTER 4

Baxter, Gail P., and Robert Glaser
  in   Investigating the cognitive complexity of science assessments. *Educational Measure-*
  press   *ment: Issues and Practice.*

DeStefano, Lizanne, P. David Pearson, and Peter Afflerbach
  1997   Content validation of the 1994 National Assessment of Educational Progress in reading:
            Assessing the relationship between the 1994 assessment and the reading framework. Pp.
            1-50 in *Quality and Utility: The 1994 Trial State Assessment in Reading: Background
            Studies,* Robert Glaser, Robert Linn, and George Bohrnstedt, eds. Panel on the Evalua-
            tion of the NAEP Trial State Assessment. Stanford, CA: National Academy of Educa-
            tion.

Greeno, James G., P. David Pearson, and Alan H. Schoenfeld
  1997   Implications for the National Assessment of Educational Progress of research on learning
            and cognition. Pp. 151-215 in *Assessment in Transition: Monitoring the Nation's Educa-
            tional Progress: Background Studies,* Robert Glaser, Robert Linn, and George
            Bohrnstedt, eds. Panel on the Evaluation of the NAEP Trial State Assessment. Stanford,
            CA: National Academy of Education.

Grouws, Douglas, ed.
  1996   *Handbook of Research on Teaching and Learning Mathematics.* New York: Macmillan.

Hamilton, Laura S., E. Michael Nussbaum, and Richard E. Snow
  1997   Interview procedures for validating science assessments. *Applied Measurement in Edu-
            cation* 10(2):181-200.

Johnson, Eugene G., Stephen Lazer, and Christine Y. O'Sullivan
  1997   *NAEP Reconfigured: An Integrated Redesign of the National Assessment of Educational
            Progress.* Prepared by Educational Testing Service, Westat, and National Computer
            Systems, August; NCES Working Paper Series No. 97-31, October. Washington, DC:
            U.S. Department of Education.

Kenney, Patricia Ann
  1999   Families of items in the NAEP mathematics assessment. In *Grading the Nation's Report
            Card: Research from the Evaluation of NAEP,* James W. Pellegrino, Lee R. Jones, and
            Karen J. Mitchell, eds. Committee on the Evaluation of National and State Assessments
            of Educational Progress, Board of Testing and Assessment. Washington, DC: National
            Academy Press.

Kenney, Patricia Ann, and Edward A. Silver
  1997   *Results from the Sixth Mathematics Assessment of the National Assessment of Educa-
            tional Progress.* Reston, VA: The National Council of Teachers of Mathematics, Inc.

Minstrell, James
  1999   Student thinking, instruction, and assessment in a facet-based learning environment. In
            Grading the Nation's Report Card: Research from the Evaluation of NAEP, James W.
            Pellegrino, Lee R. Jones, and Karen J. Mitchell, eds. Committee on the Evaluation of
            National and State Assessments of Educational Progress, Board on Testing and Assess-
            ment. Washington, DC: National Academy Press.
  1991   Facets of students' knowledge and relevant instruction. In *Research in Physics Learning:
            Theoretical Issues and Empirical Studies,* Reinders Duit, Fred Goldberg, and Hans
            Niedderer, eds., Proceedings of an International Workshop, Bremen: Germany.

Minstrell, James, and Earl Hunt
  1992   Instructional Design and Tools to Assist Teachers in Addressing Students' Understanding
            and Reasoning. Unpublished paper presented at the annual meeting of the American
            Educational Research Association, April 23, 1992.

Mislevy, Robert J.
1993   Foundations of a new test theory. In *Test Theory for a New Generation of Tests,* N. Fredericksen, R.J. Mislevy, and I.I. Bejar, eds. Hillsdale, NJ: Lawrence Erlbaum Associates, Inc.

Murnane, Richard J., and F. Levy
1996   *Teaching the New Basic Skills.* New York: Free Press.

National Academy of Education
1997   *Assessment in Transition: Monitoring the Nation's Educational Progress,* Robert Glaser, Robert Linn, and George Bohrnstedt, eds. Panel on the Evaluation of the NAEP Trial State Assessment. Stanford, CA: National Academy of Education.
1996   *Quality and Utility: The 1994 Trial State Assessment in Reading,* Robert Glaser, Robert Linn, and George Bohrnstedt, eds. Panel on the Evaluation of the NAEP Trial State Assessment. Stanford, CA: National Academy of Education.
1993   *The Trial State Assessment: Prospects and Realities,* Robert Glaser, Robert Linn, and George Bohrnstedt, eds. Panel on the Evaluation of the NAEP Trial State Assessment. Stanford, CA: National Academy of Education.
1992   *Assessing Student Achievement in the States,* Robert Glaser, Robert Linn, and George Bohrnstedt, eds. Panel on the Evaluation of the NAEP Trial State Assessment. Stanford, CA: National Academy of Education.

National Assessment Governing Board
no   *Mathematics Framework for the 1996 National Assessment of Educational Progress.*
date a Washington, DC: National Assessment Governing Board.
no   *Reading Framework for the National Assessment of Educational Progress: 1992-1998.*
date b Washington, DC: National Assessment Governing Board.
no   *Science Assessment and Exercise Specifications for the 1996 NAEP.* Washington, DC:
date c National Assessment Governing Board.
no   *Science Framework for the 1996 National Assessment of Educational Progress.* Wash-
date d ington, DC: National Assessment Governing Board.

National Council of Teachers of Mathematics
1989   *Curriculum and Evaluation Standards for School Mathematics.* Reston, VA: National Council of Teachers of Mathematics.

National Research Council
1999a   *How People Learn: New Developments from the Science of Learning.* John Bransford, Ann Brown, and Rodney R. Cocking, eds. Committee on the Science of Learning, Commission on Behavioral and Social Sciences and Education. Washington, DC: National Academy Press.
1999b   *Evaluation of the Voluntary National Tests: Phase 1 Report.* Lauress L. Wise, Robert M. Hauser, Karen J. Mitchell, and Michael J. Feuer, Board on Testing and Assessment. Washington, DC: National Academy Press.

O'Sullivan, Christine Y., Clyde M. Reese, and John Mazzeo
1997   *NAEP 1996 Science Report Card for the Nation and the States.* Washington, DC: U.S. Department of Education.

Pearson, David, and Lizanne DeStefano
1994   Content validation of the 1992 NAEP in reading: Classifying items according to the reading framework. Pp. 285-314 in *The Trial State Assessment: Prospects and Realities: Background Studies,* Robert Glaser, Robert Linn, and George Bohrnstedt, eds. Panel on the Evaluation of the NAEP Trial State Assessment. Stanford, CA: National Academy of Education.

Reese, Clyde M., Karen E. Miller, John Mazzeo, and John Dossey
1997   *NAEP 1996 Mathematics Report Card for the Nation and the States: Findings from the National Assessment of Educational Progress.* Washington, DC: U.S. Department of Education.

Resnick, Lauren B.
1987   *Education and Learning to Think.* Commission on Behavioral and Social Sciences and Education, National Research Council. Washington, DC: National Academy Press.

SCANS Commission
1991   *What Work Requires of Schools: A SCANS Report for America 2000.* The Secretary's Commission on Achieving Necessary Skills. Washington, DC: U.S. Department of Labor.

Shavelson, Richard J.
1997   On a science performance assessment technology: implications for the future of the National Assessment of Educational Progress. Pp. 103-122 in *Assessment in Transition: Background Studies,* Robert Glaser, Robert Linn, and George Bohrnstedt, eds. Panel on the Evaluation of the NAEP Trial State Assessment. Stanford, CA: National Academy of Education.

Shavelson, Richard J., Gail P. Baxter, and X. Gao
1993   Sampling variability of performance assessments. *Journal of Educational Measurement* 30(3):215-232.

Silver, Edward A., Cengiz Alacaci, and Despina Stylianou
1998   Gaining Insights into Students' Problem Solving: An Analysis of Student Responses to NAEP's Constructed-Response Questions. Presentation at the American Educational Research Association Meeting, April.

Silver, Edward A., and Patricia Ann Kenney
1994   The content and curricular validity of the 1992 NAEP TSA in mathematics. Pp. 231-284 in *The Trial State Assessment: Prospects and Realities: Background Studies,* Robert Glaser, Robert Linn, and George Bohrnstedt, eds. Panel on the Evaluation of the NAEP Trial State Assessment. Stanford, CA: National Academy of Education.

Silver, Edward A., Patricia Ann Kenney, and Leslie Salmon-Cox
1992   The content and curricular validity of the 1990 NAEP mathematics items: A retrospective analysis. Pp. 157-218 in *Assessing Student Achievement: Background Studies,* Robert Glaser, Robert Linn, and George Bohrnstedt, eds. Stanford, CA: National Academy of Education.

Sireci, Stephen G., H. Jane Rogers, Hariharan Swaminathan, Kevin Meara, and Frederic Robin
1999   An external evaluation of the content representation of the 1996 grade 8 NAEP science assessment. In *Grading the Nation's Report Card: Research from the Evaluation of NAEP,* James W. Pellegrino, Lee R. Jones, and Karen J. Mitchell, eds., Committee on the Evaluation of National and State Assessments of Educational Progress, Board on Testing and Assessment. Washington, DC: National Academy Press.

White, B.Y., and J. Frederickson
1998   Inquiry, modeling, and metacognition: making science accessible to all students. *Cognition and Instruction* 16:3-118.

CHAPTER 5

Alexander, Lamar
1991   America 2000. Washington, DC: U.S. Department of Education.

Barron, Sheila, and Daniel Koretz
in   *Interpretation and use of the NAEP Trial State Assessment Results by the Media.* Wash-
press   ington, DC: U.S. Department of Education.

Brennan, Robert L.
1998   Misconceptions at the intersection of measurement theory and practice. *Educational Measurement: Issues and Practice* 17(1):5-9.

Bullock, Cheryl Davis, and Lizanne DeStefano
   1998   A study of the utility of results from the 1992 Trial State Assessment (TSA) in reading for state-level administrators of assessment. *Educational Evaluation and Policy Analysis* 20(1):47-51.
Burstein, Leigh, Daniel Koretz, Robert Linn, Brenda Sugrue, John Novak, Eva L. Baker, and Elizabeth Lewis Harris
   1996   Describing performance standards: Validity of the 1992 National Assessment of Educational Progress achievement level descriptors as characterizations of mathematics performance. *Educational Assessment* 3(1):9-51.
Cohen, Jon, Elizabeth Greenberg, and George Bohrnstedt
   1997   NAEP Achievement Standards, Background, and Options. Unpublished paper prepared by American Institutes for Research.
Education Week
   1998   *Quality Counts.* 17(17).
Goldberg, Jeanne P.
   1998   The recommended dietary allowances: Can they inform the development of standards of academic achievement? *Applied Measurement in Education* 11(1):97-105.
Hambleton, Ronald K.
   1997   Enhancing the Validity of NAEP Achievement Level Score Reporting. Presentation at the National Assessment Governing Board Achievement Levels Committee meeting, Boulder, CO, August 20-22.
Hambleton, Ronald K., and Mary Lyn Bourque
   1991   *The Levels of Mathematics Achievement (Volume III, Technical Report).* Washington, DC: National Assessment Governing Board.
Hanser, Lawrence M.
   1998   Lessons for the National Assessment of Educational Progress from military standard setting. *Applied Measurement in Education* 11(1):81-95.
Impara, James C., and Barbara S. Plake
   1998   Teachers' ability to estimate item difficulty: A test of the assumptions in the Angoff standard setting method. *Journal of Educational Measurement* 35(1):69-81.
Jasanoff, Sheila
   1998   Science and judgment in environmental standard setting. *Applied Measurement in Education* 11(1):107-120.
Kane, Michael
   1995   Examinee-centered vs. task-centered standard setting. Pp. 119-141 in *Joint Conference on Standard Setting for Large-Scale Assessments: Proceedings Volume II.* Washington, DC: U.S. Government Printing Office.
Koretz, Daniel M., and Edward Deibert
   1995/   Setting standards and interpreting achievement: A cautionary tale from the National
   1996   Assessment of Educational Progress. *Educational Assessment* 3(1):53-81.
Lewis, D.M., D.R. Green, H.C. Mitzel, K. Braum, and R. Patz
   1998   The Bookmark Standard-setting Procedure: Methology and Recent Implications. Presentation at the National Council on Measurement in Education annual meeting, April.
Linn, Robert L.
   1998   Validating inferences from National Assessment of Educational Progress achievement-level setting. *Applied Measurement in Education* 11(1):23-47.
Linn, Robert L., and Lorrie A. Shepard
   1997   Item-by-item Standard Setting: Unintended Consequences Due to Less Than Perfect Item-correlatons. Presentation at the Council of Chief State School Officers Large-Scale Assessment Conference.

Linn, Robert L., Daniel M. Koretz, Eva L. Baker, and Leigh Burstein
   1991   *The Validity and Credibility of the Achievement Levels for the National Assessment of Educational Progress in Mathematics.* Los Angeles, CA: Center for the Study of Evaluation, University of California.
McLaughlin, Donald H., Phyllis A. DuBois, Marian S. Eaton, Dey E. Ehrlich, Fran B. Stancavage, Catherine A. O'Sonnell, Jin-Ying Yu; Lizanne DeStefano, David Pearson, Diane Bottomley, Cheryl Ann Bullock, Matthew Hanson, and Cindi Rucinski
   1993   Comparison of teachers' and researchers' ratings of students' performance in mathematics and reading with NAEP measurement of achievement levels. Pp. 283-364 in *Setting Performance Standards for Student Achievement: Background Studies,* Robert Glaser, Robert Linn, and George Bohrnstedt, eds. Stanford, CA: National Academy of Education.
Mehrens, William A.
   1995   Methodological issues in standard setting for educational exams. Pp. 221-263 in *Joint Conference on Standard Setting for Large-Scale Assessments: Proceedings Volume II.* Washington, DC: U.S. Government Printing Office.
National Academy of Education
   1997   *Assessment in Transition: Monitoring the Nation's Educational Progress,* Robert Glaser, Robert Linn, and George Bohrnstedt, eds. Panel on the Evaluation of the NAEP Trial State Assessment. Stanford, CA: National Academy of Education.
   1996   *Quality and Utility: The 1994 Trial State Assessment in Reading,* Robert Glaser, Robert Linn, and George Bohrnstedt, eds. Panel on the Evaluation of the NAEP Trial State Assessment. Stanford, CA: National Academy of Education.
   1993a   *Setting Performance Standards for Student Achievement,* Robert Glaser, Robert Linn, and George Bohrnstedt, eds. Panel on the Evaluation of the NAEP Trial State Assessment. Stanford, CA: National Academy of Education.
   1993b   *The Trial State Assessment: Prospects and Realities,* Robert Glaser, Robert Linn, and George Bohrnstedt, eds. Panel on the Evaluation of the NAEP Trial State Assessment. Stanford, CA: National Academy of Education.
   1992   *Assessing Student Achievement in the States,* Robert Glaser, Robert Linn, and George Bohrnstedt, eds. Panel on the Evaluation of the NAEP Trial State Assessment. Stanford, CA: National Academy of Education.
National Assessment Governing Board
   1997   *What Do Students Know? 1996 NAEP Science Results for 4th, 8th, and 12th Graders.* Washington, DC: U.S. Department of Education.
O'Sullivan, Christine Y., Clyde M. Reese, and John Mazzeo
   1997   *NAEP 1996 Science Report Card for the Nation and the States.* Washington, DC: U.S. Department of Education.
Pellegrino, James, Lauress Wise, and Nambury Raju
   1998   Guest editors' note. *Applied Measurement in Education* 11(1):1-7.
Reckase, Mark D.
   1998   Converting boundaries between National Assessment Governing Board performance categories to points on the National Assessment of Educational Progress score scale: The 1996 science NAEP process. *Applied Measurement in Education* 11(1):9-21.
Reese, Clyde M., Karen E. Miller, John Mazzeo, and John Dossey
   1997   *NAEP 1996 Mathematics Report Card for the Nation and the States: Findings from the National Assessment of Educational Progress.* Washington, DC: U.S. Department of Education.

Shepard, Lorrie A.
   1995   Implications for standard setting of the National Academy of Education evaluation of the
           National Assessment of Educational Progress achievement levels. Pp. 143-160 in *Pro-
           ceedings of the Joint Conference on Standard Setting for Large-Scale Assessments, Vol-
           ume II.* Presentation at the Joint Conference on Standard Setting for Large-Scale Assess-
           ments, October 5. Washington, DC: U.S. Government Printing Office.
Stufflebeam, Daniel L., Richard M. Jaeger, and Michael Scriven
   1991   Summative Evaluation of the National Assessment Governing Board's Inaugural 1990-91
           Effort to Set Achievement Levels on the National Assessment of Educational Progress.
           Prepared for the National Assessment Governing Board, August 23.
U.S. General Accounting Office
   1993   *Educational Achievement Standards: NAGB's Approach Yields Misleading Interpreta-
           tions.* GAO/PEMD-93-12. Washington, DC: U.S. General Accounting Office.

CHAPTER 6

American Institutes for Research
   1997   *Redesign Plan for a More Useful National Assessment of Education Progress,* George
           Bohrnstedt, Jon Cohen, Archie Lapointe, Roger Levine, and Christine Paulsen, eds. Pre-
           pared for National Center for Education Statistics, June, Washington, DC: American
           Institutes for Research.
Bay, Luz, Lee Chen, Bradley A. Hanson, Jay Happel, Michael J. Kolen, Timothy Miller, Mary
Pommerich, James Sconing, Tianyou Wang, and Catherine Welch
   1997   *ACT's NAEP Redesign Project: Assessment Design is the Key to Useful and Stable
           Assessment Results.* Prepared by ACT for U.S. Department of Education; NCES Work-
           ing Paper Series No. 97-30, October. Washington, DC: U.S. Department of Education.
Forsyth, Robert, Ronald Hambleton, Robert Linn, Robert Mislevy, and Wendy Yen
   1996   *Design/Feasibility Team: Report to the National Assessment Governing Board.* Wash-
           ington, DC: National Assessment Governing Board.
Johnson, Eugene G., Stephen Lazer, and Christine Y. O'Sullivan
   1997   *NAEP Reconfigured: An Integrated Redesign of the National Assessment of Educational
           Progress.* Prepared by Educational Testing Service, Westat, and National Computer
           Systems, August; NCES Working Paper Series No. 97-31, October. Washington, DC:
           U.S. Department of Education.
National Assessment Governing Board
   1997   *Bridging Policy to Implementation: A Resolution.* Washington, DC: National Assess-
           ment Governing Board.
   1996   *Policy Statement on Redesigning the National Assessment of Educational Progress.*
           Washington, DC: National Assessment Governing Board.

Appendixes

APPENDIX
A

Enhancing the Assessment of Reading

In Chapter 4, we concluded that the NAEP reading framework reflects current theory and research about reading process, but that the assessment itself does not adequately reflect the goals of the framework. It does not adequately assess several important characteristics of good readers, nor does it reflect how students' reading is influenced by interactions among reader, text, and context. In this appendix we describe more specific conclusions and recommendations designed to improve the current main NAEP reading assessment, followed by examples intended to illustrate ways of implementing the recommendations.

ASSESSMENT TASKS, ITEMS, TEXTS, AND SCORING RUBRICS

The current assessment does not adequately reflect the reading document in terms of assessment tasks, items, texts, and scoring rubrics. The assessment *tasks* confound reading purpose with type of text. It is assumed that a particular type of text always engenders a particular purpose for reading, yet it is possible, and often desirable, to read the same text for different purposes (e.g., read an informational article to understand the specific cause/effect relationships that led to a war versus to gain a general impression of the situation that led to conflict as a strategy for understanding another historical event). Students are never explicitly given a purpose for reading, forcing them to adopt an unfocused or personally constructed purpose for reading that may or may not be aligned with the focus of the comprehension items. Ultimately, purpose and focus influence comprehension. In addition, in an effort to hold *text* types more or less constant across grades and test blocks, texts used at a particular grade level may not be representative of texts students read. For example, to assess reading for literary experience, NAEP uses tales across grades 4, 8, and 12 even though this genre is rare in students' reading at the high school level.

NAEP reading *items* are designed to align with four stances of comprehension, yet research suggests that the four types are not judged to be discrete. In general, the items are developed using a 3 × 4 grid (passage type by comprehension type) for each reading selection rather than designed to meet the demands of a particular text or a focused purpose for reading. Furthermore, extended response questions often are not put to good use. In some cases they require limited thinking or writing from students (which does not improve on multiple-choice items); in other cases, the items are good but the scoring rubrics often don't require evaluation of the quality or depth of the students' written response, but rather are vague or focus on superficial elements. This is most likely a result of NAEP using a generic rubric to guide development of passage-specific rubrics.

Students should be provided with explicit and varying purposes for reading specific texts. Items should follow up on those purposes rather than being forced to fit the 3 × 4 matrix. Text types, purposes, and item types should be systematically varied across the entire NAEP assessment. The nature of the cognitive processing of text follows from a particular text and purpose for reading. Not all types of questions or levels of processing are appropriate for every text/purpose combination.

Similarly, texts should be selected to reflect what students read at a particular grade level rather than selecting text types that are held consistent across grade levels. Item formats and scoring rubrics should be appropriate to the specific questions and the depth of understanding students should demonstrate.

ASSESSING THE CONCEPTUAL FRAMEWORK

The assessment leaves many of the characteristics of effective reading described in the document unexamined or unmanipulated. For example, background knowledge, fluency, reading strategies, purpose, habits, and attitudes are not adequately assessed. Although it is true that some of these characteristics have been examined in special studies (fluency) or background questions (habits), the results have not been used to inform the larger NAEP dataset or to inform NAEP reports.

In the same way, the assessment does not adequately reflect the complex interaction among the reader, text, and context portrayed in the reading document and influential in reading performance. That is to say, that variables such as background knowledge, reading strategies, habits, comprehension (reader), text complexity, topic, comprehension items (text), and purpose for reading and classroom instructional opportunities (context) are not systematically varied or considered in a way that reflects the framework's theoretical basis, nor do they inform reporting and interpretation of student performance.

When possible, the characteristics of good readers described in the framework should be included in the large-scale portion of NAEP. When this is not feasible (because of time, money, requirements of reliable and valid assessment of these characteristics), alternative assessment materials should be used to gather data on student performance in these areas. When alternatives are used, the results should be integrated with results of the large-scale assessment, providing a more complete and more useful assessment of student performance.

To address an interactive model of reading, NAEP should develop coherent families of items to meet the demands of particular purposes for reading. Each family should include a reading selection and items that fit a particular purpose for reading the text as well as items that assess students' strategies, dispositions, and instructional experiences, as appropriate.

DATA ANALYSIS AND REPORTING

The process of data analysis treats each reading item as independent rather than analyzing the family of items around a particular reading selection as a coherent, interrelated group of items. In addition, results are reported as using a single scale, suggesting that student performance is uniform across various contexts (e.g., text types, purposes). As a result, we are not able to understand reading performance in terms of the interaction among reader, text, and context. For example, we cannot tell how well students read for different types of understanding or use various strategies when they are reading for different purposes or under different conditions. We cannot determine how these factors influence reading performance, nor can we gain insight into when students may have difficulties.

NAEP should explore alternative methods of data analysis that are based on the theoretical and empirical basis of the NAEP reading document. They should find ways to analyze and report student performance under varying conditions by treating item sets as the unit of analysis. For example, they may be able to build profiles of students' cognitive abilities as a function of various texts, tasks, and purposes for reading. At the same time, NAEP should explore ways to aggregate scores that fairly represent student performance for reporting to outside audiences.

AN EXAMPLE FROM THE 1994 NAEP READING ASSESSMENT— GRADE 8

Figure A-1 is a reading passage from the 1994 NAEP reading assessment for grade 8. In the discussion that follows, assessment material is in regular font; comments are italicized.

Section 23

The Lost People of

MESA VERDE

The Anasazi lived peacefully on the mesa for 800 years.

Then they disappeared.

By Elsa Marston

The Image Bank

In the dry land of southwestern Colorado a beautiful plateau rises. It has so many trees that early Spanish explorers called it Mesa Verde, which means "green table." For about eight hundred years Native Americans called the Anasazi lived on this mesa. And then they left. Ever since the cliff houses were first discovered a hundred years ago, scientists and historians have wondered why.

Anasazi is a Navajo word meaning "the ancient ones." When they first settled there, around 500 A.D., the Anasazi lived in alcoves in the walls of the high canyons. Later they moved to the level land on top, where they built houses of stone and mud mortar. As time passed, they constructed more elaborate houses, like apartment buildings, with several families living close together.

The Anasazi made beautiful pottery, turquoise jewelry, fine sashes of woven hair, and baskets woven tightly enough to hold water. They lived by hunting and by growing corn and squash. Their way of life went on peacefully for several hundred years.

Then around 1200 A.D. something strange happened, for which the reasons are not quite clear. Most of the people moved from the level plateau back down into alcoves in the cliffs. The move must have made their lives difficult because they had to climb back up to the plateau to do the farming. But it seems the Anasazi planned to stay in the canyon walls, for they soon filled the

GO ON TO THE NEXT PAGE

FIGURE A-1 Reading passage from the 1994 NAEP reading assessment for grade 8. Reprinted by permission.

alcoves with amazing cliff dwellings. "Cliff Palace," the most famous of these, had more than two hundred rooms.

For all the hard work that went into building these new homes, the Anasazi did not live in them long. By 1300 A.D. the cliff dwellings were empty. Mesa Verde was deserted and remained a ghost country for almost six hundred years.. Were the people driven out of their homes by enemies? No sign of attack or fighting, or even the presence of other tribes, has been found.

and beautiful pottery left behind by the Anasazi may be 1,000 years old.

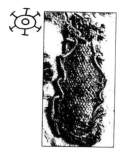

Bureau of Land Management—Anasazi Heritage Center Collections

Archaeologists who have studied the place now believe there are other reasons. Mesa Verde, the beautiful green table, was no longer a good place to live. For one thing, in the second half of the thirteenth century there were long periods of cold, and very little rain fell—or else it came at the wrong time of year. Scientists know this from examining the wood used in the cliff dwellings. The growth rings in trees show good and bad growing seasons. But the people had survived drought and bad weather before, so there must have been another reason.

As the population grew, more land on the mesa top had to be farmed in order to feed the people. That meant that trees had to be cut to clear the land and also to use

for houses and fuel. Without the forests, the rain began to wash away the mesa top.

How do we know about erosion problems that happened about eight hundred years ago? The Anasazi built many low dams across the smaller valleys on the mesa to slow down rain runoff. Even so, good soil washed away, and the people could no longer raise enough food. As the forests dwindled, the animals, already overhunted, left the mesa for mountainous areas with more trees.

And as the mesa "wore out," so did the people. It appears that the Anasazi were not healthy. Scientists can learn a lot about ancient people's health by studying the bones and teeth found in burials. The mesa dwellers had arthritis, and their teeth

were worn down by the grit in corn meal, a main part of their diet.

As food became scarce, people grew weaker. Not many lived beyond their twenties. Women died very young, and few babies survived. Living so close together in the cliff houses, where everyone was hungry and worried, the people must have suffered from emotional strain. They probably quarreled often.

In the end the Anasazi must have given up hope that things would get better.

Section 23

Families packed up and went away. Of course, the "ancient ones" did not simply disappear. They moved southeast to another area and mingled with other peoples. After a while their heritage as the people of the Mesa Verde was forgotten.

In time the trees grew back and the plateau became green once more. But, for the Anasazi it was too late. Although they respected nature and tried to farm wisely, land that was used too hard could not support them forever.

Yet in their cliff houses and crafts the "ancient ones" left us a superb monument. It is truly one of the most fascinating pictures of America's past.

WO000822

GO ON TO THE NEXT PAGE

No purpose is given for reading this informational piece. As a result, students don't have a reason to focus their reading. The following is recommended:

GLOBAL PURPOSE: This informational article is like one that you might read when doing a research report.
SPECIFIC PURPOSE: Read this informational article to understand the theories about what happened to one ancient civilization—the Anasazi.

or

You are going to write a short research report on ancient civilizations that disappeared. Read this article on the Anasazi to understand the theories scientists have for their disappearance. *(This purpose would be followed-up with another short piece on the Mayan civilization and a short writing assignment comparing the two. Students could also be asked to take notes to aid in their report writing, providing data that could be analyzed as part of a target study of students' reading and study strategies.)*

Both these purposes focus readers on theories and supporting evidence. They call for a close reading and reasoning about the text.

A logical line of questioning for these purposes would include:
   Who were the Anasazi?
   Where and when did they live?
   Why is their disappearance of interest to scientists?
   What are the theories and supporting evidence for their disappearance?

Existing Items:

1. *(Extended response)* After reading this article, what do you think is the most important information about the Anasazi?

This question doesn't have a clear focus and, as a result, elicits vague responses from students. What students determine to be most important depends on their purpose for reading.

Scoring Rationale = Initial Understanding

Initial understanding requires students to provide an initial impression or unreflective understanding of what was read.

1 = Evidence of little or no comprehension—these responses contain inaccurate information from the article or inappropriate personal opinions about the article. They do not provide any valid information or appropriate interpretation about the Anasazi as they were portrayed in the article.

3 = Evidence of full comprehension—these responses provide a specific detail or a general impression from the passage that related to some aspect of the Anasazi portrayed in the article.

(The reading assessment development panel determined that it was more appropriate to score this item with a 2-point scoring guide.)

Examples of specific statements too vague for a score of 3:
 how they stayed alive
 interesting things they made
 what they ate
 the way they lived/farmed/built houses/grew food
 they worked hard
 they had a rough life

Examples of specific statements acceptable for a score of 3:
 They left.
 They moved.

The scoring rubric is vague. Any specific text-based response is given full credit. There are only 2 credit levels - full (3) or partial (1). Ironically, "they left/they moved" is given full credit but "the way they lived/ farmed/ built houses/ grew food" are all given a score of 1. The nature of the full response does not seem to merit an extended constructed-response item.

2. *(Extended response)* The three moves made by the Anasazi are listed below. Explain the possible reasons that were suggested in the article for each move.

This question is intended to have students develop an interpretation. Although it requires students to process information across the text, it misleads them since there are no reasons given in the article for two of the moves, so answers such as "no reason given" as well as "so they could live in apartments" (which is a questionable, reader-based opinion) are given full credit. This question could be better focused to our purpose and to the interpretation of theories and evidence. The focus would be on theories for Anasazis leaving the mesa.

Scoring Rationale = Developing an Interpretation

Developing an interpretation requires students to go beyond an initial impression of a text by linking information across parts of the text or focusing on specific information.

1 = Evidence of unsatisfactory comprehension—these responses do not identify the reasons provided by the article for any of the moves that were made by the Anasazi. These responses may provide some fact about the Anasazi but do not relate them to any of the moves.

2 = Evidence of partial comprehension—these responses discuss reasons for only one or two of the moves described in the article. They receive credit for one explanation if they state that the article did not provide possible reasons for the first move.

3 = Evidence of essential comprehension—these responses identify a reason for three of the moves discussed in the article. The reasons may be brief or simple restatements of information in the article as long as they are logical and taken from the passage.

4 = Evidence of extensive comprehension—these responses identify a reason for all three moves, even though the reasons for all the moves are not explicitly discussed in the article. These responses go beyond simply restating the article to interpret some of the information provided in the article as it relates to the moves.

Unacceptable reasons for the first move:
    for protection
    for food (too vague)
    to make better houses (not specific enough)
    hard to live in a slanted house

Acceptable reasons for the first move:
    article gives no reason
    probably thought farming was better/easier
    get more rainfall
    closer to farming
    to farm on top
    ran out of room
    so they would not have to climb up and down
    hunt easier
    to build houses of stone and mortar
    so they could live in apartments

Unacceptable reasons for the second move:
    wanted to build a new place (too vague)
    because water became scarce
    top became too crowded
    reasons are not clear
    because Mese Verde life was hard
    because they had more than 200 rooms

Acceptable reasons for the second move:
    bad growing seasons
    lack of rain
    for protection
    too hot on top
    bad weather
    woods became scarce
    top became too crowded
    reasons are not clear
    because Mesa Verde life was hard
    because they had more than 200 rooms

Unacceptable reasons for third move:
    no reasons were given
    the cliffs were falling apart
    for new farm land

Acceptable reasons for third move:
    land was not useful
    for better food and water
    everyone was dying
    life was miserable
    for better farming
    living too close together
    driven out by enemies

The rubric partially confounds the completion of all three sections with the quality of the responses. Rubrics should distinguish the quality of the thinking from the quantity of responses provided.

Suggested alternate item:

The article suggests several theories about why the Anasazis left the mesa. List the theories and provide evidence from the article to support each theory.

    THEORY   *EVIDENCE*

3. *(Extended response)* If you had lived with the Anasazi at Mesa Verde, would you have preferred living on the top of the mesa or in the cliff houses built into the alcoves? Explain you preference by using information from the article.

This question directs students away from the essential information in the article. It demonstrates what happens when item writers try to develop items that fit each major category in the framework matrix. Personal response questions are probably not appropriate in the context of this particular reading passage.

4. *(Extended response)* If you could talk to the author of this article, what is one question you could ask her about the Anasazi that is not already answered in the article? Explain why you would want to know this information.

The intent of this question (seeking additional information) is reasonable for an informational "research" purpose but talking with the author is not. It would be more meaningful to ask:

What other information would you need for your report on the Anasazi? Where would you go to get it?

This not only gets at the information missing from the article, but also serves as a reading strategy item (metacognitive item) about sources of information.

This question is labeled personal response, although it might qualify equally well as critical stance. The rubric requires students to respond with an appropriate question and a clear explanation about how this additional information would be useful. Rationales such as "I would be interested" or "I want to know" are not acceptable even though students aren't given a clear purpose of reading.

5. *(Multiple choice)* Which idea from the text about the Anasazi do the photographs support?

    a. They were able to create many useful objects.
    b. Farming was probably their major source of food.
    c. Wood seems to have been their primary building material.
    d. Their life became much easier when they moved into the cliff dwellings.

There are only 2 photo sections in the reading passage—one that includes the passage title and four small photos of baskets, sandals, and pottery. These pictures are only minimally relevant to the main thrust of the text. This text is not about the culture of the Anasazi but about their unexplained disappearance. Again, this question is the result of trying to fit a particular type of question (using graphic aids) to a reading passage without regard for the passage's content or the appropriate purpose for reading it.

6. *(Extended response)* Imagine that you are living with the people of Mesa Verde during the 1200s when they left the mesa. Some of your friends and neighbors do not want to leave the area. Based on information in the article, what would you tell these people to convince them to leave?

This question overlaps with question 2—to get full credit, students must make an argument based on information from the text (same information needed in question 2). This item is labeled "critical stance" although it could just as easily be classified as "personal response." The two are obviously not distinct.

7. *(Multiple choice)* The Anasazi's life before 1200 A.D. was portrayed by the author as being

    a. dangerous and warlike
    b. busy and exciting
    c. difficult and dreary
    d. productive and peaceful

Rather than an emphasis on the date, this question should focus on the strange, unexplained change in Anasazi life—their disappearance. Before this time, their life was good, so it is difficult to explain their disappearance.

8. *(Multiple choice)* The title and photograph on the first page of the article are probably meant to make the disappearance of the Anasazi seem to be

    a. personal tragedy
    b. a terrible mistake
    c. an unsolved mystery
    d. an important political event

The best use of this photo is to help students anticipate the content of the piece and set purpose—what would they expect to read about.

9. *(Extended response)* Some people say that the Anasazi's success as a civilization may have actually caused their own decline. Using information in the article, explain why you agree or disagree with this statement.

This question does a good job of hitting the conceptual main idea and combining it with a personal response. It requires students to take a position and defend it with evidence. Although it is labeled as "personal response," it is more likely a cross between "critical stance" and "personal response."

Research About Student Learning as a Basis for Developing Assessment Materials: An Example from Science

Research about how students build their understanding of conceptual areas in science in classroom settings can inform the development of assessment materials. In particular, such investigations can serve as a foundation for the development of scoring rubrics that reflect levels and types of understanding that are based on observations of how students learn the concepts that are being assessed. In the volume of research papers that accompanies this report, Minstrell (1999) presents a synthesis of his investigations of how students build their understanding in several specific areas in the study of force and motion: (1) separating fluid/medium effects from gravitational effects, (2) average velocity, and (3) forces during interactions. Minstrell originally conducted his research to identify ways for improving the instruction of individual students in high school physics classes. We present it as an example of how information from research about student cognition and learning has application to development of large-scale assessment materials.

Table B-1 contains three examples of "facet clusters" drawn from Minstrell's research. These facet clusters are sets of related elements, grouped around a physical situation (e.g., forces on interacting objects) or around some conceptual idea (e.g., meaning of average velocity). The individual facets of students' thinking refer to individual pieces or constructions of a few pieces of knowledge and/or strategies of reasoning. They have been derived from research on students' thinking and from classroom observations by teachers. Within a cluster, facets can be sequenced in an approximate order of development. Those ending with 0 or 1 in the units digit tend to be appropriate, acceptable understandings for introductory physics. The facets ending in 9, 8 or 7 tend to be the more problem-

TABLE B-1 Three Examples of Facet Clusters

EXAMPLE A

Separating Fluid/Medium Effects from Gravitational Effects—Facets of Student Understanding

310 – pushes from above and below by a surrounding fluid medium lend a slight support (net upward push due to differences in the depth of pressure gradient)

311 – a mathematical formulaic approach ($\rho \times g \times h_1 - \rho \times g \times h_2$ = net buoyant pressure)

314 – surrounding fluids don't exert any forces or pushes on objects

315 – surrounding fluids exert equal pushes all around an object

316 – whichever surface has greater amount of fluid above or below the object has the greater push by the fluid on the surface

317 – fluid mediums exert an upward push only

318 – surrounding fluid mediums exert a net downward push

319 – weight of an object is directly proportional to medium pressure on it

EXAMPLE B

Average Speed or Average Velocity—Facets of Student Understanding

220 – average speed = (total distance covered)/(total time)

221 – average velocity = $\Delta x/\Delta t$ (together with a direction)

225 – rate expression is overgeneralized (e.g., average velocity = xf/tf)

226 – rate expression is misstated (e.g., average velocity = $\Delta t/\Delta x$ or $\Delta v/2$ or vf/2)

228 – average rate is not differentiated from another rate (e.g., velocity = speed or average velocity = average acceleration)

229 – average rate (speed/velocity) not differentiated from amount (e.g., average velocity = pf or average velocity = Δp)

TABLE B-1 Continued

EXAMPLE C

Forces During Interactions—Facets of Student Understanding

470 – all interactions involve equal magnitude and oppositely directed action and reaction forces that are on the separate interacting bodies

474 – effects (such as damage or resulting motion) dictate relative magnitude of forces during interaction

475 – equal force pairs are identified as action and reaction but are on the same object

476 – stronger exerts more force

477 – one with more motion exerts more force

478 – more active/energetic exerts more force

479 – bigger/heavier exerts more force

SOURCE: Adapted from Minstrell (1999).

atic because they represent limited understandings or, in some cases, serious misunderstandings. Those facets with middle digits frequently arise from formal instruction but may represent over- or undergeneralizations in a student's knowledge structure.

This type of systematic knowledge of the levels at which students understand and represent physical concepts, principles, and/or situations is a starting point for developing highly informative assessment materials that could be used in large-scale survey assessments such as NAEP. Figure B-1 is an example of a constructed-response item designed to probe levels of understanding from the first facet cluster in the table.

As discussed by Minstrell (1999), student responses to this item can be mapped to the facets in this cluster in a relatively straightforward manner. Students may be thinking that weight is due to the downward push by air (319), or they may believe that fluids (air or water) only push downward (318) or only push upward (317), or that fluids push equally from above, below, and all around (315), or that fluids do not push at all on objects in them (314), or that there is a differential in the push depending on how much fluid is above or below the object (316). If they do understand that there is a greater push from below than from above due to the greater pressure at greater depth, they may express it in a formulaic way (311) or with a rich conceptual description (310).

In a simple application, such facet clusters could be adapted for use as

A solid cylinder is hung by a long string from a spring scale. The reading on the scale shows that the cylinder weights 1.0 lb.

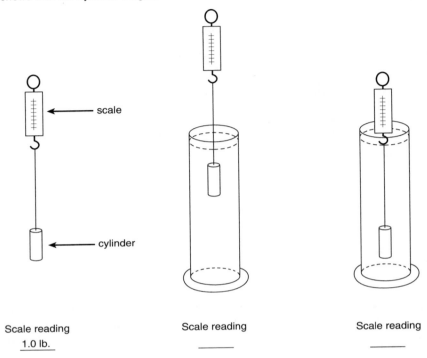

| Scale reading | Scale reading | Scale reading |
| 1.0 lb. | _____ | _____ |

About how much will the scale read if the cylinder which weighs 1.0 lbs. is submerged just below the surface of the water? What will it read when the cylinder is much deeper in the water?

Briefly explain how you decided.

FIGURE B-1 Example constructed-response item: separating fluid/medium effects from gravitational effects.

scoring rubrics if such an item were to be administered as part of a large-scale assessment, with responses reflecting facets of understanding that end in 0 or 1 being scored as correct, responses reflecting facets ending in 9, 8, or 7 being scored as incorrect, and with responses reflecting intermediate facets being scored at one or more levels of partial credit. Evaluators of students' responses must therefore be able to recognize which facet(s) are represented in a wide variety of student responses. In a large-scale scoring setting, this poses challenges for the recruitment and training of scorers.

Minstrell provides some examples of student responses and their relationship to facets of understanding in his research paper. Although this application shows how these facet clusters should be modified to adapt to current large-scale assessment scoring strategies, greater value would be realized by using the facet clusters as a basis for reporting the frequency of occurrence of various facets of understanding in students' responses and as a foundation for the types of interpretive reports we discuss in Chapter 4.

Single items such as that shown in first figure, even when coupled with qualitative evaluation frameworks such as the facet cluster in the table, seldom provide sufficient information to ascertain the specificity versus generality and appropriateness of a student's understanding. However, sets of items or item families can be constructed to assess the context specificity of understanding. Figure B-2 is a multiple-choice item that expands the analysis of medium effects in the context of the first facet cluster in the table.

These pictures show three identical blocks attached to the spring scale. In one case the block is in the water, in another it is in air, and in the third the block is in a vacuum. In the air, the scale represents 10 lbs. to the nearest 0.1 lb.

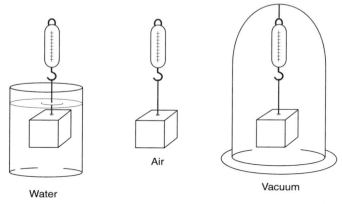

Water   Air   Vacuum

The scale readings would be

   A. about the same in all three environments.
   B. noticeably less in water but about the same in air and in a vacuum.
   C. noticeably less in air and in water.
   D. noticeably more in water and noticeably less in a vacuum.

FIGURE B-2 Example multiple-choice item: separating fluid/medium effects from gravitational effects.

By considering the response patterns across pairs or sets of items, such as those shown in the two figures, an evaluation can be provided of how much a student's understanding is tied to the specific surface situation described in a given problem. For example, for these items and this conceptual domain more generally, it is not uncommon for student understanding of the effects of a medium to achieve a more sophisticated level for the water context than the air context. Interpretable patterns of responses across items can also be obtained for other physical concepts and situations, and the use of an array of these sorts of item families in NAEP would provide a sound basis for the provision of more interpretive analyses of student performance that have been recommended throughout this report. In his research paper, Minstrell provides additional examples in multiple concept areas in the physical sciences of the application of a facet-based approach to the development of items and the evaluation of student responses.

REFERENCE

Minstrell, James
    1999   Facets of student understanding and assessment development, In *Grading the Nation's Report Card: Research from the Evaluation of NAEP*. James W. Pellegrino, Lee R. Jones, and Karen J. Mitchell, eds. Committee on the Evaluation of National and State Assessments of Educational Progress, Board on Testing and Assessment. Washington, DC: National Academy Press.

C
A Sample Family of Items Based on Number Patterns at Grade 4

In this appendix, an example of a family of items in grade 4 mathematics is presented. This information is drawn from a research paper in a volume that accompanies this report (Kenney, 1999).

NUMERICAL PATTERNS IN ELEMENTARY MATHEMATICS AND IN NAEP

The topic of patterns and relationships, and in particular numerical patterns in elementary school mathematics, is an appropriate content topic around which to create a family of items. Exploring patterns helps students in the early grades develop the ability to think algebraically (Armstrong, 1995; National Council of Teachers of Mathematics [NCTM], 1989; Reys et al., 1995). In fact, the NCTM Algebra Working Group realized that children can develop algebraic concepts at an early age and suggested that working with patterns of shapes and numbers helps to build the foundation for algebraic thinking needed in the later grades.

RELEASED NAEP PATTERN ITEMS AS THE BASIS FOR AN ITEM FAMILY

Not only did numerical pattern items appear on recent NAEP mathematics assessments, but also some of those items were released to the public. These released pattern items were not part of an item family in the assessment; instead, they appeared as single items in various parts of the assessment. However, because released pattern items and related performance data on those items were available from NAEP, it seemed reasonable to use these single items along with appropriate supplemental items to form a sample family of items.

The advantage of this method of constructing a sample family of items is that the sample family uses items that have already appeared on a NAEP assessment, and we know how students performed on them. Also, the family could be created with minimal time spent on developing original items. However, a potentially serious limitation of this method is that taking items developed individually and putting them together as a set post hoc carries with it a degree of artificiality. The ideal way to create an item family is to begin with a particular topic and information based on research about students' understanding of that topic and then build the family of items. Thus, the family of items presented here should be considered as an illustrative, but modest, example of what such a family might look like, with the understanding that better families of items should be created for future NAEP assessments. However, it is hoped that the example presented here will be used as the basis for further thought about and discussion of important features of families of items in NAEP.

NUMERICAL PATTERNS: AN ITEM FAMILY

The six items presented in this appendix constitute a proposed family of items built around the topic of numerical patterns. The set was developed according to these guidelines:

•   Each item within the set involves an increasing pattern of numbers based on a particular rule that governs the growth. In the elementary mathematics curriculum, these kinds of patterns are often referred to as "growing patterns" (e.g., Reys et al., 1995; National Council of Teachers of Mathematics, 1992). In some items, the pattern is based on constant differences between consecutive terms, and in others the pattern is based on nonconstant differences.

•   The set represents an attempt to organize the items from the easiest to the most difficult. In the case of released NAEP items, the performance data were used to determine the level of difficulty (e.g., an item for which performance was 75 percent correct was "easier" than an item for which performance was 53 percent correct). For items created especially for the set, the degree of difficulty was speculative and based solely on an educated guess.

•   In some cases, the items are presented in two formats: multiple choice and constructed response. Given that NAEP has always advocated a judicious blend of multiple-choice and constructed-response items, presenting an alternative format for items (especially those developed specifically for this paper) seemed to be appropriate. However, because of the performance differences in NAEP concerning lower percent-correct results on constructed-response items, this could affect the hierarchy of items (easiest to more difficult) within the sample set.

The source is provided for each item (e.g., a released NAEP item, an item created for the set). Following each item is a rationale about why the item was included in the item family and about the kind of information that could be obtained from performance results.

Figure C-1 summarizes the concepts and progression of the items within the sample family. Performance on these related items could provide insights into students' understanding about numerical patterns and where that understanding falters. For example, performance results could show that most fourth graders can work with patterns involving constant increases between the terms (Items 1, 2, and 3), but performance levels could be lower for items involving patterns based on nonconstant increases (Items 4 and 5) and especially for complex problems (Item 6). Performance results could also provide information on misunderstandings that students have about number patterns, with the same misunderstandings possibly occurring across items within the family. For example, some students may expect a number pattern always to have a constant difference between contiguous numbers. In this case, when faced with a pattern containing nonconstant differences, such as the number pattern in Item 4 (8, 9, 12, 17, 24, 33, 44, . . .), those students could reason that, because the difference between the last two numbers shown in the pattern is 11, then 55 (44 + 11) is the next number in the pattern. Because the next two items in the family also involve nonconstant differences, results from these items can provide additional evidence about this misunderstanding.

Some might argue that such information about students' understanding and misunderstandings of numerical patterns is already available from the NAEP mathematics assessment results. All one would need to do would be to analyze the performance results from the pattern items included on the assessment. There is a some truth to this argument, but the fact remains that most NAEP items (other than the item pairs or triples or the theme block items) are discrete; that is, each item is essentially unrelated to any other item in the assessment. Therefore, identifying the numerical pattern items in NAEP and then analyzing the performance data as if those items had been developed as an intact set is likely to result in information about students' understanding that is fragmented and difficult to interpret. The advantage of an item family is that the items were purposely developed to be related in ways that could illuminate students' understandings and misunderstanding of important mathematical concepts. Analyzing the performance data from a related set of items, then, is more likely to provide results that are connected and interpretable.

The recommendation in the 1996 NAEP mathematics framework to include families of items represents a positive direction for future NAEP mathematics assessments to take. The inclusion of families of items can increase NAEP's potential to provide important information about the depth of students' knowledge within a particular content strand and across content strands. The example presented here presents one fairly limited way in which items can be related to

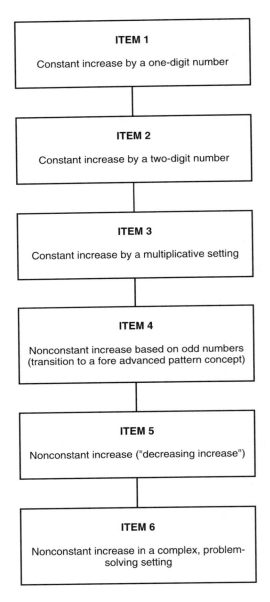

FIGURE C-1 Progression of concepts within the number pattern family of items.
SOURCE: Kenney (1999).

make a family and how the results can be analyzed to provide a more complete picture about students' understanding. The best way to develop families of items is de novo—that is, after determining in advance the desired concepts and levels of student understanding to be assessed. However, as illustrated in the example, it is possible to use existing NAEP materials as the foundation for building families. We recommend that future assessment developers build item families that better reflect the intentions for families of items described in the 1996 NAEP mathematics framework document.

AN EXAMPLE FAMILY OF ITEMS

ITEM 1

Version 1: Multiple choice

8, 14, 20, 26, 32, ...

If the pattern shown continues, which of the following numbers would be next in the pattern?

A. 34
B. 36
C. 38
D. 40

Version 2: Constructed response

Write the next two numbers in the number pattern.

8   14   20   26   32   ____   ____

Version 3: Multiple-choice set within a context

Emily started her stamp collection with 8 stamps and added the same number of stamps to her collection each week. If she had 14 stamps after the first week, 20 stamps after the second week, and 26 stamps after the third week, how many stamps would she have after the fourth week?

A. 28
B. 32
C. 38
D. 40

Based on an example from Kenney and Silver (1997: 270).

Rationale for Item 1

This item would appear first in the family to determine the "floor" effect—that is, nearly all the fourth-grade students should be able to produce a correct answer based on the constant difference of 6 between the numbers in the pattern. The first version (multiple choice, no context) would best serve this purpose. The other versions are presented here as additional examples of simple pattern items based on single-digit, constant differences between consecutive numbers. The last version set within a context could possibly be too difficult to appear as the first item in the set, but its multiple-choice format could make it more accessible to fourth-grade students.

ITEM 2

Original NAEP item

In 1990 a school had 125 students. Each year the number of students in the school increases by 50. Fill in the table to show the number of students expected for each year.

Year	Number of Students
1990	125
1991	——
1992	——
1993	——

Source: 1992 NAEP mathematics assessment   [calculator use permitted]

Performance results:

All three answers correct:	51 percent
Any two answers correct:	3 percent
Any one answer correct:	9 percent
At least one answer correct:	63 percent

Version for the item family

In 1990 a school had 125 students. Each year the number of students in the school increases by 50. Answer the questions based on the table.

Year	Number of Students
1990	125
1991	——
1992	——
1993	——

1. How many students will the school have in 1991?
    Answer: _____

2. Complete the table to show the number of students expected for 1992 and 1993.

Rationale for Item 2

A version of the 1992 NAEP item would appear next in the item family because, although the pattern of numbers is still constantly increasing, the increase itself is a double-digit number. Despite the fact that the increase is a multiple of both 5 and 10 and that the increase is given in the problem, this item is considered as a step up from the first problem because of its constructed-response format and the need to work with a pattern involving a two-digit number increase.

The NAEP version, however, should be modified so that more information can be obtained from student responses. In particular, the original NAEP item asked for three numbers in the pattern based on a given constant increase of 50 students. The results showed that just over half the fourth-grade students gave completely correct responses. However, the results did not reveal which of the three numbers was the most difficult to obtain. The version proposed for the item family could remedy this situation by providing information on whether the students understood that the enrollment increases in the first year by 50 students, and then by that same number in each of the next two years.

ITEM 3

Original NAEP item pair

Items 1 and 2 refer to the table below:

Column A		Column B
12	→	3
16	→	4
24	→	6
40	→	10

1. What is a rule used in the table to get the numbers in column B from the numbers in column A?

    A. Divide the number in column A by 4.
    B. Multiply the number in column A by 4.
    C. Subtract 9 from the number in column A.
    D. Add 9 to the number in column A.

Column A		Column B
120	→	

2. Suppose 120 is a number in column A of the table. Use the same rule to fill in the number in column B.

Source: 1992 NAEP mathematics assessment   [calculator use permitted]

Performance results:
    Item 1:   42 percent selected correct choice (A)
    Item 2:   24 percent obtained correct answer of 30

Version 1 for the item family: Division

The next questions use the following table:

Column A		Column B
12	→	3
16	→	4
24	→	6
40	→	10

Write the rule used to get the numbers in column B from the numbers in column A.
Rule:_____

Column A		Column B
120	→	

Suppose 120 is a number in column A of the table. Use the rule you wrote to fill in the number in column B.

Version 2 for the item family: Multiplication

The next questions use the following table:

Column A		Column B
12	→	3
16	→	4
24	→	6
40	→	10

Write the rule used to get the numbers in column A from the numbers in column B.
Rule: _____

Column A	Column B
	30

Suppose 30 is a number in column B of the table. Use the rule you wrote to fill in the number in column A.

Rationale for Item 3

The third item in the family represents a transition from patterns based on addition of a constant to patterns based on multiplicative models. This item would reveal whether students understand that patterns of differences could be based on arithmetic operations other than addition. The original NAEP item was discussed in an earlier section of this paper, and it had some flaws from the lack of analysis of performance results on both parts of the item pair together. In particular, the results did not completely reveal the degree of consistency between the rule selected by students and whether they used that rule to answer the second question.

Using one of the revised versions, both of which are constructed-response questions, perhaps we can better relate the students' description of the rule in part 1 and their use (or misuse) of that rule in part 2. For example, in version 1 for students who answered "Divide the number in Column A by 4," but who wrote "3" in Column B in the second part of the problem, we could more accurately attribute this incorrect answer to a place-value error or perhaps to carelessness. For other students who wrote the correct rule, but who answered "480" in the second part, it is likely that their error involved multiplying instead of dividing.

With respect to the two versions suggested for the family, one version might be preferable over the other depending on whether the multiplicative model or the division model is more easily recognized by students. Both versions could be pilot-tested to answer this question, but only one version would be included in the family.

ITEM 4

Version 1: Multiple choice

8, 9, 12, 17, 24, 33, 44, ...

If the pattern shown continues, which of the following numbers would be next in the pattern?

A. 53
B. 55
C. 57
D. 59

Version 2: Constructed response

Write the next two numbers in the number pattern.
8   9   12   17   24   ____   ____

Source: Created as an example for this report.

Rationale for Item 4

The fourth item, presented in two versions (multiple choice and constructed response), serves as a transition between numerical patterns based on constant increases to those based on nonconstant increases. In an important way, nonconstant increases are in themselves a pattern within a pattern. For example, the pattern in the item (8, 9, 12, 17, 24, 33, 44, ...) also has a pattern of increases (1, 3, 5, 7, 9, ...)—the set of odd numbers. Because the notion of nonconstant increases is likely to be difficulty for some fourth-grade students, basing the nonconstant increases on the set of odd numbers could make the item more accessible. Also, the operation used to create the pattern is again simple addition.

As noted earlier in the paper, this item and the ones that follow could provide evidence about an important misunderstanding about patterns; that is, the notion that all patterns (even those that are based on nonconstant differences) contain pairs of numbers that have a constant difference. For item 4 in the family, it is likely that some students could choose B (55) for the multiple-choice version or write 31 and 38 as the next two numbers in the pattern for the constructed-response version. In both cases, such responses show evidence of changing the nonconstant increase to a constant increase based on the difference between the last two numbers shown in the pattern.

ITEM 5

Original NAEP item

Puppy's Age	Puppy's Weight
1 month	10 lbs.
2 months	15 lbs.
3 months	19 lbs.
4 months	22 lbs.
5 months	?

John records the weight of his puppy every month in a chart like the one shown above. If the pattern of the puppy's weight gain continues, how many pounds will the puppy weigh at 5 months?

A. 30
B. 27
C. 25
D. 24

Source: 1992 NAEP mathematics assessment

Performance results:
Choice A	12 percent
Choice B	24 percent
Choice C	29 percent
Choice D*	32 percent

*correct response

Note: Four percent of the students did not answer this item, and it had a 20 percent "not reached" rate (i.e., 20 percent of the students in sample left this item and all items that followed it blank).

Version for the item family

Puppy's Age	Puppy's Weight
1 month	10 lbs.
2 months	15 lbs.
3 months	19 lbs.
4 months	22 lbs.
5 months	?

John records the weight of his puppy every month in a chart like the one shown above. Suppose the pattern of the puppy's weight gain continues.

1. How many pounds did the puppy gain from 1 month to 2 months?
   Answer: _____

2. How many pounds did the puppy gain from 2 months to 3 months?
   Answer: _____

   If the pattern of the puppy's weight gain continues, how many pounds will the puppy weigh at 5 months?
   Answer: _____

Rationale for Item 5

This item within the family has the potential to be the most difficult question to this point. Results from the original NAEP version of the item showed that about the same percent of students selected choice C (25 pounds) as selected the correct choice D (24 pounds). This error pattern shows that some students may expect a number pattern to have a constant difference between some contiguous numbers: that is, in the puppy problem, students retained the 3-pound weight gain between the third and fourth months and used it as a constant to calculate the weight at 5 months (22 + 3 = 25). Also, the high omitted and not-reached rate suggests that some fourth-grade students thought that this problem was so difficult that they did not even try to answer it.

The version proposed for the item family attempts to make the question more accessible to students. It is scaffolded so that students must identify the first two nonconstant differences between the weights, in the hope that students will more easily recognize that the weight gains are decreasing between consecutive months. The final question involves a transition from the nonconstant differences to the actual weight of the puppy.

As for Item 4 in the family, this item has the potential to provide additional evidence of the misunderstanding about nonconstant increases. Despite the attempt at scaffolding, students could still change to a constant increase and answer 25 pounds or some other number based on a constant increase in weight.

ITEM 6

Original NAEP item

A pattern of dots is shown below. At each step, more dots are added to the pattern. The number of dots added at each step is more than the number added in the previous step. The pattern continues infinitely.

(1st step)   (2nd step)   (3rd step)

```
                                                          • • • •
                               • • •                      • • • •
        • • •                  • • •                      • • • •
```

2 dots   6 dots   12 dots

Marcy has to determine the number of dots in the 20th step, but she does not want to draw all 20 pictures and then count the dots.

Explain or show how she could do this and give the answer that Marcy should get for the number of dots.

Source: 1992 NAEP mathematics assessment—grade 8   [calculator use permitted]

Performance results:
  Extended response   5 percent
  Satisfactory response   1 percent
  Partial response   6 percent
  Minimal response   10 percent
  Incorrect response   63 percent

Note: Sixteen percent of the eighth-grade students did not answer this question.

Version for the item family

A pattern of dots is shown below. At each step, more dots are added to the pattern. The number of dots added at each step is more than the number added in the previous step. The pattern continues and does not stop.

(1st step)	(2nd step)	(3rd step)
		• • • •
	• • •	• • • •
• • •	• • •	• • • •
2 dots	6 dots	12 dots

How many dots would be in the 4th step? Show how you got your answer.

Marcy has to determine the number of dots in the 10th step, but she does not want to draw all 10 pictures and then count the dots.

Explain or show how she could do this and give the answer that Marcy should get for the number of dots in the 10th step.

Rationale for Item 6

The original NAEP item, called Marcy's Dot Pattern in NAEP reports (e.g., Dossey et al., 1993), was administered to students in the 1992 eighth grade sample as an extended constructed-response question in the algebra and functions content strand. As shown by the performance results, this question was difficult for the eighth-grade students: only 6 percent produced a response that was scored as satisfactory or extended. However, the fact that the item was last in an item block with previous items having little or no connection to number patterns could have affected performance levels. How would students have performed if this question, or an appropriate version thereof, appeared in a family of items devoted to number patterns?

Given the structure of the family of items describe thus far, it seemed reasonable to think about including an adaptation of the Marcy's Dot Pattern as the culminating item in the family. As the culminating item, it has characteristics based on work done on the previous items. For example, Marcy's Dot Pattern involves a pattern of nonconstant differences between the number of dots in each step and requires students to identify the rule that underlies the pattern. The version for the item family begins with an introductory question about the number of dots in the fourth step as a way to introduce students to the problem. Here, it would be reasonable for students to draw the fourth figure so that they can better understand the pattern. The next part of the problem is similar to that given to students in the eighth grade sample, but the steps are reduced from the 20th step to the 10th step. This last decision needs careful thought, however, because drawing 7 more sets of dots is more accessible than drawing 17 more sets. Pilot-testing could reveal the differences between working with the 10th step or a step further out in the pattern of dots.

REFERENCES

Armstrong, B. E.
   1995   Teaching patterns, relationships, and multiplication as worthwhile mathematical tasks. *Teaching Children Mathematics* 1: 446-450.
Dossey, John A., Ina V. Mullis, and C.O. Jones
   1993   *Can Students Do Mathematical Problem Solving?: Results from Constructed-response Questions in NAEP's 1992 Mathematics Assessment.* Washington, DC: National Center for Education Statistics.
Kenney, P.A.
   1999   Families of items in the NAEP mathematics assessment, In *Grading the Nation's Report Card: Research from the Evaluation of NAEP*, James W. Pellegrino, Lee R. Jones, and Karen J. Mitchell, eds. Committee on the Evaluation of National and State Assessments of Educational Progress, Board on Testing and Assessment, Washington, DC: National Academy Press.
Kenney, Patricia A., and Edward A. Silver
   1997   Probing the foundations of algebra: Grade 4 pattern items in NAEP. *Teaching Children Mathematics* 3(6):268-274.
National Council of Teachers of Mathematics
   1992   *Curriculum and Evaluation Standards for School Mathematics Addenda Series, Grades K-6: Fourth-Grade Book.* Reston, VA: National Council of Teachers of Mathematics.
   1989   *Curriculum and Evaluation Standards for School Mathematics.* Reston, VA: National Council of Teachers of Mathematics.
Reys, R. E., M.N. Suydam, and M.M. Lindquist
   1995   *Helping Children Learn Mathematics,* Fourth edition. Boston: Allyn and Bacon.

D
Exploring New Models for Achievement-Level Setting

In Chapter 5, we suggested exploring models for achievement-level setting in which judgments focus on aggregates of student performance data, rather than on the accumulation of many item-level judgments. We also recommended the use of normative and external comparative data to assist in ensuring the reasonableness of the achievement-level cutscores. In this appendix, we provide the initial conceptual framing for a model of achievement-level setting for NAEP that relies on the solicitation of judgments about aggregates of student performance data and on the use of comparative data to help ensure the reasonableness of the results. We emphasize that this model has not been pilot-tested, even on a small scale; therefore, we have no empirical basis for evaluating its merits. However, we hope that this collection of ideas can stimulate discussion of alternatives for future achievement-level-setting efforts.

CONCEPTUAL DESCRIPTION OF ONE POSSIBLE MODEL

Step 1: Framework Development and Item Authoring

The first step in this model calls for simultaneous development of frameworks and preliminary achievement-level descriptions in NAEP disciplines. The subject-matter experts who develop NAEP frameworks would include individuals who are well positioned to describe the knowledge and skills that students performing at the basic, proficient, and advanced levels should exhibit at each of the grades assessed.

During assessment development, assessment materials (including draft scoring rubrics) would be developed to reflect the knowledge and skills addressed by the preliminary achievement-level descriptions. Items and tasks would be constructed to specifically assess the knowledge and skills described in the preliminary achievement-level descriptions. Rubrics would be constructed to permit assessment of students' levels of understanding relative to the specified knowledge and skills.

Step 2: Item Mapping and Generation of Anchor Descriptions

After the assessment is administered, all items would be mapped onto the NAEP proficiency scale. The process of item mapping (described by O'Sullivan et al., 1997:6-9) results in the hierarchical ranking of items (or, in the case of constructed-response items with multiple scoring levels, the ranking of levels of responses to items) along the NAEP proficiency scale, with easiest items near the bottom of the scale and more difficult items at the top of the scale.

Following item mapping and based on the evaluation of the items and item-level data, a group of educators and other experts in the discipline (and including framework developers) would develop descriptions of the knowledge and skills that correspond to performance at selected points along the NAEP proficiency scale. For example, by analyzing the collection of items that map at or near selected points on the proficiency scale, behavioral anchor descriptions of aggregated student performance at increments along the scale could be developed.

Figure D-1 illustrates this second step, providing an illustrative set of behavioral anchor descriptions along the NAEP proficiency scale. These were developed using 1996 NAEP science assessment data from grade 8. The center column of the figure shows the NAEP proficiency scale at 20-point intervals from 80 to 260. Also shown are points along the proficiency scale for various percentiles for the grade 8 NAEP student population (e.g., 5 percent of the student population had a proficiency of 89 or below; 50 percent of the student population had a proficiency of 153 or below). The mean proficiency of the national grade 8 student population (148) also is shown.

The left-hand column shows behavioral anchor descriptions that we developed based on items that mapped within a $\pm$ 5-point interval around each of the anchor points on the diagram. For example, the behavioral anchor description at 160 represents a description of the aggregate of knowledge and skills achieved by students correctly answering the items that mapped between 155 and 165 on the proficiency scale (or, for constructed-response items, generating responses that correspond to scoring levels that mapped between 155 and 165). This set of behavioral anchor descriptions provides a view of student achievement arrayed along the NAEP proficiency scale.

If the developers who wrote the frameworks and preliminary achievement-level descriptions were able to lay out reasonable expectations for student performance in those descriptions, and *if* assessment materials were developed and student responses scored with the differences in levels of student performance on the preliminary achievement-level descriptions in mind, then the behavioral an-

260: Justify selection of experimental procedures; explain and apply complex biological and physical concepts.

260

- % at or above Level 350 – Integrates Specialized Scientific Information (1996 NAEP science age 13 long-term trend)

240: Predict changes to outcomes based on changes in variables; apply knowledge to explain observations of biological and physical phenomena; evaluate cost/benefits of energy sources; understand additional sophisticated concepts (e.g., biomagnification, why seasons occur)

240

- Singapore 95th percentile – TIMSS

220: Design straightforward experiments to test hypotheses; describe differences between models and real-world phenomena; apply results of experiments to answer specific questions; understand additional science concepts (e.g., properties of light, formation of rock layers, cell structure).

220
99th percentile: 219

95th percentile: 202

- % at or above Advanced – 1996 main NAEP math
- Japan 95th percentile/Russia 95th percentile – TIMSS

200: Evaluate multiple pieces of information and draw conclusions; provide explanations of biological and physical occurrences; explain results of experiments; some understanding of more sophisticated concepts (e.g., evolution, inheritance, formation of precipitation).

200
90th percentile: 192

- Singapore 75th percentile – TIMSS
- % at or above Level 300 – Analyzes Scientific Data and Procedures (1996 NAEP science age 13 long-term trend)

180: Carry out multi-step lab tasks to completion; extrapolate from provided data; understand how models can represent real-world phenomena; consistently measure length accurately; understand some underlying physical and biological causes of environmental changes.

180
80th percentile: 178
75th percentile: 174

- Japan 75th percentile – TIMSS
- % at or above Proficient – 1996 main NAEP math
- Singapore 50th percentile – TIMSS
- Maine 1996 main NAEP science mean scale score =163 (highest state mean)

160: Perform a series of simple physical tests and evaluate the results; usually measure length accurately; interpret information in a single graph but not in relation to information in a related graph; full understanding of certain life, physical, and earth science concepts; partial understanding of others.

160
60th percentile: 160
50th percentile: 153
National Mean: 148
40th percentile: 143

- Japan 50th percentile – TIMSS
- Russia 50th percentile – TIMSS
- % at or above Level 250 – Applies General Scientific Information (1996 NAEP science age 13 long-term trend)

140: Read and compare multiple pieces of information in a single graph; set up first steps in an experiment; partial understanding of some life, physical, and earth science concepts.

140
30th percentile: 133
25th percentile: 128

20th percentile: 121

- % at or above Basic – 1996 main NAEP math
- California 1996 main NAEP science mean scale score = 138
- Russia 25th percentile – TIMSS

120: Interpret data displayed in a graph; correctly carry out a series of physical tests, including chemical soil tests; understand some basic concepts in life science; partial understanding of some real-world physical phenomena.

120

10th percentile: 104

100: Identify plants as producers of food using the sun's energy; understand some basic ecological principles; perform some parts of a soil water-holding capacity test.

100
5th percentile: 89

- % at or above Level 200 – Understands Simple Scientific Principles (1996 NAEP science age 13 long-term trend)

80: Read a simple graph; record results of observations and measurements in a table; perform and interpret the results of simple physical tests; calculate the average of two measurements.

80

- % at or above level 150 – Knows Everyday Science Facts (1996 NAEP science age 13 long-term trend)

FIGURE D-1 Illustrative achievement-level-setting data. Plots of TIMSS percentiles are approximations. SOURCES: 1996 main NAEP science (O'Sullivan et al., 1997); 1996 main NAEP mathematics (Reese et al., 1997); 1996 long-term trend NAEP (Campbell et al., 1997); 1995 TIMSS grade 8 science (Beaton et al., 1996).

chor descriptions should bear at least some general similarities to the preliminary achievement-level descriptions. For example, it would be reasonable to expect that the level of knowledge and skills described in the preliminary achievement-level description for advanced performance would be reflected more frequently in the behavioral anchor descriptions at the upper end of the proficiency scale than in the middle or lower portions of the scale. We would not necessarily expect, however, that there would be a tight and complete correspondence of the behavioral anchor descriptions with the preliminary achievement-level descriptions. Since in this model the preliminary descriptions serve primarily as guides for assessment and scoring rubric development, a lack of correspondence between behavioral anchor descriptions and preliminary achievement-level descriptions can be accommodated, as described in later steps of the model.

Step 3: Mapping of Comparative Data

After the administration is completed, internal and external comparative data also can be mapped onto the NAEP proficiency scale. As illustrated in the right-hand column in the example in Figure D-1, these types of data could include mean proficiencies of various states participating in the assessment. Achievement-level data from other NAEP grade 8 assessments, achievement data from countries participating in TIMSS, and data from behavioral anchoring in the NAEP long-term trend assessments could also be mapped to corresponding percentile locations on the scale. While such direct comparisons of the latter three data collections to main NAEP science have serious limitations (Johnson, 1997; National Research Council, 1999), these data do provide some basis for comparison, since the sample of students assessed in main NAEP science, other main NAEP subjects, long-term trend NAEP assessments, and the TIMSS assessments all were nationally probability samples. (We recognize that one problem with mapping these comparative data directly on a diagram such as Figure D-1 is that this representation may suggest a stronger linkage between NAEP and other data collections than actually exists.)

Step 4: Achievement-Level Setting

In the fourth step, judges would be impaneled (including grade-level educators, disciplinary experts, and policy makers) to set standards by reviewing three kinds of data: (1) distribution data showing the percentage of students scoring at or above each score increment (i.e., the percentiles displayed in Figure D-1), (2) the behavioral anchor descriptions developed in Step 2, and (3) comparative benchmark data such as that described in Step 3. These performance benchmarks help place NAEP results in a broader context and should include comparison data from other assessments when appropriate and when they are available. Raters with differing expertise and policy interests would be assembled to perform the setting of achievement levels. Ideally, this group would include members of the National Assessment Governing Board so that the discussions and decisions of the group of raters could be directly reflected in NAGB's decisions about the final achievement levels.

A variety of strategies could be employed to help raters utilize information such as that displayed in Figure D-1 in setting achievement levels. We describe key steps of one possible strategy here.

Raters should first consider the behavioral anchor descriptions and determine which descriptions best represent basic, proficient, and advanced performance. Raters would be guided by the policy descriptions, the preliminary achievement-level descriptions, and their own judgments about what constitutes basic, proficient, and advanced performance. Once a general proficiency range has been determined (e.g., that the 120-140 anchor descriptions describe basic performance, but the 160 description is proficient, and the 100 description is below basic), raters would examine where individual items mapped to more narrowly determine the specific proficiency at which a cutscore would be set. The key feature of this strategy is that raters would first consider aggregate data, and then move to item data only after having determined the general features of what constitutes basic, proficient, and advanced performance.

After these initial achievement-level cutscores are determined, raters would then examine normative data (percentiles) and comparative benchmark data to evaluate the reasonableness of the cutscores, and to inform the magnitude of any adjustments in cutscores that might be deemed necessary based on that evaluation. All raters, including subject-matter experts, policy makers, and members of the National Assessment Governing Board, would evaluate the reasonableness of the cutscores jointly, and together agree on any needed adjustments.

Once raters finalize their cutscores, the results would be forwarded to the full NAGB for review and approval (or adjustment). In their review, NAGB would have the full array of data displayed in Figure D-1 available to inform their decision making, as well as the raters' rationale for any adjustments made to their initial cutscores based on the evaluation of normative and comparative data. The rationale for decisions made by NAGB to adjust achievement levels submitted to them by the raters should be clearly described in the reports of achievement-level results.

Step 5: Revising the Achievement-Level Descriptions

After the final achievement levels are approved by NAGB, the achievement-level descriptions would then be revised (using behavioral anchoring techniques) to match the knowledge and skills represented by the items that map on the NAEP proficiency scale within the range of proficiencies associated with each of the final achievement levels.

This concept is not without its own challenges. For example, the processes of item mapping and developing behavioral anchor descriptions have been the subject of some controversy (Forsyth, 1991). In particular, there is no universally accepted rule regarding where on the NAEP proficiency scale an item should be mapped: at the point where 50 percent of the students respond correctly? 65 percent? 80 percent? Ongoing research, some of it conducted for NAEP, has not resolved this issue.

If the ideas presented here are explored further, they undoubtedly would undergo significant revision. We do believe further discussion of the features of this model is warranted, as this method relies on rater judgments about aggregates of achievement data, permits evaluation of reasonableness using normative and comparative data, fosters joint participation in standard setting by policy makers and educators, and may result in a more easily understood achievement-level-setting process.

REFERENCES

Beaton, Albert E., Michael O. Martin, Ina V. S. Mullis, Eugenio J. Gonzalez, Teresa A. Smith, and Dana L. Kelly
  1996   *Science Achievement in the Middle School Years.* Chestnut Hill, MA: Center for the Study of Testing, Evaluation, and Educational Policy, Boston College.
Campbell, Jay R., Kristin E. Voelkl, and Patricia L. Donahue
  1997   *NAEP 1996 Trends in Academic Progress: Achievement of U.S. Students in Science, 1969 to 1996; Mathematics, 1973 to 1996; Reading, 1971 to 1996; and Writing, 1984 to 1996.* NCES 97-985. Washington, DC: U.S. Department of Education.
Forsyth, R.A.
  1991   Do NAEP scales yield valid criterion-referenced interpretations? *Educational Measurement: Issues and Practice* (Fall):3-9.
Johnson, Eugene G.
  1997   A TIMMS-NAEP Link. Unpublished paper prepared for the U.S. Department of Education, Washington, DC.
National Research Council
  1999   *Uncommon Measures: Equivalence and Linkage of Educational Tests*: Michael J. Feuer, Paul Holland, Meryl W. Bertenthal, F. Cadelle Hemphill, and Bert F. Green, eds. Committee on Equivalence and Linkage of Educational Tests, Board on Testing and Assessment. Washington, DC: National Academy Press.
O'Sullivan, Christine Y., Clyde M. Reese, and John Mazzeo
  1997   *NAEP 1996 Science Report Card for the Nation and the States.* Washington, DC: U.S. Department of Education.
Reese, Clyde M., Karen E. Miller, John Mazzeo, and John Dossey
  1997   *NAEP 1996 Mathematics Report Card for the Nation and the States: Findings from the National Assessment of Educational Progress.* Washington, DC: U.S. Department of Education.

Biographical Sketches

JAMES W. PELLEGRINO *(Chair)* is the Frank W. Mayborn professor of cognitive studies at Vanderbilt University's Peabody College of Education and Human Development. He has been a faculty member at the University of Pittsburgh and at the University of California, Santa Barbara. His research focuses on the application of cognitive theory and information technologies to the analysis of children's and adults thinking and learning, and the implications for assessment design and instructional practice. He has a B.A. in psychology from Colgate University and M.A. and Ph.D. degrees in experimental psychology from the University of Colorado.

GAIL P. BAXTER is a research scientist at the Educational Testing Service and, while serving on the committee, was an assistant professor in the School of Education at the University of Michigan. She has developed and evaluated science performance assessments and published books and reports examining the psychometric qualities of hands-on assessments. She has a B.A. in psychology from Queens University, an M.A. in psychology from Eastern New Mexico University, and a Ph.D. in education from the University of California, Santa Barbara. She is currently working with teachers and scientists in several school districts to develop curriculum-embedded assessments that can be used to inform classroom practice.

NORMAN M. BRADBURN is the Tiffany and Margaret Blake distinguished service professor in the Department of Psychology and professor in the Harris Graduate School of Public Policy Studies at the University of Chicago. He is also senior vice president for research at the National Opinion Research Center. He has conducted research on the application of cognitive psychological principles to the study of response error and is an authority on nonsampling errors in surveys. He has written extensively on questionnaire design. He has bachelor's degrees from Oxford University and the University of Chicago. He has an M.A. in clinical psychology and a Ph.D. in social psychology, both from Harvard University. He is former chair of the National Research Council's Committee on National Statistics.

THOMAS P. CARPENTER is professor of curriculum and instruction at the University of Wisconsin-Madison and acting director of the National Center for Improving Student Learning and Achievement in Mathematics and Science. His research integrates the study of teaching and learning in mathematics. He has a B.S. in mathematics from Stanford University, an M.A. in mathematics from San Diego State University, and a Ph.D. in curriculum and instruction from the University of Wisconsin-Madison. He is a former editor of the *Journal for Research in Mathematics Education*, and he participated in writing interpretive reports of the first four NAEP mathematics assessments.

ALAN COLLINS is principal scientist at Bolt, Beranek and Newman, Inc., and a professor of education and social policy at Northwestern University. He has B.B.A., M.A., and Ph.D. degrees (the latter in psychology) all from the University of Michigan. His research program focuses on cognitive information processing and education. He has published extensively on techniques for analyzing human dialogues to determine how human tutoring and inferential question-answering strategies can be integrated into intelligent tutoring systems.

PASQUALE J. DEVITO is director of the Office of Assessment of the Rhode Island Department of Education and adjunct professor at the University of Rhode Island. He formerly served as a member of the National Academy of Education's Select Panel for the Evaluation of the NAEP Trial State Assessment. His research interests lie in the area of educational measurement, evaluation, and policy and he has published numerous articles in this field of interest. He has an A.B. in psychology, an M.Ed. in educational psychology, and a Ph.D. in educational research, measurement, and evaluation, all from Boston College.

STEPHEN B. DUNBAR is professor of educational measurement and statistics in the College of Education at the University of Iowa. He has served on the Board of Directors of National Council on Measurement in Education and is a senior author of the *Iowa Tests of Basic Skills*. He has contributed substantially to the professional literature in the areas of achievement testing and evaluation of performance-based assessments. He has a B.A. in English from the University of

Wisconsin-Madison and an A.M. in applied linguistics and a Ph.D. in educational psychology from the University of Illinois at Urbana-Champaign.

LARRY V. HEDGES is the Stella M. Rowley professor of education and the social sciences at the University of Chicago, where he previously served as chair of the Department of Education. Statistical methods for combining evidence from replicated research studies and statistical models in cognitive psychology are his primary focus of research. With Ingram Olken, he is author of *Statistical Methods for Meta-Analysis.* He is currently on the editorial board of *New Directions in Program Evaluation, The Journal of Educational Statistics,* and *The Behavioral and Brain Sciences.* He has a B.A. in mathematics from the University of California, San Diego, and an M.A. in statistics and a Ph.D. in mathematical methods in educational research from Stanford University.

LEE R. JONES *(Study Director)* is a senior program officer in the Board on Testing and Assessment of the National Academy of Sciences/National Research Council. Prior to joining the NAS/NRC, he was executive director of College Board Programs and program director for assessment development for the Advanced Placement Program at Educational Testing Service. He has a B.S. in biology from Indiana University of Pennsylvania, and an M.S. and a Ph.D. in biology from Utah State University. He has served on the biology faculties at Middlebury College, Mercer University, and Emory University.

SHARON LEWIS is director of research at the Council of Great City Schools. She has bachelor's degrees in psychology and secondary mathematics and an M.A. and a Ph.D. in evaluation and research from Wayne University. Her expertise is in the use of assessment data and shaping educational policy.

RODERICK J.A. LITTLE is professor and chairman of the Department of Biostatistics at the University of Michigan. With D.B. Rubin, he is the author of *Statistical Analysis with Missing Data.* The focus of his research is missing values in multivariate statistical analysis. He has a B.A. in mathematics from Cambridge University, and an M.Sc. in statistics and operational research and a Ph.D. in statistics, from London University.

KAREN J. MITCHELL is a senior program officer in the Board on Testing and Assessment at the National Academy of Sciences/National Research Council. Previously she was at RAND, where she conducted research on student assessment, education reform, and education policy. She has a B.A. in early childhood and elementary education from Wesleyan College and M.S. and Ph.D. degrees both in educational research methodology, from Cornell University.

ELSIE G. J. MOORE is associate professor in the Department of Psychology in Education at Arizona State University. Much of her research focuses on socialization and cognitive development, psychoeducational assessment, life-span developmental psychology, and behavior genetics. She has a B.A. in psychology and philosophy from Elmhurst College and M.A. and Ph.D. degrees from the University of Chicago, both in human development. She has written numerous books, monographs, and chapters on the role of ethnicity and social class in explaining children's test performance.

NAMBURY S. RAJU is a distinguished professor and director of the Center for Research and Service in the Institute of Psychology at the Illinois Institute of Technology. He has published extensively in the areas of differential item functioning, validity generalization, and test utility analysis models. His research focuses on large-scale testing applications in educational and personnel testing. He is a fellow of the Evaluation and Measurement Division and the Society for Industrial and Organizational Psychology Division of the American Psychological Association. He has a B.A. from Madras University and M.S. from Purdue University. He also has a M.S. and a Ph.D. from the Illinois Institute of Technology.

MARLENE SCARDAMALIA is professor in the Department of Measurement, Evaluation and Computer Applications at the Ontario Institute for Studies in Education, University of Toronto. She is also the head of the university's Center for Applied Cognitive Science. Her research focuses on strategies and schemata for building complex knowledge, the development of knowledge-building architecture for computer-supported learning, interactive environments for promoting learning, networking environments, and telelearning networks. She serves on the editorial boards of seven journals in general and special education. She has a B.A. in English from Clarion State College, an M.S. in educational research and educational psychology from Bucknell University, and a Ph.D. in applied psychology from the University of Toronto.

GUADALUPE VALDÉS is professor in the School of Education and the Department of Spanish and Portuguese at Stanford University. Dr. Valdés has a B.A. in Spanish from the University of West Florida and M.A. and Ph.D. degrees from Florida State University, both in Spanish. She has written numerous books, monographs, and chapters on bilingualism, language use in bilingual settings, and the teaching and learning of second languages.

SHEILA W. VALENCIA is an associate professor in the College of Education at the University of Washington. Much of her research focuses on the use of literacy portfolios both to improve teaching, learning, and communication and for large-scale assessment. She has a B.S. in remedial education and an M.Ed. in reading disabilities from the State University of New York at Buffalo and a Ph.D. from the University of Colorado in curriculum and instruction and reading education.

LAURESS L. WISE is president of the Human Resources Research Organization (HumRRO). He has a B.S. in mathematics and psychology from Stanford University and a Ph.D. in mathematical psychology from the University of California, Berkeley. In addition to his administrative responsibilities, he remains active in the research on testing and test use policy. His current projects include work on validity and equating for the state assessment in Kentucky and selection testing for the Federal Aviation Administration. He served on the National Academy of Education's Panel for the Evaluation of the NAEP Trial State Assessment and currently serves on a research and development advisory committee for the College Board. He recently served as co-principal investigator for the National Research Council's evaluation of the development of the voluntary national tests and as a member of its Committee on Linkage and Equivalency.

Index

A

Accommodations/adaptations, 51, 88-89, 91-112 (passim), 191
  Americans with Disabilities Act, 88
  Goals 2000: Educate America Act, 10, 88, 96
  individualized education plans, 88, 94, 99-100
  Individuals with Disabilities Education Act, 88
  items read orally to poor readers, 13, 95, 99, 105
  test administration procedures, 91, 92, 99-100
Accountability, 2, 10, 19, 23, 27
  students with disabilities/English-language learners, 88, 91, 94, 107, 109, 110-111, 112
Achievement-level descriptions, 114, 128, 134-139, 141, 152-154, 163-173 (passim)
  preliminary, 119, 134-135, 165, 170, 176-179, 182, 183, 256, 257, 259, 260
Achievement levels, 2, 7, 9, 10, 17, 20, 25, 72, 73, 162-184
  cost factors, 8
  definitional issues, 54, 124, 137-138, 139, 169-170, 186
  frameworks and assessment development process, 115, 116, 117, 121, 124-125,
  128, 134, 135-140, 143-147 (passim), 152-154, 158, 159, 160, 192, 194, 195, 196
  reporting, 2, 6, 7, 25-31, 32, 33, 72, 73, 135, 162, 163-165
  special studies, 16, 57, 110
  use of NAEP results, 2, 31, 171, 176, 180, 182, 184, 246
  see also Mathematics achievement; Performance standards; Reading achievement; Science achievement; Writing achievement
Achievement-level setting, 2, 7, 31, 48, 116, 134-135, 152, 162, 163-168, 171, 176, 179-184, 186, 246, 256-261
  anchoring, 2, 170-171, 173, 177, 257-261
  Angoff procedure, 165, 166, 168
  NCES role, 167, 175-176, 187, 196
  see also Cutscores
Administration procedures, testing, 12-13, 65
  costs, 78
  grade- vs age-level testing, 13, 14
  individual testing, 12-13, 99
  item response time, 13, 62, 99, 128, 130-131
  items read orally due to poor readers, 13, 95, 99, 105
  professional administrators, 13, 82, 86
  state vs national NAEP, 82, 85

267

students with disabilities/English-language learners, 91, 92, 99-100

see also Group testing

Administration schedules, testing, 18, 121, 191, 192-193, 195

Administrative factors, *see* Governance factors; School-level measures

Advanced achievement levels, 2, 7, 64, 147, 152, 163, 164-171, 173, 174, 175, 180, 183, 186, 256, 259, 260

Advanced placement, 165, 167, 169, 174

Advisory Council on Education Statistics, 53

African Americans, 44, 62

Age factors, 12, 13, 79

   grade- *vs* age-level testing, 13, 14, 192-193

   see also Grade-level factors

Alexander-James Panel, 2, 15

American College Testing, 19, 168-169, 190

American Institutes for Research, 190

Americans with Disabilities Act, 88

Analysis methods, 20, 189, 193, 196

   coordinated system of education indicators, 45, 49-51 (passim), 55-56

   costs, 78

   current NAEP, 35, 58, 62, 63-64, 65, 67, 68-70, 71, 78

   frameworks and assessment development process, 116, 117

   reporting metrics, 72

   secondary data, 42

   streamlining NAEP design, 4, 14, 62, 63-64, 65, 67, 68-70, 71, 78, 79

   students with disabilities/English-language learners, 101, 104, 108, 110

   text analysis, 43, 49, 219-220

   video analyses, 43, 46, 48, 194

   see also Computer-based testing and analysis; Content coverage and analysis; Item analysis and development

Anchoring, 2, 170-171, 173, 177, 257-261

Angoff procedure, 165, 166, 168

Applied Measurement in Education, 11

Arts achievement, 193-194

Assessment development process, 2, 4, 5-6, 33, 67, 92, 114-161, 190-191, 194, 195, 220-236

   achievement levels, 115, 116, 117, 121, 124-125, 128, 134, 135-140, 145-147, 152-154, 158, 159, 160, 192, 194, 195, 196; *see also* "mathematics

achievement" *and* "*science achievement*" *infra*

   constructed-response items, 115, 122, 123, 128-129, 132, 146, 149, 150, 153-154

   contractors, 115, 116, 118, 119, 136, 148-150, 190, 192-193, 195

   defined, 115

   funding, 149-150, 151, 155, 191

   governance, 117-118, 134-135

   interpretive information, 114, 116, 137, 153, 154-157, 159, 160-161

   item analysis and development, 117, 118-119, 122-123, 125, 128-137, 142, 149-155, 160, 219-236, 256-257

   knowledge and skills measures, 115, 121, 125, 126, 127, 128, 131-133, 138, 139, 140, 156, 159, 233, 256-257

   large-scale assessments, 114, 125, 128, 133, 136, 147-149, 156, 158, 159, 161, 194

   main NAEP, 114, 118-121, 126-128, 136, 194, 195, 259

   mathematics achievement, 118, 121, 122-124, 126-127, 132, 136, 142

   NCES role, 115, 116, 118, 122, 134, 148-149, 154

   performance standards, 114, 115, 118, 123, 125, 133, 142-143, 146, 149, 155, 159, 220, 257, 259-260

   reading achievement, 118, 119, 120, 122, 123, 127-128, 132, 133, 136, 141-142, 219-230

   reporting procedures, 114, 117, 121, 128, 135, 145-146, 151, 154-160 (passim), 221

   science achievement, 116, 118, 126, 129-130, 132-133, 134, 136, 142, 143-144, 231-236

   scoring, 114, 117, 118, 119, 125, 132, 133-134, 135, 136, 146, 149, 150, 153-154, 156, 160, 161, 219-220, 226-227, 234-235, 257

   summary scores, 116, 117, 121, 128, 139, 152, 154

   task measures, 119, 128, 132, 136, 139, 142-144, 146, 149, 153-154, 160, 219-220

   see also Field tests; Item analysis and development

Assessment in Transition: Monitoring the Nation's Educational Progress, 25, 124

Association of State Assessment Programs, 97

B

Background variables, 34
  instructional, 65
  students, 35, 40, 42, 64, 95, 119, 122, 149, 188, 190, 220
  teachers, 40, 41, 43
Balanced incomplete blocks, 62, 63, 66
Barometer information, *see* Descriptive information
Bias, *see* Error of measurement
Bilingual education, 91, 98-101 (passim), 104, 105
  translated versions of NAEP, 95, 97, 100, 101, 111
Black persons, *see* African Americans

C

Center for Equity and Excellence, 98
Civics, 18, 61, 136
Class size, 26, 44
Cognitive factors and theory, 6, 7, 19-20, 128, 133, 137-141, 143-146, 166
  see also Knowledge and skills measures; Learning theory; Problem solving
Common Core of Data, 36-37, 51
Computer-based testing and analysis, 32, 63, 148, 194
The Condition of Education, 35
Constructed-response items, 80, 136, 166, 174
  frameworks and assessment development process, 115, 122, 123, 128-129, 132, 146, 149, 150, 153-154
  main *vs* trend NAEP, 79
  national NAEP, 80
  nonresponse rates, 123
Content coverage and analysis, 12, 27, 48-49, 70, 79, 118
  text analysis, 43, 49, 219-220
Contextual data, *see* Interpretive information
Contracts and contractors, 17, 31, 68, 82, 116, 118, 136, 150, 166, 168, 177, 191, 195, 196
  administration of testing, state *vs* national, 82
  Educational Testing Service, 14, 17, 31, 93, 118, 119, 148-149, 150, 190
  frameworks and assessment development process, 115, 116, 118, 119, 136, 148-150, 190, 192-193, 195

KPMG Peat Marwick LLP, 25, 66, 69, 70, 78
  NAEP, redesign/transitional, 148, 175, 187, 189-196 (passim)
  National Computer Systems, 119
  RAND, 40, 46
  scheduled contracts and administration by framework, 192-193, 195
  WESTAT, 17, 119
Coordinated system of education indicators, 4, 6, 8, 20, 22-55, 73, 158, 186, 187, 188
  analysis methods, 45, 49-51 (passim), 55-56
  costs of, 51-52, 53
  curriculum, 23, 40, 41, 43, 54
  data collection, 4, 6, 8, 20, 22-55, 106
  Department of Education role, 23-24, 34, 50, 53-54
  frameworks, 24, 33, 38, 40, 47, 51-55 (passim)
  funding, 23, 41, 42, 44, 53
  governance, 45, 51-54
    NAGB, 22-25, 31, 187
  international components, 42, 43, 46, 158, 188
  interpretive information, 4, 23, 24, 25, 27-55, 45, 115
  knowledge and skills measures, 23-24, 47
  large-scale assessments, 24, 34, 47, 51, 54, 188
  NCES, 31, 34-38, 40-41, 45-46, 49-54, 187
  new paradigm NAEP, 46-47, 48, 55, 84, 85, 109, 110, 146-147, 151, 158, 187-197
  pedagogy, 23, 40-43 (passim), 46, 47-49, 54
  reporting procedures, 25-26, 73
  sampling, 45, 46, 47, 49, 50-51, 107
  skills measures, 24, 47
  standards, general, 23, 45
  state-level factors, 45-46
  students with disabilities/English-language learners, 106, 107
  task measures, 23, 24, 33, 47, 54
  validity issues, 40, 46
Core NAEP, 7, 47, 57, 78, 80, 82, 84, 85, 147-149, 153, 155, 158, 181-182, 187, 188, 194
  students with disabilities/English-language learners, 109, 110, 112
  see also Mathematics achievement; Reading achievement; Science achievement; Writing achievement
Cost and cost-benefit factors, 8, 10, 78
  elementary/secondary school expenditures, data on, 35

indicator systems, 38, 51-52, 53
  NAEP design, general, 3, 8, 62, 78, 84,
    149-150, 151
  national/state systems separate, 66, 78, 82,
    85
  sampling designs, 62, 66
  state-level indicators, 62, 66, 78, 82, 85
  students with disabilities/English-language
    learners, 8, 107-108, 111
  trend NAEP, 78
  see also Accountability; Funding
Council of Chief State School Officers, 17, 40,
  46, 53, 96, 98
Council of the Great City Schools, 53
CSEI, *see* Coordinated system of education
  indicators
Cultural bias, 63
Curriculum, 6
  cognitive theory and, 19-20
  coordinated system of education indicators,
    23, 40, 41, 43, 54
  high school, 80-81
  NAEP design and, 12, 16, 20, 58, 79, 80-81
  special studies, 16, 57
  standards, 10, 179, 153
  students with disabilities/English-language
    learners, 111
*Curriculum and Evaluation Standards for
  School Mathematics*, 10, 122
Cutscores, 64, 166, 167-171, 173-177 (passim),
  180, 182, 183, 256, 260

D

Databases, 50-52, 196
Data collection, general, 4, 11, 14, 20, 23, 196,
  259
  coordinated system of education indicators,
    4, 6, 8, 20, 22-55, 106
  frameworks, 115, 150
  mixed methods of, 43, 45, 47-49, 54
  NAGB objectives, 25
  national *vs* state, 65
  streamlining NAEP design, 4, 7, 65, 68, 73,
    76, 79-82, 84, 190, 196
  students with disabilities/English-language
    learners, 87, 96, 104, 106, 107, 108,
    112, 113
  see also Large-scale assessments; Sampling
Data presentation, *see* Reporting procedures

Demographic factors, 1, 152, 19
  performance measures, 27, 163
  reporting, 1-2, 27, 31, 34, 163
  socioeconomic status, 14, 50
    poverty, 14, 44
  social indicator systems, 3, 24, 38-39, 152,
    153
  summary scores, 14
  students with disabilities/English-language
    learners, 89-90
  see also Age factors; Gender factors; Race/
    ethnicity; Urban/rural factors
Department of Education, 1, 3, 187
  coordinated system of education indicators,
    23-24, 34, 50, 53-54
  English-language learners, 105, 106
  students with disabilities, 106, 109
  see also Contracts and contractors; National
    Center for Education Statistics; *terms
    beginning "Office of..."*
Department of Education Organization Act, 88
Descriptive information, 3, 8, 27-32, 33, 57, 72,
  114, 128, 164, 197
  cost factors, 8
  students with disabilities, 101
Design/Feasibility Team, 66, 72, 78-79, 190
Difficulty level, *see* Item difficulty
Dimensionality of data, 63, 70
Disabilities, *see* Learning disabilities; Students
  with disabilities
Dropouts, 57, 81, 86

E

Early Childhood Longitudinal Study, 36-37, 46,
  110, 188
Economic factors, *see* Cost and cost-benefit
  factors; Funding; Poverty;
  Socioeconomic status
*Educating One and All: Students with
  Disabilities and Standards-Based
  Reform*, 91, 94
Educational indicators, 4, 9, 10, 19, 154
  summary scores, 128
  see also Coordinated system of educational
    indicators
Educational Longitudinal Study, 36-37
Educational Testing Service, 14, 17, 31, 93,
  118, 119, 148-149, 150, 190
Education Commission of the States, 14

Education Counts, 38
Education reform, 2, 9-10, 19, 20, 25-27
    (passim), 118, 153
    coordinated system of education indicators,
       41
    see also Accountability
Education Week, 172
Elementary and Secondary Education Act, 14
English-language learners, 7-8, 14, 19, 20, 26,
    87-113, 134, 186, 191
    accommodations/adaptations, 51, 88-89, 91-
       112 (passim), 191
    analysis methods, 101, 104, 108, 110
    bilingual education, 91, 98-101 (passim),
       104, 105
       translated versions of NAEP, 95, 97,
          100, 101, 111
    coordinated system of education indicators,
       106, 107
    core NAEP, 109, 110, 112
    cost factors, 8, 107-108, 111
    data collection, 87, 96, 104, 106, 107, 108,
       112, 113
    defined, 87(n.1)
    demography of, 89-90
    educational indicators, 88, 106, 114
    field tests, 98-101
    funding, 108, 109
    Goals 2000: Educate America Act, 10, 88,
       96
    grade-level factors, 90
    historical perspectives, 5, 92-98
    identification/classification, 102, 104-105,
       106, 113
    inclusion, 45, 92, 93, 95, 97-104, 106, 109,
       111-113, 191
    interpretive information, 5, 87, 99, 106, 112
    large-scale assessments, 88, 89, 91-93, 96,
       97, 98, 104, 105, 106-109, 110, 112-
       113
    legislation, 10, 88, 96, 106, 108
    mathematics achievement, 98-101, 103, 110
    NCES role, 91, 93, 94, 97, 105, 106, 109,
       191-192
    numbers by grade level, 90
    participation, 5, 19, 57
    performance standards, 87, 89, 94
    reading achievement, 94, 110
    regional factors, 89-90
    reporting procedures, 108, 111
    sampling, 101, 102, 103, 106, 107

    school-level measures, 89-90
    skills measures, 104-105
    standards, general, 5, 87, 89, 91, 92, 94, 98-
       102, 109, 111-113
    state role, 88, 93, 94, 97, 98, 104, 106, 109,
       110
    summary scores, 106
    test administration procedures, 91, 92, 99-
       100
    TIMSS, 44
    translated versions of NAEP, 95, 97, 100,
       101, 111
    urban/rural factors, 89-90
    validity issues, 88, 91, 95, 106, 109-111
    see also Hispanic students; Participation,
       students with disabilities/English-
       language learners
Equality of Opportunity Surveys, 50
Error of measurement, 63, 69, 82-83, 86, 118,
    175
    probability sampling, 62, 64, 66, 68-69, 175
Estimation procedures, 58, 76, 80, 86, 175
Evaluative information, 3, 4, 7, 8, 11, 27-33
    (passim), 57
    teacher evaluation of NAEP, 77-78, 129-
       130
    see also Achievement levels; Performance
       standards
Extended-response items, 128, 132, 136, 140,
    149, 150, 155, 190-191, 194, 220,
    225, 226, 229, 230

F

Family factors, 27, 34, 41, 42, 44
Federal government
    national curriculum, 13-14
    standards, general, 10
    see also Department of Education; Funding;
       Legislation
Field tests, 51, 117, 118, 119, 133-134, 136,
    150, 194
    reporting procedures, tables/displays, 71
Fit of items, 63, 69, 70, 101, 118, 122-123,
    125, 128-132, 220, 221, 229
Focused Reports, 65
Focus on NAEP, 65
Foreign countries, *see* International
       perspectives; *specific countries*
Foreign-language speakers, *see* English-
       language learners

Frameworks, 2, 4, 5-6, 17, 114-161, 165, 194, 257
 achievement levels, 115, 116, 117, 121, 124-125, 128, 134, 135-140, 145-147, 152-154, 158, 159, 160, 192, 194, 195, 196; *see also other "mathematics achievement" and "science achievement" infra*
 analysis methods, 116, 117
 constructed-response items, 115, 122, 123, 128-129, 132, 146, 149, 150, 153-154
 contractors, 115, 116, 118, 119, 136, 148-150, 190, 192-193, 195
 coordinated system of education indicators, 24, 33, 38, 40, 47, 51-55 (passim)
 data collection, 115, 150
 design streamlining, 57, 58-61, 62, 65-66, 77
 funding, 149-150, 151, 155, 191
 governance, 117-118, 134-135
  NAGB, 116, 118, 127, 194, 196
 interpretive information, 114, 116, 137, 153, 154-157, 159, 160-161
 item analysis and development, 117, 118-119, 122-123, 125, 128-137, 142, 149-155, 160, 219-236, 256-257
 knowledge and skills measures, 115, 121, 125, 126, 127, 128, 131-133, 138, 139, 140, 156, 159, 233, 256-257
 large-scale assessments, 114, 125, 128, 133, 136, 147-149, 156, 158, 159, 161, 194
 main NAEP, 114, 118-121, 126-128, 136, 194, 195, 259
 mathematics achievement, 118, 121, 122-124, 126-127, 132, 136, 142
 national NAEP, 59-60
 NCES role, 115, 116, 118, 122, 134, 148-149, 154
 performance standards, 114, 115, 118, 123, 125, 133, 142-143, 146, 149, 155, 159, 220, 257, 259-260
 reading achievement, 118, 119, 120, 122, 123, 127-128, 132, 133, 136, 141-142, 219-230
 reporting procedures, 114, 117, 121, 128, 135, 145-146, 151, 154-160 (passim), 221
 scheduled contracts and administration by framework, 192-193, 195
 science achievement, 116, 118, 126, 129-130, 132-133, 134, 136, 142, 143-144, 231-236

 scoring, 114, 117, 118, 119, 125, 132, 133-134, 135, 136, 146, 149, 150, 153-154, 156, 160, 161, 219-220, 226-227, 234-235, 257
 summary scores, 116, 117, 121, 128, 139, 152, 154
 task measures, 119, 128, 132, 136, 139, 142-144, 146, 149, 153-154, 160, 219-220
 trend NAEP, 77-78, 192, 194
From Data to Information, 40, 41, 49-50
Funding, 19
 coordinated system of education indicators, 23, 41, 42, 44, 53
 framework and assessment development process, 149-150, 151, 155, 191
 students with disabilities/English-language learners, 108, 109
 see also Accountability; Contracts and contractors; Cost and cost-benefit factors

G

Gender factors, 2, 68, 152, 169
Geography achievement, 18, 61, 136, 166
Goals 2000: Educate America Act, 10, 88, 96
Governance factors, 17-19
 coordinated system of education indicators, 45, 51-54
 frameworks and assessment development process, 117-118, 134-135
 reporting, 19, 31, 72, 164, 172, 190
 see also National Assessment Governing Board
Government role, *see* Federal government; Local government; State government
Grade-level factors, 13, 14, 15, 31, 172-173, 192-193
 see also Age factors
Graduate Record Exam, 93
Group testing, 12-13
 group tasks, 47, 138

H

Hawkins-Stafford Elementary and Secondary School Improvement Amendment, 35
High School and Beyond, 31, 46
High school students, 44, 80-81, 85, 86, 186
 dropouts, 57, 81, 86

Hispanic students, 44, 62, 95, 99
  bilingual education, 91, 98-101 (passim),
    105, 110
  translated versions of NAEP, 95, 97, 100,
    101, 111
Historical perspectives, 1-2, 9-15, 19, 163
  achievement measures, 4
  contextual data, 24
  indicator systems, 38
  sociopolitical context, 9-11
  students with disabilities/English language
    learners, 5, 92-98
History, as academic subject, 18, 32, 52, 61,
  136, 166

I

Improving America's Schools Act, 2, 10, 11,
  17, 24, 88, 122, 162, 175, 196
*Improving Schooling for Language-Minority
  Children: A Research Agenda*, 91
Inclusion, 45, 92, 93, 95, 97-104, 106, 109,
  111-113, 191
*The Inclusion of Students with Disabilities and
  Limited Proficient Students in Large-
  Scale Assessments: A Summary of
  Recent Progress*, 92
Indicator systems
  costs of, 38, 51-52, 53
  general, 38-39
  purposes saved by 1, 3-4, 9, 10, 27-32, 34,
    35-39, 42-45, 186; *see also*
    Accountability
  social, 3, 24, 38-39, 152, 153
  see also Coordinated system of educational
    indicators
Individualized education plans, 88, 94, 99-100
Individual-level measures, *see* Student-level
  measures
Individuals with Disabilities Education Act, 88
Individual testing, 12-13
  students with disabilities/English language
    learners, 99
Institute on Educational Governance, Finance,
  Policy Making, and Management, 53
Institute on Student Achievement, Curriculum,
  and Assessment, 52
Instruction, *see* Pedagogy
Instructional Reports, 65
Integrating Federal Statistics on Children, 40
International perspectives, 2, 15, 85, 110

coordinated system of education indicators,
  42, 43, 46, 158, 188
sociopolitical trends, 9-10
TIMSS, 36-37, 40, 42-44, 46, 48, 110, 169,
  174, 188, 259
Interpretive information, 6, 9, 19
  cost factors, 8
  coordinated system of education indicators,
    4, 23, 24, 25, 27-55, 45, 115
  frameworks and assessment development
    processes, 114, 116, 137, 153, 154-
    157, 159, 160-161
  mass media, 9-10, 12, 25-30, 68, 71, 171
  streamlining NAEP design, 4, 5, 57, 64, 65,
    67-68, 71, 72, 73, 81, 86, 190
  students with disabilities/English-language
    learners, 5, 87, 99, 106, 112
  see also Descriptive information;
    Evaluative information
IRT, *see* Item response theory
Item analysis and development, 4, 7, 14, 62-64,
  69, 178-179, 192
  anchoring, 2, 170-171, 173, 177, 257-261
  fit of items, 63, 69, 70, 101, 118, 122-123,
    125, 128-132, 220, 221, 229
  frameworks and assessment development
    process, 117, 118-119, 122-123, 125,
    128-137, 142, 149-155, 160, 219-236,
    256-257
  matrix sampling, 13, 62, 68
    balanced incomplete blocks, 62, 63, 66
    see also Field tests
Item authoring, 256-257
Item difficulty, 13, 14, 100-101, 110, 119, 139,
  166, 174-175, 179, 238, 243, 245, 257
Item families, 146, 156-157, 160, 193, 237-255
Item mapping, 51, 169, 233, 257-259, 260-261
Item response theory, 62-64, 69, 72, 95, 101

J

Jackknife methods, 64, 69

K

Knowledge and skills measures, 5, 6, 12, 13,
  19-20, 27, 77
  coordinated system of education indicators,
    23-24, 47
  English-language learners, 104-105

frameworks and assessment development
    process, 115, 121, 125, 126, 127, 128,
    131-133, 138, 139, 140, 159, 233,
    256-257
main NAEP, 4-5, 15-16, 77, 78-80
main *vs* trend NAEP, 77
see also Task measures
KPMG Peat Marwick LLP, 25, 66, 69, 70, 78

L

Language factors, *see* Bilingual education;
    English-language learners
Large-scale assessments, 3-10 (passim), 21
    achievement-level setting, 182
    coordinated system of education indicators,
        24, 34, 47, 51, 54, 188
    frameworks and assessment development
        processes, 114, 125, 128, 133, 136,
        147-149, 156, 158, 159, 161, 194
    streamlining NAEP design, 56, 57, 70, 80,
        84
    students with disabilities/English-language
        learners, 88, 89, 91-93, 96, 97, 98,
        104, 105, 106-109, 110, 112-113
Learning disabilities, 88, 95, 104, 108, 110
    Office of Special Education and
        Rehabilitative Services, 91
Learning theory, 5-6, 19-20, 128, 137, 138-141,
    151, 160
LEAs, *see* School districts
Legislation, 10
    Americans with Disabilities Act, 88
    Department of Education Organization Act,
        88
    Elementary and Secondary Education Act,
        14
    Goals 2000: Educate America Act, 10, 88,
        96
    Hawkins-Stafford Elementary and
        Secondary School Improvement
        Amendment, 35
    Improving America's Schools Act, 2, 10,
        11, 17, 24, 88, 122, 162, 175, 196
    Individuals with Disabilities Education Act,
        88
    National Education Statistics Act, 52
    Perkins Act, 88
    students with disabilities/English-language
        learners, 10, 88, 96, 106, 108

Literacy, *see* English-language learners;
    Reading achievement; Writing
    achievement
Local Education Authorities, *see* School
    districts
Local factors and trends, 4
    age- *vs* grade-level testing, 14
    streamlining testing, 81-82
    see also School-level measures
Local government
    national curriculum, 13
    standards, 56
Longitudinal studies, 31, 34, 36-37, 39, 42, 43,
    46, 85, 110, 158
    see also specific studies

M

Main NAEP
    frameworks and assessment development
        process, 114, 118-121, 126-128, 136,
        194, 195, 259
    knowledge measures, 4-5, 15-16, 77, 78-80
    mathematics achievement, 15, 17, 28-30,
        65, 77-78, 80, 84, 118, 119, 125, 126-
        127, 132, 156, 157, 171, 192-193
    national trends, 15-16, 56, 57, 58, 65
    performance standards, 4-5, 15-16, 77, 78-
        80
    reading achievement, 15, 17, 65, 80, 84,
        118, 120, 125, 127-128, 133, 171,
        192-193, 219
    reporting, 163, 171
    science achievement, 15, 17, 28-30, 65, 77-
        78, 80, 84, 116, 118, 121, 125, 126,
        157, 168, 192-193, 259
    state, 15, 16, 56, 57, 58, 65-66
    students with disabilities/English-language
        learners, 103
    trend *vs*, 4-5, 15-16, 58, 63, 64, 65, 73-80,
        84, 85
    writing achievement, 15, 17, 65, 80, 84,
        192-193
Market-basket reporting, 72, 189
Mass media, 9-10, 12, 25-30, 68, 71, 171
Mathematics achievement, 7, 10, 27, 52, 58,
    60, 65
    English-language learners, 98-101, 103, 110
    frameworks and assessment development
        process, 118, 121, 122-124, 126-127,
        132, 136, 142

item families, 237-255
main NAEP, 15, 17, 28-30, 65, 77-78, 80, 84, 118, 119, 125, 126-127, 132, 156, 157, 171, 192-193
NAEP administration schedule, 18
National Council of Teachers of Mathematics, 122, 155, 193
national NAEP, 18, 60, 63, 73, 75, 77
new paradigm NAEP, 84
reporting, 28, 58, 59, 73, 171, 172
standards, 10, 166, 171, 172, 176
state NAEP, 82
students with disabilities, 103
TIMSS, 36-37, 40, 42-44, 46, 48, 110, 169, 174, 188, 259
trend NAEP, 15, 17, 18, 60, 63, 73, 75, 77, 80, 84, 102
trend *vs* main NAEP, 73, 75-80 (passim)
see also Achievement levels; Core NAEP
Matrix sampling, 13, 62, 68
balanced incomplete blocks, 62, 63, 66
Minority groups, *see* Race/ethnicity
Mixed methods of data collection, 43, 45, 47-49, 54
Multiple assessment strategies, 4, 6, 7, 47, 57, 66, 73-80
Multiple-choice items, 12, 118, 128-129, 136, 146, 150, 174, 229, 230
guessing/nonresponse, 13, 64
item response theory, 63
main *vs* trend NAEP, 79
Multiple-methods NAEP, 6, 7, 8, 10, 46, 47, 66, 80, 81, 84, 85, 109, 110, 124, 147-156 (passim), 158, 181-182, 186, 188, 190, 193, 194

N

NAEP Facts, 65
NAEP Redesigned, 148-149
NAEP *Report Cards,* see *Report Cards*
National Academy of Education, 7, 25-26, 66, 67, 122, 137
performance standards, 167, 168, 174
students with disabilities/English-language learners, 92, 94, 96, 98
National Assessment Governing Board, 1, 2, 3, 11, 17, 65-66, 185, 189
achievement-level setting, 165-166, 168-171, 173-174, 175, 180, 182, 183, 187, 191, 196, 260

coordinated system of education indicators, 22-25, 31, 187
Design/Feasibility Team, 66, 72, 78-79, 190
frameworks and assessment development process, 116, 118, 127, 194, 196
NAEP objectives, general, 24-25, 78-79, 162, 189-190
reporting, 31, 72, 164, 172, 190
state government role, 25, 65-66
National Assessment of Educational Progress, *see* Core NAEP; Main NAEP; Multiple-methods NAEP; National NAEP; New paradigm NAEP; State NAEP; Trend NAEP
National Association of State Test Directors, 53
National Center for Education Statistics, 1-3, 17, 185, 189
achievement-level setting, 167, 175-176, 187, 196
coordinated system of education indicators, 31, 34-38, 40-41, 45-46, 49-54, 187
data collection, general, 36-37, 196
frameworks and assessment development process, 115, 116, 118, 122, 134, 148-149, 154
reporting procedures, 31, 154, 196
students with disabilities/English-language learners, 91, 93, 94, 97, 105, 106, 109, 191-192
see also Contracts and contractors
National Center for History in Schools, 52
National Center for Improving Student Learning and Achievement in Mathematics and Science, 52
National Center for Research on Evaluation, Standards, and Student Testing, 52, 97, 98
National Center for Research on the Organization and Restructuring of Schools, 53
National Center for the Improvement of Early Reading Achievement, 52
National Center for the Study of Teaching and Policy, 53
National Center on Education Outcomes, 92
National Center on Increasing the Effectiveness of State and Local Education Reform Efforts, 53
National Computer Systems, 119
National Council of Teachers of Mathematics, 122, 155, 193

National Education Longitudinal Study, 36-37, 44, 46, 50, 51, 110, 188
National Education Statistics Act, 52
National Governors' Association, 15, 172
National Household Education Survey, 35-36
National Longitudinal Survey of Youth, 44
National NAEP, 15-16, 56, 57, 58-60, 63, 65, 73
    administration of testing, 82
    constructed-response items, 80
    costs, 66, 78, 82, 85
    frameworks, 59-60
    main NAEP, 15-16, 56, 57, 58, 65
    mathematics achievement, 18, 60, 63, 73, 75, 77
    multiple assessments, 73-77
    pedagogy, 16, 58
    reading achievement, 16, 18, 59, 73-75, 77
    reporting, 1-2, 14, 71
    sampling, 59-60, 62, 66
    science achievement, 18, 60, 63
    state *vs*, 65, 81-84, 85
    writing achievement, 16, 18, 59
National Research and Development Center on English Learning and Achievement, 52
National Science Education Standards, 10
National trends, 5, 19, 46-46
    coordinated system of education indicators, 45-46
    main NAEP, 15-16, 56, 57, 58, 65
    NAEP results reporting, 1-2, 14
    NAGB objectives, 24
    sampling, 59-63, 68, 194
    standards and goals, 10
    streamlining, 81-84, 189
    students with disabilities/English-language learners, 110
    see also National NAEP
A Nation at Risk, 1, 9, 14
The Nation's Report Card, 15, 154, 172
NCES, *see* National Center for Education Statistics
New paradigm NAEP, 46-47, 48, 55, 84, 85, 109, 110, 146-147, 151, 158, 187, 189, 194-196
Newspapers, *see* Mass media
Non-native English speakers, *see* English-language learners
Nonresponse rates, 64, 80

O

Office of Bilingual Education and Minority Languages, 91
Office of Civil Rights, 91
Office of Education Research and Improvement, 46, 91, 94
Office of Special Education and Rehabilitative Services, 91
Office of the General Counsel, 91
Open-ended items, 22, 146
    see also Extended-response items

P

Participation, students with disabilities/English-language learners, 5, 19, 57, 87-89, 91-113 (passim)
    accommodations/adaptations, 51, 88-89, 91-112 (passim), 191
    Goals 2000: Educate America Act, 10, 88, 96
Pedagogy
    coordinated system of education indicators, 23, 40-43 (passim), 46, 47-49, 54
    national NAEP, 16, 58
    teacher background, 40, 41, 43
    trend NAEP, 77
    video techniques, instructional methods analysis, 43, 46, 48, 194
Performance standards, 3, 17, 19, 20, 23, 44, 48, 162-184, 196
    advanced level, 2, 7, 64, 147, 152, 163, 164-171, 173, 174, 175, 180, 183, 186, 256, 259, 260
    defined, 162-164
    demographic factors, 27, 163
    frameworks and assessment development process, 114, 115, 118, 123, 125, 133, 142-143, 146, 149, 155, 159, 220, 257, 259-260
    history of, 15
    main NAEP, 4-5, 15-16, 77, 78-80
    reporting of, 2, 6, 7, 25-31, 32, 33, 72, 73, 162, 163-165
    students with disabilities/English-language learners, 87, 89, 94
    see also Achievement levels; Constructed-response items; Cutscores; Extended-response items; Task measures

Perkins Act, 88
Policy Statement on Redesigning the National Assessment of Educational Progress, 11
Political factors, 9-11, 13-15, 19, 20, 23, 25-26, 31, 38-39
　stakeholders, 3, 25, 80
　see also Accountability; Education reform
Poverty, 14, 44
Preliminary achievement-level descriptions, 119, 134-135, 165, 170, 176-179, 182, 183, 256, 257, 259, 260; *see also* Achievement-level descriptions
Press, *see* Mass media
Private School Universe Study, 36-37
Problem solving, 47, 57, 121, 127, 136-137, 138, 140, 146

Q

Quality Counts, 172

R

Race/ethnicity, 14, 50, 79, 169
　African Americans, 44, 62
　bilingual education, 91, 98-101 (passim), 105, 110
　cultural bias, 63
　Hispanics, 44, 62, 95, 99
　translated versions of NAEP, 95, 97, 100, 101, 111
　trend NAEP, 44, 79
RAND, 40, 46
Reading achievement, 7, 65, 166
　frameworks and assessment development process, 118, 119, 120, 122, 123, 127-128, 132, 133, 136, 141-142, 219-230
　items read orally due to poor readers, 13, 95, 99, 105
　main NAEP, 15, 17, 65, 80, 84, 118, 120, 125, 127-128, 133, 171, 192-193, 219
　NAEP administration schedule, 18
　NAEP mandate, 24
　national NAEP, 16, 18, 59, 73-75, 77
　new paradigm NAEP, 84
　oral, 16
　reporting, 31-32
　state-level trends, 26, 59

　students with disabilities/English-language learners, 94, 110
　text analysis, 43, 49, 219-220
　time factors, reading passages, 122
　trend NAEP, 15, 17, 18, 59, 63, 73-75, 77, 80, 84
　see also Achievement levels; Core NAEP
Reform of education, *see* Education reform
Reform Up Close, 40
Regional factors and trends
　English-language learners, 89-90
　NAEP results reporting, 1, 14, 19, 152
Report Cards, 8, 65, 71, 72, 73, 107, 121, 152, 154, 163, 170, 172
Reporting metrics, 72, 84, 86, 159, 162, 164, 171, 189
Reporting procedures, 1-2, 8, 20, 25-26, 64-65, 66, 67-68, 70-73, 86, 196
　achievement levels, 2, 6, 7, 25-31, 32, 33, 72, 73, 162, 163-165
　coordinated system of education indicators, 25-26, 73
　costs, 78
　demographic factors, 1-2, 27, 31, 34, 163
　field tests, tables/displays, 71
　frameworks and assessment development process, 114, 117, 121, 128, 135, 145-146, 151, 154-160 (passim), 221
　governance, 19, 31, 72, 164, 172, 190
　market-basket reporting, 72, 189
　mathematics achievement, 28, 58, 59, 73, 171, 172
　national NAEP, 1-2, 14, 71
　NCES role, 31, 154, 196
　performance standards, 2, 6, 7, 25-31, 32, 33, 72, 73, 162, 163-165
　reading achievement, 31-32
　regional trends, 1, 14, 19, 152
　scoring and scoring criteria, 72, *see also* Summary scores
　standards-based, 2, 7, 25-26, 33, 162, 163-165, 167-168, 171-173, 182, 184
　students with disabilities/English-language learners, 108, 111
　state NAEP, 2, 10, 14, 15, 26, 31, 68, 71
　timeliness, 67, 71, 152, 154
　trend NAEP, 73, 163
　see also Descriptive information; Evaluative information; Interpretive information

Rural areas, *see* Urban/rural factors

S

Sampling, 2, 4, 11, 13, 14, 17, 20, 45, 46, 47, 49, 50-51, 56, 57, 58-63, 64, 66, 68, 86, 161
    coordinated system of education indicators, 45, 46, 47, 49, 50-51, 107
    cost factors, 62, 66
    dropouts, 81, 86
    errors, 82-83
    probability sampling, 62, 64, 66, 68-69, 175
    jackknife methods, 64, 69
    matrix sampling, 13, 62, 68
    balanced incomplete blocks, 62, 63, 66
    national NAEP, 59-60, 62, 66
    national trends, other, 59-63, 68, 194
    state-level, 59-62, 65-66, 68, 83, 85, 194
    state *vs* national NAEP, 83, 85
    students with disabilities/English-language learners, 101, 102, 103, 106, 107
    time factors, 69
    see also Demographic factors; Error of measurement; Race/ethnicity
Scaling, 4, 56, 66, 67, 72, 80, 101, 111, 117, 154, 163, 261
Scholastic Aptitude Test, 50, 93
School districts, 10, 82, 104
School-level measures, 27, 34, 39, 40, 41, 42, 45, 46, 47, 51
    English-language learners, 89-90
Schools and Staffing Survey, 36-37, 41, 51
Science achievement, 7, 10, 27, 60, 65, 78, 80, 259
    database, 50
    frameworks and assessment development process, 116, 118, 126, 129-130, 132-133, 134, 136, 142, 143-144, 231-236
    main NAEP, 15, 17, 28-30, 65, 77-78, 80, 84, 116, 118, 121, 125, 126, 157, 168, 192-193, 259
    NAEP administration schedule, 18
    national NAEP, 18, 60, 63
    new paradigm NAEP, 84
    standards, 10, 166, 168-171, 178-179
    TIMSS, 36-37, 40, 42-44, 46, 48, 110, 169, 174, 188, 259
    trend NAEP, 15, 17, 18, 60, 63, 80, 84, 259
    see also Achievement levels; Core NAEP

Scoring and scoring criteria, 67, 192
    frameworks and assessment development process, 114, 117, 118, 119, 125, 132, 133-134, 135, 136, 146, 149, 150, 153-154, 156, 160, 161, 219-220, 226-227, 234-235, 257
    levels and types of knowledge, 6
    multicategory, 67
    nonresponse rates, 64, 80
    reporting, 72
    state *vs* national NAEP, 82-83
    see also Cutscores; Summary scores
Second-language speakers, *see* English-language learners
Sex differences, *see* Gender factors
Social indicator systems, 3, 24, 38-39, 152, 153
Socioeconomic status, 50
    poverty, 14, 44
Sociopolitical factors, *see* Demographic factors; Political factors
Spanish-speaking students, *see* Hispanic students
Special studies, 16, 57, 110
Special Study Panel on Education Indicators, 35, 37, 38, 40-41
Standards, general, 19, 20, 27, 126
    coordinated system of education indicators, 23, 45
    curriculum, 10, 179, 153
    mathematics achievement, 58, 59, 73
    NAEP history, 12, 15
    reporting, standards-based, 2, 7, 25-26, 33, 162, 163-165, 167-168, 171-173, 182, 184
    science achievement, 10, 166, 168-171, 178-179
    students with disabilities/English-language learners, 5, 87, 89, 91, 92, 94, 98-102, 109, 111-113
    see also Achievement-level descriptions; Achievement levels; Achievement-level setting; Performance standards; Preliminary achievement-level descriptions; Scoring and scoring criteria
State Collaboratives on Assessment and Standards Project, 40, 46
State government, 19
    costs, 78
    curriculum reform, 13, 153
    evaluation of programs, 11
    NAGB and, 25, 65-66

national curriculum, 13
National Governors' Association, 15, 172
standards, 10, 56
students with disabilities/English-language
learners, 88, 93, 94, 97, 98, 104, 106,
109, 110
State-level factors and trends, 4, 5, 23, 26, 189
age- *vs* grade-level testing, 14
coordinated system of education indicators,
45-46
main NAEP, 15, 16, 56, 57, 58, 65-66
reading achievement, 26, 59
sampling, 59-62, 65-66, 68, 83, 85, 194
sociopolitical factors, 10
State NAEP, 14, 15, 16, 45-46, 56, 57, 58, 65-
66, 192-193
cost factors, 62, 66, 78, 82, 85
national NAEP *vs*, 65, 81-84, 85
objectives, 24
reporting, 2, 10, 14, 15, 26, 31, 68, 71
sampling, 59-62, 65-66, 68, 83, 85, 194
streamlining, 81-84
Student-level measures, 40, 42, 43, 45, 46
Students with disabilities, 5, 7-8, 14, 19, 20,
87-113, 134, 191
accommodations/adaptations, 51, 88-89, 91-
112 (passim), 191
accountability, 91, 94
achievement levels, 88, 107, 109, 110-111,
112
administration procedures, testing, 91, 92,
99-100
analysis methods, 101, 104, 108, 110
coordinated system of education indicators,
106, 107
core NAEP, 109, 110, 112
cost factors, 8, 107-108, 111
curriculum, 111
data collection, 87, 96, 104, 106, 107, 108,
112, 113
demography of, 89-90
Department of Education role, 106, 109
NCES, 91, 93, 94, 97, 105, 106, 109,
191-192
educational indicators, general, 88, 106, 114
funding, 108, 109
Goals 2000: Educate America Act, 10, 88,
96
historical perspectives, 5, 92-98
identification/classification, 102, 104-105,
106

inclusion, 45, 92, 93, 95, 97-104, 106, 109,
111-113, 191
individualized education plans, 88
interpretive information, 5, 87, 99, 106, 112
large-scale assessments, 88, 89, 91-93, 96,
97, 98, 104, 106-109, 110, 112-113
legislation, 10, 88, 106, 108
NCES role, 91, 93, 94, 97, 105, 106, 109,
191-192
participation, 5, 19, 57, 87-88
performance standards, 87, 89, 94
reading achievement, 94, 110
reporting procedures, 108, 111
sampling, 101, 102, 103, 106, 107
standards, 5, 87, 89, 91, 92, 94, 98-102,
109, 111-113
validity issues, 88, 91, 95, 106, 109-111
see also Learning disabilities
Students with limited English proficiency, *see*
English-language learners
Student/teacher ratios, 44
Summary scores, 1-2, 6
demographic trends, 14
error of measurement, 63
frameworks and assessment development
process, 116, 117, 121, 128, 139, 152,
154

T

Task measures, 4, 12, 192
coordinated system of education indicators,
23, 24, 33, 47, 54
framework and assessment development
process, 119, 128, 132, 136, 139, 142-
144, 146, 149, 153-154, 160, 219-220
group, 47, 138
streamlining NAEP design, 67, 68, 71, 81,
86
see also Extended-response items
Teacher background variables, 40, 41, 43
Teacher evaluation of NAEP, 77-78, 129-130
Teaching methods, *see* Pedagogy
Technical Review Panel, 11, 166
Test administration procedures, *see*
Administration procedures, testing
Text analysis, 219-220
textbooks, 43, 49
Third International Mathematics and Science
Study, 36-37, 40, 42-44, 46, 48, 110,
169, 174, 188, 259

Time factors
    administration schedules, 18, 121, 191, 192-193, 195
    assessment development processes, 124, 136, 159, 160
    item response time, 13, 62, 99, 128, 130-131
    reading passages, 122
    reporting of results, 67, 71, 152, 154
    sampling, 69
Trend NAEP, 4, 27, 56, 58, 65, 84, 85
    achievement levels, 4-5, 15-16, 56, 58, 77, 78-80
    cost factors, 78
    frameworks, 77-78, 192, 194
    main *vs*, 4-5, 15-16, 57, 58, 63, 64, 65, 73, 77, 78-80, 84, 85
    mathematics achievement, 15, 17, 18, 60, 63, 73, 75, 77, 80, 84, 102
        new paradigm, 47, 194
    race, 44, 79
    reading achievement, 15, 17, 18, 59, 63, 73-75, 77, 80, 84
    reporting, 73, 163
    sampling, 66
    science achievement, 15, 17, 18, 60, 63, 80, 84, 259
    writing achievement, 15, 17, 18, 59, 63, 80, 84
Trends in Academic Progress, 65
Trial State Assessment, 25, 94, 96-98 (passim), 174

U

Urban/rural factors
    English-language learners, 89-90
Use of NAEP results, 11, 20, 25-31, 39, 114, 181, 256

achievement levels, 2, 31, 171, 176, 180, 182, 184, 246
mass media, 9-10, 12, 25-30, 68, 71, 171
school districts, 104
stakeholders, 3, 25, 80

V

Validating National Curriculum Indicators, 40, 46
Validity issues, 11, 122, 153, 167-168, 173, 176-177, 182, 189, 221, 226
    analysis and scaling models, 67
    content, 12
    coordinated system of education indicators, 40, 46
    students with disabilities/English-language learners, 88, 91, 95, 106, 109-111
Validity Studies Panel, 11
Video techniques, instructional methods analysis, 43, 46, 48, 194

W

WESTAT, 17, 119
Writing achievement, 7, 59, 65
    main NAEP, 15, 17, 65, 80, 84, 192-193
    NAEP administration schedule, 18
    NAEP mandate, 24
    national NAEP, 16, 18, 59
    new paradigm NAEP, 84
        extended performance, 16
    trend NAEP, 15, 17, 18, 59, 63, 80, 84
    trend *vs* main NAEP, 79, 80
    see also Core NAEP